Church of
Ringshall

The Anglo Saxon name of Ringshale means "secluded spot or nook of Hring" or "round shelter for cattle"

Dedicated to my husband, John, and my family

First published 2000
by LeverPress Limited.

Written and compiled by Maureen June Wills
Copyright © 2000

All rights reserved.
No part of this book may be reproduced by any means or transmitted or translated into a machine language, without the written permission of the author.

ISBN 0-9539084-0-2

Designed and printed by LeverPress Limited, Ipswich, England.

ACKNOWLEDGEMENTS

*F*irst of all, I want to thank my husband, John, for all his support. Writing a book is almost like pregnancy. Towards the end the excitement surrounding the expected event turns to trepidation as the mother wonders 'how things will turn out'. Like most expectant fathers, my husband has encouraged me and steadied my fears, not just for nine months, but three years; the longest gestation in history.

Special thanks to Marian Cole for all her hard work on the word processor, and her encouragement. She has been fantastic. Special thanks to David Hitchcock, and to my husband, John, who both spent hours reading the manuscripts and painstakingly corrected any errors. Special thanks also to my friend, Daphne Gadsden, for illustrating the book covers. I owe a particular debt of gratitude to Andrew Toomey who helped me with typing, and took many lovely photographs and produced several interesting drawings. Special thanks to Michael Poll who supplied some very important material, and to Elizabeth Hitchcock who was very helpful in supplying material. Special thanks also to Warrant Officer (Retd) Terry Betchley, MBE of Wattisham Base without whose help the text re Wattisham Base would have been impossible; and to Jon Durrant for his clever cartoons and excellent drawings, and to Lisa Cresswell for her clever cartoons. My thanks also to Kate Chantry, Service Archivist at Ipswich Record Office, who made the difficult task of copyright much easier. Special thanks to Geoff and Sheila Durrant, who have been a fount of encouragement, as has John Waspe, who introduced me to some lovely people, and was ALWAYS ready and eager to help me in gaining information for my book. Special thanks to my son Mark Wills, and to my daughter-in-law Collette Wills, who helped in gaining necessary materials.

I am indebted to many people who have generously given up the time to talk to me. Without them this book would have been impossible to write. May I say THANK YOU to each and every one of you.

Other people that warrant particular mention, are: John Herrington and staff at Gainsborough Library; Hilary Platts, Ipswich Library; Judi Barnes; Audrey Coventry; Otto Glaser; Brian J Bell, MBE of Old Pond Publishing – "From Sickle to Satellite"; Roy Tricker; David Butler; Christine Darton, local Mobile Library; David Hopgood ("Hopgoods, Stowmarket"); Rev. Kit Gray, St. Catherine's Church, Ringshall; Peter Watson; David Ford; Her Majesty's Stationery Office, Norwich; Mary Moore of Suffolk County Council; Lt. Col. (Rtd.) Peter Coombe, of Wattisham Base; Clare Secret of Ringshall Parochial Council; Ipswich Record Office. Finally, special thanks to Gordon Leggett, Jo Gardiner and staff of LeverPress, Ipswich. Gordon Leggett gave me good and much appreciated advice.

i

FOREWORD

This book, "Chronicles of Ringshall" cannot go to print without a big thank you to Maureen Wills for the many hours of hard work and dedication she has given, in collecting and compiling information to produce this marvellous edition of Ringshall's past and present: well done Maureen!

And also many thanks to the residents and non residents for pictures and information.

This book will be enjoyed, we are sure, by present and future generations to come.

Ringshall Parish Council (1999)

Over 100 copies of this book were bought by the parish council to be distributed free of charge to the residents of Ringshall.

This book is based on an idea put forward by John Hitchcock.

St. Catherine's Church, Ringshall
Photograph taken by Peter Watson of Lower Farm Road, Ringshall

Contents

1. In the Beginning. 1
2. St. Catherine's Parish Church 11
3. Ringshall Village Hall 29
4. School Days through the Years 38
5. Historical Houses 48
6. Chapel Farm. 80
7. The Farm Houses 120
8. More Tales from the Farms 138
9. When Ringshall had a Village Shop 180
10. Tooting and Hull meet Ringshall 193
11. Recollections and Changing Times 207
12. Wattisham Airfield 236
13. Last – but not Least 246

The author at work!

The author has attempted to trace copyright owners. Where inadvertent infringement has been made, she apologises.

1
In the Beginning

The following extract about the village of Ringshall comes from "The Manors of Suffolk", Vol.2 by W. A. Copinger, MA, LLD, FSA, FRSA (1908).

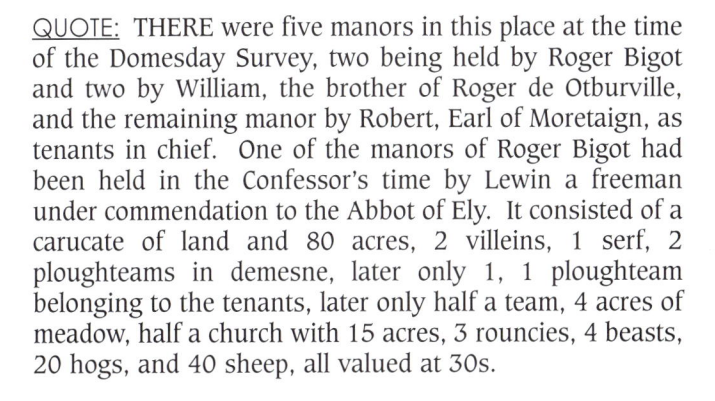

QUOTE: THERE were five manors in this place at the time of the Domesday Survey, two being held by Roger Bigot and two by William, the brother of Roger de Otburville, and the remaining manor by Robert, Earl of Moretaign, as tenants in chief. One of the manors of Roger Bigot had been held in the Confessor's time by Lewin a freeman under commendation to the Abbot of Ely. It consisted of a carucate of land and 80 acres, 2 villeins, 1 serf, 2 ploughteams in demesne, later only 1, 1 ploughteam belonging to the tenants, later only half a team, 4 acres of meadow, half a church with 15 acres, 3 rouncies, 4 beasts, 20 hogs, and 40 sheep, all valued at 30s.

By the time of the Survey the details had varied considerably, and the value had been increased to 50s. At that time there were 4 bordars, the serf had disappeared, the ploughteams in demesne from 1 had again risen to 2, but of the tenants there was but half a team, the rouncies had increased by 1, the beasts had gone up to 18, the hogs to 40, the sheep to 100, and there were then 30 goats.

The second manor of Roger Bigot had been held by a freeman named Grim in the Confessor's time, with 100 acres, under commendation to the Abbot of Ely. There were attached to the manor 4 acres of meadow, a ploughteam and a half, 1 rouncy, and 3 beasts, valued at 20s.

By the time of the Great Survey there was no ploughteam, but the value was placed at 30s. Both of the above manors were held by William de Burnoille of Roger Bigot, and the King and the Earl had the soc.

This William de Burnoille also held under Bigot what in earlier days had been held by four freemen. Lewin, Roger Bigot's predecessor, had commendation over two, who were called Frodo and Leuric. The other two, called Lustwin and Edwic, were not under his commendation. These freemen had 50 acres and ploughteam, and an acre of meadow, all valued at 12s and the King and the Earl had the soc. It paid in a gelt 15d. It was a league long and half a league in breadth.

One of the two manors of William, brother of Roger de Otburville, was held in the Confessor's time by Godwin a freeman, with a carucate of land and 40 acres, 1 villein, 2 ploughteams, 4 bordars, 6 acres of meadow, wood sufficient for 8 hogs, half a church with 12 acres, 4 rouncies, 13 hogs, 60 sheep, and 32 goats, valued at 47s. of this land, one under commendation to the Abbot of St Edmunds held at this time 11 acres. At the time of the Survey there was only half a ploughteam and the rouncies had come down to 1. Of the manor Hugh then held 40 acres, valued at 5s included in the above valuation.

The second of the manors was held in Saxon times by a freeman named Uluric with 80 acres, 1 ploughteam, and 4 acres of meadow, valued at 20s. By the time of the Survey the value was but 8s and the manor was held by Fulco of William, the King and the Earl having the soc. Amongst the same tenant in chief's holdings were two small ones here which he held in demesne. One consisted of 18 acres and also formerly half a ploughteam, valued at 3s and had been held in the Confessor's time held by a freeman named Trumwin, and the other of 5 acres valued at 12d which had in Saxon times been held by Edric, a freeman under commendation to William de Otburville's predecessor.

A fifth manor here was held in demesne by Robert, Earl of Moretaign, and consisted of 30 acres, which Ulmar, a freeman, had formerly held with 2 bordars, 2 acres of meadow, and 1 ploughteam, valued at 10s. In this holding was included the twelfth part of a church in Battisford. The only other holding mentioned in the Survey was 4 acres, formerly held by a freeman named Booty, valued at 10d. It was held in chief by Earl Robert, and the King and the Earl had the soc.

Manor of Ringshall

This was the manor of Saxon Lewin and of Norman Bigot, held under the latter at the time of the Survey by William de Burnoille or Burnaville. He continued to hold in the time of Henry II for we find that William de Burnaville and Alice his wife gave the church and tithes of this parish to the priory of the virgin Mary and St Andrew in Thetford, and King Henry II at the request of Hugh Bigot confirmed the said gift. The manor passed from the last mentioned William to his son and heir, Sir Geoffrey de Burnaville, and from him to his son and heir, Sir Robert de Burnaville. Sir Robert was succeeded by his son and heir Robert, and he by his son and heir, Sir William de Burnaville.

In 1363 we learn that the heirs of Richard de Burnaville held here, and in 1381 Simon Blyant probably held the manor, for he did homage "for land formerly held by Robert de Burnaville". John Blyant next held, and died in 1523, when the manor passed to his son and heir, Richard Blyant, who died without lawful issue.

The manor was then acquired by Sir Richard Gresham, Knt., who died in 1548, when it passed to his son and heir, Sir John Fresham, Knt., who died in 1560, when it went to his brother and heir, Sir Thomas Fresham. Amongst the Chancery proceedings in the time of Queen Elizabeth will be found an action by William Gresham against Francis Cuddon and Thomas Cuddon for relief against an alleged fraud relating to this manor, of which Sir Thomas Gresham was then stated to be seised for life with divers remainders over.

Sir Thomas Gresham died in 1579, when the manor vested in William Gresham, who in 1583 had licence to alienate to William Rowe and Thomas Byarde, who sold to John Barker and others in 1587. John Barker died in 1609, and the manor passed to his eldest son, Sir Robert Barker, KB of Grimston Hall, Trimley St Martin, and on his death passed to Sir Thomas Barker, his eldest son by his second wife. Sir Thomas Barker resided at Ringshall Hall, and sold the manor to his youngest brother, William Barker who was an alderman of the City of London.

On the death of William Barker the manor passed to his son and heir, William Barker, of Bocking Hall, who was created a Bart by King Charles II in 1676. He married Elizabeth, sixteenth child of Sir Jerome Alexander, Knt., one of the Justices of the Common Pleas in Ireland. Sir William died in Ireland, and was succeeded by his eldest son, Sir William Barker, 2nd Bart of Bocking Hall. He married Catherine Teresa (eldest daughter and coheir of Samuel Keck, one of the Masters in Chancery), who died in 1736, and was buried in the parish church of Ringshall.

Sir William survived until 1746, and the hall and manor were in 1750 sold to Peter Lefebure, and on his death in 1753 passed to his widow Elizabeth. In 1761 the hall and manor were vested in William Watson and Jonathan Watson, of Bury St Edmunds. This last gentleman was an F.R.S., a Justice of the Peace, Deputy

Lieutenant for the County, and major of the East Suffolk Militia, and in 1783 sold the hall and manor to William Wollaston, of Finborough Hall, who held his first court 19th Oct 1784, and died in 1797. It is quite possible that he sold the manor before his death, certainly in 1786 he offered it for sale with four freehold farms in Ringshall and one in Battisford of the yearly rent of £400, with a large wood containing 50 acres. As, however, William Wollaston is said to have destroyed the manor house in 1788, he probably did not sell to Alexander Adair till this year. The manor was subsequently acquired by Alexander Adair, who held a court 22nd May 1822, and died in 1834, when it passed to his son William Adair, who held courts 29th Oct. 1835, and 21st Sept 1836, and the manor has since devolved in the same way as the Manor of Cratfield le Roos, in Blything Hundred, and is now vested in Sir Frederick Edward Shafto Adair, 4th Bart of Flixton Hall, Bungay.

Manor of Charles Hall

This was the Lordship of the Saxon Grim and of William de Burnoille under Roger Bigot at the time of the Domesday Survey.

In 1270 it was vested in Thomas Charles, a member of the Bentley family of this name, who had a grant of market and fair here at that date, and free warren in 1285. Amongst the Abbreviation of Pleas there is a finding in 1288 that Ranulph de la Wade de Rudgessale, William and Nicholas, his sons, trespassed on the free warren of this Thomas Charles, at Ringshall, and the King had £11 for forfeiture in the said warren. In 1301 the manor was conveyed by deed poll from Sir William Charles to his son, Sir Edward Charles, Knt., who was succeeded in the lordship by his son and heir, William Charles. In 1339 William Charles, son of the last named William Charles, granted the reversion of the manor to Sir John de Stonore, Knt. The next we hear of the manor was that Henry Wentworth died seised of it in 1482, when it passed to his son and heir, Roger Wentworth. After vesting in one John Boxted it passed to Sir Richard Gresham, and on his death in 1548 went to his widow Isabella for life.

She died in 1565, when the manor passed to Sir Richard's son, Sir Thomas Gresham, and from that time has passed in the same course as the main manor. Charles Hall is a common farmhouse, with a chimney of early date and a moat.

Manor of Rawlins

This was no doubt one of the manors of William, brother of Roger de Otburville, and probably held by Brian, son of Aunsel, who held half a knight's fee in Ringshall in the time of Henry III. In another place in the Testa de Nevill he is referred to as Brian de Ringeshall, and as holding his half knight's fee of Margaret de Ripariis.

We find the manor subsequently vested in Sir Richard Gresham, Knt., who died seised in 1545, and it has since apparently devolved in the same course as the main manor, being now vested in Sir Frederick Edward Shafto Adair, 4th Bart. In 1588 a fine was levied of this manor by Robert Barker and others against William Gresham and others.

Manor of Rockells or Willisham and Rockells

This was the other manor of William, brother of Roger de Otburville, or Auberville, the Domesday tenant in chief. We have information as to the descent from the Conquest to the time of Edward I in the Quo Warranto Rolls when Richard de la Rokele and Robert de Willasham claimed view of frankpledge and assize of bread and beer in Ringshall. They then showed that William de Daundevill or Auberville or Otburville came over with the Conqueror. He is no doubt the same with the Domesday tenant in Chief.

From this William the manor descended to William and Jordan as heirs. William died without issue, and his moiety of the manor passed to his brother and heir Peter, who gave the same to William de la Rokele, the father of Richard de la Rokele, while the other moiety of the manor, that of Jordan, descended to his daughter and heir, Matilda, and from her to her son and heir, Robert, and from him to his son and heir, Ralph, and from him to his son and heir, Ralph, and from him passed to his son and heir, Robert de Willakesham, who is said to have held one fee of Margery de Ripariis. The share of William de la Rokele passed to his son and heir, Sir Richard de la Rokele.

We find in Ringshall a chapel belonging to the priory of Norwich, settled on this cell at Hoxne in 1294 when it was returned by the oath of Luke, the parish chaplain of Ringshall, that this was a free chapel belonging to the prior of Norwich Cathedral, who assigned it to his cell of St Edmund at Hoxne; that it was endowed with 32 acres of land and two parts of all the tithe, corn and hay of the ancient demesne of Sir Richard de la Rokele and Robert de Wyllakysham and their tenants in Ringshall, the tithes being then of 30s per annum value, all of which were confirmed by the Bishop. In 1313 Robert Guer, chaplain, had the whole assigned to him for life, paying 30s per annum, serving the chapel thrice a week, and keeping the houses in repair.

Amongst the ancient deeds in the Court of Chancery preserved in the Public Record office is a grant by John, son of Elias de Ochotte, of Ryngeshall, to his Sir

"Richard de Rokele", Knt., of land in the parish of Ringshall in a field called "Bydwodescroft", in Ringshall, between the road leading from Brecete to Needham, and the town-house of the prior of Hoxne. The deed is dated at Ringshall, Tuesday the morrow of the Circumcision, 5th Edw. II.

Sir Richard de la Rokele was succeeded by John de la Rokele, and we subsequently find the Rokele share vested in John de Copeldyke, who died in 1327. In 1359 a fine was levied of the manor by Gilbert de Illeye and Johanna his wife against John de Copeldyke and Johanna his wife, the John being probably a son of the last mentioned lord.

The Davy MSS say that in 1428 the manor vested in W. Burys. In this same year, 1428, we also find the share of Ralph Wylasham vested in one Thomas Cook. A century later the manor became vested in Sir Richard Gresham, who died seised in 1548, when it passed to his widow Isabella for life, and on her death in 1565 vested in Sir Richard's son, Sir Thomas Gresham.

Amongst the Calendar to Pleadings of the Duchy of Lancaster in the time of Philip and Mary, an action will be found between the King and Queen and Thomas Gresham as to a claim to relief and knights' fees in Ringshall.

Sir Thomas Gresham died in 1579, from which time the devolution of the manor is apparently identical with the main manor, being now vested in Sir Frederick Edward Shafto Adair, 4th Bart. UNQUOTE

The above may contain unfamiliar words whose meanings are shown below:

Carucate Measure of land that could be ploughed by 8 oxon and 1 plough in a year.

Villein Peasant cultivator attached to a manor.

Demesne Land not held by subordinate tenant.

Rouncies Land holding villagers.

FACTS AND FIGURES

1270 Grant of market and fair to Thomas Charles to be held on Charles Hall Manor.

EDUCATION

1833 1 Sunday School established 1821 (66 attend)
1891 School attended by 22 children
1912 Public Elementary school, average attendance 20

POOR RELIEF

1776	£96. 14s. 0d	spent on poor relief	**1830**	£361. 7s. 0d	spent on poor relief
1803	£120. 17s. 6d	" "	**1832**	£459. 7s. 0d	" "
1818	£317. 1s. 0d	" "	**1834**	£300. 7s. 0d	" "

OCCUPATIONS

1550-1599 1 husbandman
1600-1649 10 yeomen, 2 husbandmen, 1 sawyer
1650-1699 15 yeomen, 3 husbandmen, 1 clerk, 1 millwright
1831 84 in agriculture, 2 in retail trade, 1 professional, 15 in domestic service, 1 other
1844 2 shoemakers, 11 farmers
1912 Sub-postmaster, teacher, 15 farmers, shopkeeper, grocer

POPULATION

1086	20	Recorded	
1327	18	Taxpayers paid £2. 18s.	
1524	22	Taxpayers paid £5. 8s. 6d	
1603	136	Adults	
1674	33	Households	
1676	Not recorded		
1801	257	Inhabitants	
1831	337	Inhabitants	
1851	371	Inhabitants	
1871	304	Inhabitants	
1901	243	Inhabitants	
1931	225	Inhabitants	
1951	1,111	Inhabitants	) *These figures probably*
1971	1,218	Inhabitants	) *include part of*
1981	968	Inhabitants	) *Wattisham base*
1997	350	Inhabitants	

SOME OF RINGSHALL'S RESIDENTS IN 1855

BIRD, Ebenezer – Grocer and Draper
BLYTHE, Mr William
CHARLES, Rev. Samual MA – Curate
DICKERSON, Daniel – Shoemaker
DRIVER, Maria – Shopkeeper
PARKER, Rev. Charles, Fred MA – Rectory

FARMERS

BEAUMONT, Isaac
COOPER, James, Charles Hall
COOPER, Jonathan
GIBBONS, Thomas
HARVEY, William
HAYWARD, Thomas, Ringshall Hall
HICKS, Mrs Catherine
HITCHCOCK, John
HORNE, Daniel
KNOCK, William
LAFLIN, Hannah
LAFLIN, Jonathan
MAKENS, John
MAKENS, Robert
MUDD, Thomas
NUNN, Samuel
POWLING, Charles
ROUSE, Benjamin

SOME OF RINGSHALL'S RESIDENTS IN 1874

BAXTER, Miss Elizabeth – Parochial Schoolmistress
CARTER, Robert – Farmer
COOPER, Jonathan – Farmer, Charles Hall
EMSDEN, Benjamin – Rake and Hurdle Maker
GIBBONS, Thomas and William – Farmers
GOODERHAM, George Creasy – Farmer, Red House Farm
GREEN, Abraham – Farmer and Landowner
HAWKINS, Rev Edward William, MA – Rector, The Rectory
HAYWARD, Thomas – Farmer, The Hall
HITCHCOCK, Joseph Ennals, Farmer and Landowner, Chapel Farm
HITCHCOCK, Susan (Mrs) – Farmer and Landowner
KNELL, Rev Albert – Baptist Church
LAPLIN, Jonathan – Farmer
LAPLIN, Mary (Mrs) – Farmer
MAKENS, John – Farmer, Cattle Dealer and Landowner
MAKENS (Mrs) – Farmer, Cattle Dealer and Landowner
MANN, David – Grocer and Draper
PLANTON, John – Farmer
TRICKER, John – Farmer
WILDEN, James – Grocer, Draper and Boot and Shoemaker
WILSON, James – Postmaster

RINGSHALL (1885)

– Taken from the History, Gazetteer and Directory of Suffolk

A school is held in premises purchased by the rector and parishioners, and attended by about 40 children.

Post Office at Mr James Wilden's. Letters arrive at 8.30 am and are despatched at 5.30 pm to Stowmarket, but Needham Market is the nearest Money Order Office.

SOME OF RINGSHALL'S RESIDENTS IN 1885

BAKER, Charles – Farmer
CARTER, Robert – Farmer, Hill Farm
COOPER, James – Farmer, Stoke Farm
COOPER, Jonathan – Farmer & Landowner, Charles Hall & Cambs
DAVES, Robert – Farm Bailiff
DICKERSON, Daniel – Shoemaker
EMSDEN, Charles – Farm Bailiff, Chapel Farm
GARNER, Jas – Farm Bailiff, Bradley's Farm
GIBBONS, William – Shopkeeper
GOODERHAM, George Creasy – Farmer, Red House & Crow Croft, Wattisham
HAYWARD, Thomas – Farmer, The Hall
HAWKINS, Rev Edward William – Rector, The Rectory
HITCHCOCK, Ennals – Farmer & Landowner
HITCHCOCK, Joseph Ennals – Farmer & Landowner, Chapel Farm & Brockford
KEEBLE, Edward – Farmer
KNELL, Rev Albert – Baptist
LABRAM, Miss L – Ntnl School Mistress
LAPLIN, Mary (Mrs) – Farmer
MAKENS, Abraham & John – Farmers & Landowners
MAKENS, Robert – Farmer & Cattle Dealer
MAKENS, (Mrs) – Farmer, Cattle Dealer & Landowner
MANN, David – Grocer and Draper
PAGE, Harry – Farmer; & Norton; and Blacksmith, Gt Bricett
PARKES, Thomas – Thatcher
SQUIRRELL, Robert – Farmer: & Cambs
TRICKER, Jno – Farmer, The Boarded House
WILDEN, Jas – Grocer, Draper, Shoemaker & Sub-Postmaster

SOME OF RINGSHALL'S RESIDENTS IN 1925

DURRANT, Walter Edward – Farmer
EMSDEN, Benjamin – Farmer
FELLINGHAM, Edward – Farmer, Poplar Farm
GARROD, Charles – Farmer
GILBERT, Albert Edward – Farmer
GOODERHAM, Alfred – Farmer, Red House and Boarded House
GOODING, Herbert – Farmer, Charles Hall
HALL, Frank – Shopkeeper and Carrier
HITCHCOCK, William C – Farmer and Landowner, Chapel Farm
LAFLIN, Olive (Mrs) – Farmer
LONG, Harry (exors of) – Farmer, Ringshall Hall
LONG (Mrs) – Ringshall Hall
MAKENS, Spencer – Farmer
MAKENS (Miss) – Hill House
MARRIOTT, Frederick Walter – Farmer
PALMER, William – Farmer
PARTRIDGE, Arthur Edward – Farmer
TAYLOR, Rev John Kinnersley MA – Rector, The Rectory
WASPE, Annie (Mrs) – Farmer
WRIGHT, Maurice – Farmer, Hill House Farm

A blacksmith at work

2
St Catherine's Parish Church

Who was Saint Catherine?

The story of St Catherine is a short and tragic one. She lived in the fourth century, and was the daughter of the King of Cyprus, an island in the Eastern Mediterranean. She died in Alexandria, city and seaport of Egypt, at the hands of Emperor Maxentius.

Emperor Maxentius, a tyrannical ruler, was determined that Catherine would worship his gods, but she had no intention of paying homage to false idols. The furious Emperor ordered four spiked wheels to be set up and her young body crushed between them.

Saint Catherine was one of the most popular saints in the middle ages. Eighty churches are dedicated to her in England.

The College of St Catherine, Oxford has a spiked wheel in its arms. The distinctive catherine wheel emblem may be found in Combe-In-Teignhead, Devon, Lessingham, Norfolk, Westhall, Suffolk and All Saints College, Oxford.

Two villages in England are named after her, Catherington, in Hampshire, and St Catherine, Avon.

On the 5 November we mainly think of Guy Fawkes (1570-1606), a Yorkshire Catholic, who with Catesby and other conspirators, planned to blow up the Houses of Parliament.

Fireworks are lit, with the small catherine wheels usually tied to posts. Not many people realise the tragic story behind this particular firework.

NOTE: Some of the above facts were obtained from the book
***"Discovering Saints in Britain"**, by John Vince.*

St Catherine's Parish Church, Ringshall

The Church

Ringshall is a spread-out agricultural village in the heart of the Suffolk countryside and in this cosy corner stands St Catherine's Church. The Church lies back from the road on a slight incline. Surrounded by meadows, the immediate feeling is of peace and tranquillity.

A church existed here when the Domesday Survey was compiled, and some of the present building apparently dates from that time. Most of the building was reconstructed in the fifteenth century, when in 1430 the tenor bell was hung in the tower which probably dates back to early Norman times. The West end tower contains the two bells which are hung for swing chiming. As previously mentioned, the tenor bell was cast circa 1430 by Richard Hille, a London Founder, Robert Phelps.

The bell frame is of timber construction and was originally designed to house three bells, although according to the notes from John Taylor (Bell Founders) Ltd, the larger pit which is in the eastern half of the tower appears never to have carried a bell.

The ancient arcaded font may well have been installed in early Norman times. The circular column was reinforced in the nineteenth century by the insertion of little columns. One can so easily visualise generations of local families grouped around this font celebrating their babies' entry into the church (over seven-hundred years).

The interior of the church is formed as a single cell – meaning no break between Nave and Chancel. The Nave has arched braced tie beams, the ends of which protrude through the external walls and are secured with needles surmounted by king posts which support a central runner. The Chancel has a fine hammer beam roof on which are the initials of Richard Borsall who, over five-hundred years ago, was the benefactor who paid for its reconstruction. In more recent times, 1878, a year was spent in bringing the church fabric into a good state of repair when the roof was stripped to inspect the timbers before replacing the original tiles and removing a plastered ceiling to leave the main roof trusses over the Chancel much as Richard Borsall saw them so long ago; and while this work was being done opportunity was taken to restore to their former size the lovely window embrasures which in the early Victorian era had been partially bricked up to fit the then more modern smaller windows. The East window keeps green the memory of Charles Frederick Pepper who ministered here for 51 years from 1819 to 1870. This work was directed by Mr R M Phipson and his oak porch is a very good reproduction of a 14th century design. The doorway was inserted about 1300 and is still a very solid construction. The inner arch is round headed and so it may possibly have replaced a Norman original. The East and South East windows are filled with glass by Clayton and Bell (1870). The Resurrection and Christ with St Mary Magdalene in the garden, in one, and Christ as The Good Shepherd and the Light of the World, in the other. All the church furniture dates from the 1870s and is as solid as the rest of the building. When standing in the church one is aware of the extreme thickness of the walls, this edifice was built to last. The line of an earlier roof is marked on the East face of the tower.

During the turbulent times of the Tudors, the Church changed its allegiance, first from the

I have taken information from various sources to compile this article on St Catherine's Parish Church. They are:

- *The Popular Guide to Suffolk Churches Bk2 by D P Mortlock.*
- *Various church documents supplied by Ringshall Parochial Church Council.*
- *A brochure, entitled A Short History of St Catherine's Parish Church, supplied by Ringshall Parochial Church Council and Suffolk Records Office.*

Pope to Henry VIII and Edward VI as supreme heads of the Church. Henry died on 28th January 1547 and the consumptive Edward died in 1553. The older daughter of Henry VIII then succeeded to the throne. Mary turned the Church again to Rome. With the death of Mary and the ascension of Elizabeth to the throne, the more protestant outlook returned which has continued to the present time.

The Second World War and the adjacent Royal Air Force Station at Wattisham sadly filled a new section of the churchyard with the flower of the youth of that Service to whose memory we can only give our heartfelt thanks for their splendid and heroic defence of this country. In the older part of the churchyard, names recur of many distinguished residents whose descendants are still living in the village, or nearby hamlets today.

It is said that a painting existed on the wall above the South door which was supposed to have depicted the "Seven works of Mercy". No trace of this can now be found at the present time, but about the middle of the last century a description of its appearance was given in a certain publication.

St Catherine's Church is a very small but very appealing building. Because of its age, we get a feeling of strength and continuity. It stands alone surrounded by farmland, erect, proud and honourable. Let us hope this lovely church is preserved for posterity.

Notes of Interest Re: St. Catherine's Church

The church has nave with centre aisle, chancel, tower at west end. Vestry under tower. South porch. The porch was restored in 1974 in memory of Mrs Last, former headmistress of the local village school.

- *BUILDING MATERIALS* Flint with stone cornices, copings etc. Roof of red tile. There is cement rendering to many parts of exterior walls. Interior walls are all plaster. Floors are of concrete and tiles.

- *APPROXIMATE DATE OF VARIOUS PARTS* Norman onwards. Tower and slit windows and south door arch are Norman. Roof to Nave is 14th century, to Chancel is 16th century. The present structure is therefore 12th to 16th century.

- The maintenance and repair of the whole church is the responsibility of the Church Council.

- The Department of the Environment gave a grant of £6,045 on 25th September, 1979 towards major repairs to the Tower, etc.

The organ is a small, one manual instrument (no pedals). A "Cassons patent" by Positive Organ Co. of London W1. There are foot pedals, but an electric blower mechanism is now fitted.

- *PICTURES* Black and white print of "Light of the World", on the North wall. Two pictures given July 1981 by Mrs Mary Cobbold, a) "the Pilgrim's Journey", b) The "Broad and Narrow Way".

- The churchyard surrounds the church, although mainly to the north-east. It is approximately two acres and is surrounded by a hawthorn hedge for which the church is responsible. There is a right of way along the approach road leading down to the Battisford-Ringshall road. This was given to the church in exchange for the original right of way that used to lead to the church through the grounds of Ringshall Hall. The new section of the churchyard (about half an acre), was consecrated on 5th June, 1942. The access road was made with a part grant from East Suffolk County Council.

- *STAINED GLASS WINDOWS*
  East Window "To the Glory of God and in memory of Charles Frederick Parker, MA, Rector 1819-1870". Two panels with tracery above. Depict the risen Christ, one panel with the Angel, the other with Mary.

  South (Chancel) Window "To the Glory of God and in memory of Edward L. Hesp, Died June 18th, 1870. Two panels with tracery above. Depict Christ, one as the Good Shepherd, one in the setting of Revelation 3, verse 20.

- *MEMORIAL TABLETS AND LEDGER SLABS*
  (In brass)　In memory of Elizabeth, the beloved wife of the Rev C. F. Parker, Rector of this parish. Eldest daughter of the late Rev Joseph Eyre, and the affectionate mother of two surviving sons. Trusting in her Redeemer, she died in Torquay, May 4th, 1856 aged 72 years. (North wall of Sanctuary).

  (In marble)　Near this place are interred the bodies of Mrs Elizabeth Watson, daughter of Josiah Bullock of Faulkbourn Hall, Essex wife of Jonathan Watson of Bury St Edmunds who died June 20th, 1763 in the 38th year of her age; leaving to her afflicted husband and seven orphans the inconsolable regret of so great a loss.

  Also on November 7th, 1803 were here deposited the remains of the said Jonathan Watson, Esq, FRS formerly one of His Majesty's Justices of the Peace Deputy Lieutenant for this county, and Major of the East Suffolk Militia, who died 31st October, 1803 in the 84th year of his age.

	Also two of their children, George and Ann. The former died November 12th, 1766 aged 6. The latter died December 13th, 1766 aged 7.
(In brass)	To John Willis (South wall – Lancet window). Died 18th October, 1982. This Lancet window was restored in 1985.
(In brass)	To Harold Dagley (South wall – in vestry). Died 16th January, 1982. Tower access was provided 1983.

In memory of...Alfred G. Gooderham, and William E. Palmer. For many years churchwardens of this church.

In memory of...Mr W. E. Palmer. For many years churchwarden of this church.

In memory of...Violet K. Gibbons 1981.

In memory of...Mrs Elizabeth Hobson who died at Stoke Farm, Ringshall on 26th August, 1944 aged 79 years.

In memory of...Kenneth Gordon Allardice, aged 21 years. Missing 15th December, 1940 while serving as a bomber pilot in the RAFVR.

In memory of...Anna Maria Partridge, Stoke Farm, Ringshall. Aged 89 years. 1957.

In memory of...Zoe Mullett who died 1990 (Curtains by south chancel door).

There are four memorial stones set in the Vestry floor. Two stones are dedicated to members of the Chapman family, one stone is dedicated to William Peppen, Clerk, who died in March, 1789 aged 68 years. The inscription on the fourth stone is unclear.

NOTE: All the aforementioned information came from the Ringshall "Terrier and Inventory". Supplied by Clare Secret, Churchwarden.

Ringshall Church and
'Wire' Pond - 1948

Rectors of St. Catherine's Church, Ringshall

- *NOTE: These dates are believed to be correct.*

  When the names of two rectors occur in the same year, one was of the Free Chapel, (remains of which can be seen in grounds of Chapel Farm, Ringshall)

  *This list of rectors obtained from the **Ipswich Record Office**.*

Rector	Year
Robertus Pres: de Ringesela	1200 AD
John de Cokefield	1306
William de Redemelde }	1318
John de Thetford }	
William Aylmer	1320
Roger de Downe	1361
John Elys }	1390
Thomas Andimer }	
Thomas Bose	1402
John Joneson }	1414
William Benet }	
William Jenkel	1419
John Grey	1420
John Springold	1437
Roger Boorne }	1497
William Baker }	
Thomas Peerson	1504
Robert Bossall	1514
Robert Bossall	1572
William Cage	1576
William Keble	1611
George Peppen	1659
James Peppen	1689
William Peppen	1707
William Malkin	1741
William Peppen	1744
Thomas Hay	1789
Henry Rowe	1790 died 2 Sept 1819
Charles Parker – Pembroke College, Oxford	1819
Parsonage rebuilt	**1820**
Edward William Hawkins	1878 AD
Edward Hawkins	1878 – 1906 AD
G. Cuthbert Blaxland	1907 – 1926
C. V. Taylor	1926 – 1932
John Vincent-Fernie	1932 – 1947
Haydn Price-Jones	1947 – 1969
John Youden-Duffie	1969 – 1971
Hugh Cartwright	1971 – 1975
Brian Short	1975 – 1978
Harry Chapman	1978 – 1993
Christine (Kit) Gray	1994 –

From "The East Anglian Miscellany" – 1910
Ringshall Church Registers

QUOTE: These entries from the Ringshall registers show the feeling of the Rector, and perhaps of the people, too, with respect to the Prayer Book ...

The Rev. W. Keble, B.D., Rector 1600-1659.
1645   The Prayer Book forbidden
1649   The Great Rebellion (1649)
1660   (May 29) The Restoration
1662   The Prayer Book ordered

- Rev W Keble, appointed in reign of James I, confirmed to the commonwealth, but evidently continued a Royalist at heart.

- John Bird was buried May 20, 1660, B.C.P.

Interior of St. Catherine's Church - 12th November 1978. Photograph by Jim Staines of Hadleigh. Church records

- John Bartlett of Brissett, and Anna Robinson, of Woolpit, were married in Ringshall Church May the last 1660, B.C.P.
- James, son of Richard Manning, and Elizabeth, his wife was buried in Ringshall churchyard July 28, 1660, B.C.P.

These three B.C.P. were added in different ink, showing that the Prayer Book had already begun to be used.

- John, the son of William Balderge, and Susan, his wife, was baptised in Ringshall church at ye font by the Book of Common prayer, May ye 10, 1660.
- Further entries added to "by ye B.C.P." until Oct. 1662, when the new Prayer Book was authorised. UNQUOTE

By H H Bartrum, Alpheton Rectory

CONTRIBUTED BY THE REV. KIT GRAY

There has probably been a church at Ringshall for most of the past Millennium, parts of the present church building can be dated back to around 1175, and there is evidence of a building prior to that. For all those years the church has been a centre for worship and celebration, for local and national thanksgiving and mourning. It has marked the significant moments in the life of individuals and of the village, and so the church registers and the churchyard record much of the village's history: the coming and goings of families, the arrival of the RAF and so on.

The Rectory was originally the house now named 'The Grange'. The 'Old Rectory' was built in 1949 and housed the rector until about 1978. It was then considered 'unsuitable', ie, too run down and too large to manage, and the then rector, Harry Chapman, moved to Barking. Over recent years the parish has shared the rector with various sets of local parishes, such as Little Finborough, Great Bricett, Battisford and Barking.

My arrival in 1994 marked even more changes. The unofficial parish group now comprises Battisford, Great Bricett, Ringshall, Willisham and Offton. A new Rectory has been built at Willisham. And I am a woman!

I have now been in ministry for nearly 25 years. I began as a Lay Worker, then Deaconess, in Huddersfield, West Yorkshire. I was ordained Deacon in 1987, whilst assistant Chaplain to Nottingham University. I then moved to Suffolk, to

The Rector of St. Catherine's, Kit Gray officiating at the Baptism of James Walters, son of Ian and Susan Walters

Rushmere, on the outskirts of Ipswich from where I was eventually priested in 1994, together with twenty-one other women. Shortly afterwards I was appointed here.

Although I grew up in London, I had spent nearly every school holiday with a family in the country and it is where I am most happy. I don't pretend to understand all the rural issues of our day, but I am interested in them and committed to the best of rural life.

Like many villagers I am nostalgic about the days when every parish had its vicar wandering around, and knowing everyone (and possibly interfering in everything!). I wish I had the time to do that; instead I regret having to rush around so much. But then I notice that most other people are doing the same. We cannot turn the clock back. Most of us now have cars and use them. Increased mobility brings with it increased opportunities; we can all have more than enough to fit into one week, and choices have to be made. Life appears to be a lot faster now; and it can be less secure. We are told that people are likely to keep changing their careers, and possibly their partners. Nothing is certain.

One change is that the church is no longer at the centre of village life in Ringshall, that role is now taken by the new village hall. However the church is still valued as a centre of faith and worship. Thanks to its faithful members, it is kept open, and used regularly on Sundays. It is the scene of larger celebrations at Harvest and Christmas and the place where children are baptised, people are married and the dead are laid to rest, alongside the countless generations that have gone before.

The church is a witness to eternal values, a sign that God does not change and his love for us is never ending. I am pleased to be a part of it and privileged to share in the life of the village, and in the lives of those who live here.

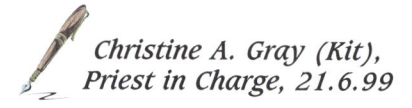

Christine A. Gray (Kit),
Priest in Charge, 21.6.99

For King and Country – Parish of Ringshall (Church Plaque)

A record of the names of the men of this Parish who served their country in H.M. Forces during the Great War 1914-1919.

(It must be noted that although there was a cessation of hostilities on November 11th, 1918 (Armistice Day), the Treaty was signed on 28th June, 1919 in the Palace of Versailles, between Germany and the Allies which terminated the war of 1914-1918. This explains the date on the church plaque. The Royal Palace of Versailles was built by Louis XIII and XIV).

Robert **BARTON**
Bertie **BARTON**
Wilfred **BARTON**
Shadrach **BARTON**
Christopher **BARTON**
Ewan Christopher **BLAXLAND**
John **BUTTON**
Frederick **CALEY**
Walter **CALEY**
John **EMSDEN**
Walter Ernest **FRANCIS**
Thomas William **FRANCIS**
John William **GAME** †
Frederick Robert **GERRARD**
Thomas Willie **GIBBONS**

Percy Wilfred **GOODCHILD**
Bailey Arthur **GOODCHILD**
Bertie Benjamin **GOODCHILD**
Edward Frank **HALL**
Clement **HITCHCOCK**
Stanley W. H. **HOLDER**
Calab T. O. **HOLDER**
Harold Noble **LONG**
George **MOWLES**
James **MOWLES**
Walter **MOYES**
William **MOYES**
Arthur **SPARKES**
Walter Jack **THORPE**
Ernest Edward **WASPE** †

Note: *The cross denotes those who died.*

For King and Country – Parish of Ringshall

A record of the names of the men of this parish who served their country in H.M. Forces during the 1939-1945 war.

The Second World War ended on 7th May, 1945. The Japanese war ended on 15th August, 1945.

Eddie **FELLINGHAM**	Ronnie **SMITH**
John **GIBBONS**	Francis **THOMPSON**
Bill **KEEBLE**	Frank **THORPE**
Albert **LAST**	John **THORPE**
Clifford **LAST**	Felix **WILDEN**
Jack **SMITH**	

The following names are of service personnel who died during the 1914-1918 and 1939-1945 wars:

First World War 1914-1918
From the Parish of Ringshall:
  Gunner **WASPE**, Royal Field Artillery
  Naval Rating J. W. **GAME**, Royal Naval Division

Second World War 1939-1945
From the Royal Air Force, Wattisham:
  Flight Sergeant **BRAY**
  Sergeant **BROADLEY** (Royal New Zealand Air Force)
  Aircraftman **BETTS**
  Aircraftman **DAVISON**
  Sergeant **GILMORE**
  Warrant Officer **GRAVES** (Royal Canadian Air Force)
  Sergeant **HUMPHREY** (Royal Canadian Air Force)
  Flight Sergeant **LLOYD** (Royal Australian Air Force)
  Flying Officer **MACE**
  Sergeant **MARTIN**
  Sergeant **RICHARDSON**
  Sergeant **WHITFIELD**

The following names are of service personnel who have died since 1945 and are buried in Ringshall churchyard:

Flying Officer **ADAM**
Flight Sergeant **ALLEN**
Flight Lieutenant **BAKER**
Senior Aircraftman **BUSHELL**
Chief Technician **DAVIS**
Flying Officer **DERWIN**
Flying Officer **ENGLAND**
Flight Lieutenant **FOULKS**
Flying Officer **GARSIDE**
Flight Lieutenant **HATCH**
Flying Officer **LAW**
Senior Aircraftman **LAWFORD**
Corporal **MUNRO**
Flight Lieutenant **MURDOCK**
Staff Sergeant Anthony Paul **NICHOLS**
Flying Officer **OGG**
Flight Lieutenant **ORR**
Sergeant **RICE**
Chief Technician **WAITE**
Leading Aircraftman **WELSH**
Flight Lieutenant **WOOD**

NOTE: The parents of Flying Officer England present Ringshall Church with a pedestal arrangement of flowers every Christmas in memory of their son.

Local Marriages 1786 – 1961

Thomas Brown **SCOTT** and Rachel Letita **MANN**, both of Ringshall . . . . 14th Feb. 1786

John **WILLIAMS** of Stonham Parva, and Sarah Ann **HAYWARD** of Ringshall . . . . 9th Nov. 1841

Henry Edward **MOORE** of Bricett and Sophia **HAYWARD** of Ringshall. . . . . 6th Oct. 1846

Charles **CRACKNELL** of Paddington (Mx.) and Jane **COOPER** of Ringshall, minor . . . . 9th Dec. 1846

William **BAKER** of Combs and Elizabeth **MEAKENS** of Ringshall. . . . . 28th Oct. 1847

John **HITCHCOCK** and Maria **BLYTH**, both of Ringshall . . . . . . 19th Dec. 1849

Jonathan **COOPER** and Elizabeth **ROUSE**, both of Ringshall . . . 26th May 1851

John Long of **MILDEN**, and Sarah **MAKENS** of Ringshall. . . . . . 1st Aug. 1853

Jonathan **LAFLIN** and Mary **OTTEWIL**, widow, both of Ringshall .18th Oct. 1853

Jonathan **LAFLIN** of Ringshall and Sarah **MULLEY** of Lt. Stonham . . . . 17th Nov. 1859

Henry Percival **CHENERY** of Offton, widower,
and Marianne **MEAKINS** of Ringshall .... 5th June 1860

George Creasy **GOODERHAM** of Barking and Emma **MEAKINS**
of Ringshall... 15th Oct. 1864

William Hayward **BAKER** of Combs and Maria **HAYWARD**
of Ringshall... 3rd July 1865

Spencer Thomas **CRACKNELL** of Wickham Market and
Louisa **HAYWARD** of Ringshall........................... 16th Feb. 1867

Thomas Farrar **PERKINS** of Baylham and
Sophia Elizabeth **HAYWARD** of Ringshall .... 27th Dec. 1867

William **HATTEN** of Gt Finborough and Esther **COOPER**
of Ringshall, minor .... 7th July 1874

Maggie **HOBSON** of Ringshall and Harry John **ROME** of
All Saints, Basingstoke (Ha.).......................... 28th Mar. 1923

Leslie Edward **LILLISTONE** of Stowmarket and
Freda Rosamund **GOODING** of Ringshall .... 30th Apr. 1943

Kenneth Charles **WILDING** of Stowmarket, widower,
and Florence Winifred **PALMER** of Ringshall .... 13th Sept. 1944

Edward Thomas Peter **ASTBURY** of St. Aidens, Carlisle,
County Cumberland, and Katherine Joyce **GIBBONS**
of Ringshall .... 11th Nov. 1948

Frank Stanley **LAFLIN**, and Betty Alice **WASPE**
both of Ringshall..................................... 20th Dec. 1951

Brian Thomas **KEELING** of Gt Bricett, and
Elenore Maria Josephine **HAUKE** of Detmond, West Germany
married in Ringshall Church .... 11th Mar. 1959

Joseph **NIXON** of Seaton, County Cumberland, minor,
and Janet Gertrude **RISEBROW**, minor of Ringshall ..... 27th Mar. 1961

NOTE: *The aforementioned taken from Survey of Parish Records
– Suffolk Record Office – Ipswich Branch, County Hall, Ipswich.
March, 1979. Supplied by Clare Secret, Churchwarden, Ringshall.*

This is a copy of a letter, in part, from the Home Office to the Vicar of the Church of St Catherine, concerning the removal of German remains interred in the local churchyard. Date of letter 11 October 1962.

"Sir

With reference to the Home Office letter of 8th November, 1966, about the Agreement concluded between the Government of the United Kingdom and the Government of the German Federal Republic regarding German war graves in the United Kingdom. I am directed by the Secretary of State to say that the Volksbund have now begun the work of removal from burial grounds in England and Wales and to send you a copy of the licence and relevant schedule which has been issued for the removal of the remains at present interred in the burial ground(s) under your control."

The following is a copy of a letter from Volksbund Deutsche Kriegsgraberfursorge (German War Graves Commission). Date of letter 16th November 1962 to Rev' Price-Jones.

"Dear Sir

With reference to the letter (LA/1) of August 1962 addressed to you from our headquarters in Maidenhead, I have to inform you that we hope to effect the exhumation and removal of the remains of German servicemen in Ringshall during the period 19th to the 25th November, 1962.

A representative of this Commission will contact you personally or by telephone at least two days prior to the commencement of the work of exhumation, and I would be most grateful if you would then notify the relevant medical officer of health.

The only name mentioned is that of P SCHMIDT who died 25th February, 1941."

From "The East Anglian Miscellany" – 1910

Ringshall Church Registers

The following is an entry from the registers of Ringshall Church.

QUOTE: The ancient and most reverend Divine, Mr William Keble, Bachelor in Divinity, and Fellow of St. Benedict's College in Cambridge, Rector of Ringshall by the space of fifty years and upwards, being four score and one years of age, who was a Pastor most faithful in the service of his master Jesus Christ, most loyal to his Prince, very peaceable and exemplary amongst his parishioners, very pitiful and charitable towards the poor, very charitable to strangers, and most courteous to all honest-minded men, finished his natural life the sixteenth day of February between an eleven and twelve of the clock in the night, and was buried February the 18th, 1659. And his funeral sermon and Christian burial were dispensed by Mr Fairfax, Minister of Barking. UNQUOTE

*The above was compiled by **H H Bartrum**.*
Modern translation.

From "The East Anglian Miscellany" – 1910

Ringshall Church Registers

QUOTE: Mr George Peppen, Master of Arts of Queenes Colledge, Cambridge, Rector of Tobdock (Copdock), and Vicar of Washbrooke, under the Patronage of the Right Worshipful Thomas Bedingfield, of Darsham, in the Countie of Suffolk, Knight, succeeded his Father-in-law, Mr William Keble, by the marriage of his daughter, Susan (who by his last Will and Testament bequeathed the Advowsioner, Patronage, right of Patronage, nomination, gifts, P'sentation and of all disposition of the Rectory of the Parish Church of Ringshall in Suffolk, to his daughter, Susan) immediately after his decease. UNQUOTE

*The above was compiled by **H H Bartrum**.*

The Rev. J. Youden-Duffie, Rector of St Catherine's Church, Ringshall, in 1969, showing a display of Dutch tulips, cheeses and pottery, arranged in one of the church windows, part of the church's Tulip Festival, to Mrs D. R. Maddock, wife of the Bishop of Dunwich, right, and Mrs R. C. Riches, secretary to the church council

Admiring the blooms, are, left to right, Mrs K. Goodchild, Mrs E. Coleman and Mrs G. Goodchild

Quite a few familiar faces here! Outside St Catherine's Church, 1998
(Photograph taken by Peter Watson, Lower Farm Road, Ringshall)

3
Ringshall Village Hall

We are very privileged in Ringshall to have a most attractive village hall, situated on the Village Green. Let us trace its beginning in prose and photographs, which hopefully will bring back memories to all who helped in its planning and construction.

A few points to note....

- The site was presented to the village on a hundred year lease by C G Hitchcock & Son, who also cleared the site and laid the car park.

- The hard core and stone for the car park was donated by Wattisham airfield, who at the time were converting the airfield from RAF to Army Air Corps use.

- The sum of £18,000 was raised from the sale of the original village hall to Mr John Alborough (the former owner); the property has now been sold on to the Hitchcock family.

- The Village Hall Management Committee (which was formerly The Amenities Fund) and the local people of Ringshall raised between £2,000 and £3,000 by various fund raising events.

- £10,000 and the interest derived from this sum was bequeathed to the village towards a new hall by a local benefactor.

- Mid Suffolk District Council made a grant of £36,666.

- Suffolk County Council through their Suffolk Provision to Assist Rural Communities scheme gave a grant of £5,504.

- Ringshall Parish Council gave £39,000 (money which was collected via the parish precept over a number of years for this purpose).

- 'Rural Action' gave a grant of £1,300 towards the landscaping.

The upper part of the sign was the handiwork of Alison Card.

The hall was built by Seamans of Stowmarket. Work started on 21 March 1994. The date stone was laid on 21 May 1994. Construction was completed by the end of September, followed by furious painting and kitchen fitting by the villagers.

Spot Len and Gwen Le Grice – both former members of the Amenities Fund Committee

The Building Of Ringshall Village Hall – Opened 22 October 1994

The photographs and captions supplied by David Secret, trace the construction of the new Hall from the empty playing field (village green).

The site (the old Hall can be seen to the right of the white houses)

It all started here....

And it's too late to move it now!

.......nearly there!

District Councillor Tuffy Turner pauses from his enjoyment of a glass of wine long enough to lay the date stone

31

Head teacher of the local school, Mrs Sally Green, brought some of her pupils along to place a time capsule under the floor of the new Hall. Pupils and staff made the capsule, which contains photographs of the school, lists of contemporary music, pieces of school projects and pencils; to show what life was like in 1994.

Pupils of Ringshall School place their time capsule

Mid Suffolk Councillor Tuffy Turner looking very jolly in a colourful suit, joined Mr Graham Card, Chairman of the Village Hall Management Committee, for the block laying ceremony. The local residents of Ringshall clearly enjoyed the Opening Ceremony carried out with great aplomb by Tuffy Turner on 22 October 1994.

Spot Robert Willis – he was chairman of the Parish Council when work started and had the honour of signing the Contract

Village Hall Opening

The hall was opened on Saturday 22 October 1994 by Councillor Tuffy Turner, and marked the beginning of a celebratory week of events.

Most people paid attention to what was being said...

Part of the gathering at the official opening

Some hinted that it was time for the food!

The gentleman in the red shirt was Lewis Hart, the Contract Manager of Seamans (Builders)

Were you there?

District Councillor, Tuffy Turner and his princess perform the official opening

33

The Old Village Hall
Compiled by Paul Laflin of 8 Coronation Glebe, Ringshall

The following text and photographs showing the old Village Hall were compiled by Paul Laflin. He has produced his own very interesting and well researched 'History of 4 Buildings in Ringshall', and has kindly given permission for certain extracts to be shown in this book. Paul's research into local history was carried out while still a pupil at Ringshall School. The Laflin family have lived in this village for many generations and Paul is undoubtedly very proud of his ancestral lineage.

The old Village Hall – circa 1993

Old Village Hall

In 1874 a school was held in the premises purchased by the rector and parishioners and was attended by 40 children. By 1891 the school was attended by 22 children. In 1896 the school was attended by 48 children and a Miss Sarah Curtis was head mistress.

My Great Nan who is 88 attended Ringshall School in 1911. At Ringshall School religious education was taught every day and they knew the Bible off by heart. The attendance by 1912 was only 20 children. When a bigger school was needed the building was turned into the Parish Rooms. The Parish Rooms became the Village Hall in 1979. Toilet facilities were improved and general repairs were made.

Hadleigh Weekly News 8.12.78
A newspaper cutting speaking of a Parish Council meeting
and the decision that the Parish Rooms are to become the Village Hall.

Parish room to be village hall

AT a recent meeting of Ringshall Parish Council, it was announced that completion of the purchase of the parish room from the parochial church council will take place on January 2.

After that date, provisions will be made by the parish council to effect improvements by providing toilet facilities and general repairs of this property to make it suitable as a village hall.

This is a picture showing the original fireplace

In 1994 the Parish Council sold the property to John Alborough who has converted it into an office.

This picture shows the original brick walls and the fact the village hall was built on a dirt floor and had no footings

35

Bennetts Farmhouse

Bennetts Farmhouse is situated on Bildeston Road, Ringshall. It was built in the 15th or early 16th century.

> **This is a description of the Farmhouse. I found it at the Records Office in Ipswich.**
>
> TM 05 SW   RINGSHALL   Bildeston Road
> 5/158   Bennetts Farmhouse
> 1.10.85   Grade II
>
> House, C15 or early C16 with C17 and C19 alterations. 1 storey and attics. 3-cell plan. Timber-framed: the front wall encased in mid C19 red brick, other walls plastered. Thatched roof, half-hipped at left hand end. Axial C17 chimney of red brick. One C19 gabled casement dormer. C19 small-plane casements and boarded entrance door. A central open hall has had its open truss removed, but most of the smoke-blackened coupled-rafter roof remains; there is evidence for a former crownpost system. The right hand cell also has a smoke-blackened roof, suggesting that the partition wall was not of full height. An inserted floor in the hall and a chimney in the former cross-passage are C17 alterations. Framing largely concealed.

The farmhouse was originally owned by the Fowler Trust. Members of the Laflin family have occupied Bennetts Farmhouse for many years. When looking at the censors records we found that many Laflin families lived in Ringshall and as the censor records for villages do not contain street or house names we relied mostly on family information for this report.

This picture shows what the house looks like now

In 1896 an Oliver Laflin, a local farmer lived in Ringshall. His family tree:-

OLIVER (Husband)   **JANE** (Wife)

CHARLES (Son)   **PHILIP** (Son)

SALLY (Daughter)   **SARAH** (Daughter)   **MILLICENT** (Daughter)

He would have been my great, great grandfather. During the 1900s his son Philip lived in Bennetts Farmhouse. Philip's family tree:-

PHILIP (Husband)   **KATE** (Wife)

ARCHIE (Son)   **MAY** (Daughter)   **GEORGE** (Son)

BESSIE (Daughter)   **FRANK** (Son)   **ANNIE** (Daughter)

VIOLI (Daughter)   **BERTIE** (Son)   **KENNETH** (Son)

ROLAND (Son)   **MOLLY** (Daughter)

Many Laflins are buried in Ringshall churchyard This is a picture of Philip and his wife Kate's gravestone

Philip was a farmer on the land. He would have been my Great grandfather. Philip and his wife brought his family up in Bennetts Farmhouse. Philip died in 1961 and when his wife Kate died in 1969 two of their sons, Kenneth & Roland continued to live in the farmhouse. Kenneth died in 1984. Roland and his sister Molly bought Bennetts Farmhouse in 1987. Roland died in 1991. The house is now owned by Molly, my Great Aunt. The house has had many changes and doesn't look anything like it would originally.

My family tree:-

My Great, Great Grandfather	OLIVER & JANE
My Great Grandfather	PHILIP & KATE
My Grandfather	BERTIE & BERYL
My Dad	STEPHEN & ROSEMARY
Me and My Brother	PAUL & GARY

4
School Days through the Years

This is an extract from the *"East Anglian Daily Times"*, dated 25th October 1983

The School days of Mr H. Gooch at the "Old Schoolhouse", Ringshall

In his own words it reads as follows:

"I went to a small school in Ringshall where there were two women teachers. I learned to read, write and do arithmetic the hard way with one teacher, while the other taught and cared for the five year old pupils.

Discipline was very strict, children had the cane for "simple things we did wrong" such as copying from the child at the next desk.

To write we used slate pencils, ink wells were fitted to desks. We were not allowed to speak to one another during lessons and had the cane if we were late for school. Some had long distances to walk. I had to walk four miles to school.

My mother had no sympathy if we got the cane – she said we must have deserved it!"

The old school at Ringshall, circa 1899

Mrs Daisy Steward – Deputy Head
Ringshall Primary 1952-1967

Mrs Daisy Steward was born in Westerfield but her parents then moved to Needham Market. In 1939 her parents had a bungalow built in Barking and named their new home "Broad Oaks". It must have been one of the last properties constructed in the area before the advent of the Second World War when all private building came to an abrupt halt. Mrs Steward moved into this bungalow with her husband on the death of her parents, and she lives there to this day.

She always wanted to teach, and commenced her career in a school in Dagenham, Essex. Her mother subsequently became seriously ill, and she managed to obtain a teaching post at Barham School. After a spell at the primary school at Hintlesham, she got married in 1935. Her new husband firmly believed that wives should stay at home, but fate intervened only two weeks after the wedding. The head mistress of Great Bricett school was taken ill, and her husband asked Mr Steward if his wife would like to take her place for a few days. This she duly did, but unfortunately, the head mistress died unexpectedly and Mrs Steward stayed for the continuation of the term. She continued her career as a 'supply' teacher to various schools until 1941 when her only son, Peter, was born. She left to devote herself to husband, son and home for the next eleven years.

In 1952 she decided it would be a suitable time to pick up her teaching career. She obtained a post at Barking school, but was only there for one term when she was asked to go as Deputy Head at the new primary school at Ringshall under the headship of Mrs Barber. Mrs Steward was to stay here until her eventual retirement fifteen years later.

During her years in this school she taught 1,729 children. Many adults in the area remember her still, and she often gets warm acknowledgements when meeting former pupils.

When the school took in its first pupils in September, 1952 it consisted of four classrooms, but later a large extra room was built onto the back of the school, and eventually two portable classrooms were added. The school was growing fast. Pupils came from Ringshall, Wattisham, Great Bricett and Offton.

Mrs Steward is a firm believer in the Early Morning Assembly, and daily scripture lessons. The discipline at Ringshall school was very good and the cane very rarely used.

She remembers a little Polish girl from Wattisham called Christine Halque. Her parents at the time could hardly speak English, but their daughter managed to get a scholarship. Mrs Steward noticed that this little girl would always clap her hands together and say a short prayer over her food when she collected her plate, and also when she sat down at the table. When Mrs Steward remarked on this, Christine replied that her parents were living in the town of Cracow in Poland when the Germans invaded. During that time, life was very hard for the people, and such awful privation is never forgotten. The family felt their survival was a miracle from God, and every day they said their prayers and thanked the Lord for all the good things in their lives. The more fortunate of us do take the good things in life for granted. Another former pupil went on to become a highly qualified teacher in Dorset and appeared on television in "Mastermind" with Magnus Magnusson.

On her retirement in December 1967, Mrs Steward received gifts from the managers, parents and pupils. On behalf of the parents and managers, Mrs Clement Hitchcock presented her with a suitcase, and on behalf of the children she was presented with a tea service from the Headmaster, Mr Hart. The suitcase was very handy as Mrs Steward and her husband spent the next few years travelling extensively.

Mrs Steward was a joy to talk to and my time with her 'flew by'. She was delighted to talk about Ringshall School and it was obvious she felt great affection for the school and the numerous pupils she taught. She has suffered some ill health in the last few years, but her interest in the world around her remains undiminished. We had a few chuckles over her reminiscences, and although she claimed her memory was not so good now, I found her stories and anecdotes belied this statement. My afternoon with her was thoroughly enjoyable.

Could this be lunch time?

By Lisa Cresswell of Stowmarket

Barking Village School

This photograph featured here with the accompanying letter, was submitted by Mr. Ernie Thorpe of Home Farm, Barking to the East Anglian Daily Times, Monday 9th December, 1991.

"Sir, this photograph is of Barking School boys over 60 years ago. Headgear is strategically placed for instant donning after the "photo call". This avoided falling victim to a malady referred to as "the pip", although one or two hardy souls who discounted hats never seemed to fall victim.

An incident illustrating the "pip" theory occurred during an annual school "treat" to Felixstowe. I was sitting by the bus driver, Mr Kerridge, and emulating him, removed my cap. Mother from the rear of the bus quickly passed word for me to reinstate my headgear.

Those who went without head-covering in this era were referred to as the "Hatless brigade".

"Where did you get that hat?" was in the Top Ten."

A group of school boys at
Barking Village School – 1925

Philip Hamblett (centre, with
tie), Wilfred Hamblett
(second right, with tie), Felix
Wilden (fifth from left)

A group of boys at
Barking Village
School – 1927

Ringshall Primary School

Ringshall Primary School was
opened in September 1952.
The final cost was £45,000
(forty-five thousand pounds).
Front view

Ringshall Primary
School.
Back view

Tea in the New School to Celebrate the Coronation – 1953

(Far left – from bottom) Maureen Wilden, Jack Thorpe (father to Frank and John Thorpe), Frank Thorpe, Anne Thorpe (Frank's wife), Mr George Grimwood.
(Middle – from bottom) Ada Braybrook, Arthur Braybrook, ?, John Thorpe, ?, ?, Arthur Coleman (Ted's father), Ted Coleman.
(Far right – from bottom) Pauline Gibbons, Brian Gibbons, Wendy Gibbons, Derek Quinton, Jimmy Wilden

This photograph shows some of the pupils at Ringshall School in July 1954 enjoying a well earned break in the sunshine

Members of staff at Ringshall School in the early years

From left: Mrs Ruegg, Mrs Rissi, Mrs Steward, Mrs Barker (Headmistress). The names of the members of staff at end of row cannot be recalled

Pupils at Ringshall Primary School – Circa 1968

Top Row L to R: Mr Bradley, ?, ?, Graham Spall, ?, Anne Coleman, Vanessa Keeling, Linda Wodsley, ?, Martin Webber
2nd Row L to R: ?, ?, Julie Cornforth, Karen Reeve, Rachel Vyvyen, ?, ?, Christopher Laflin, Stephen Wilson, ?, Jeremy Morphew
Bottom row L to R: ?, John Bates, ?, ?, ?, ?, ?, Elain Thorpe

Evening Star - 27.3.1984
A newspaper cutting describing a visit to the fire station.

SEVENTEEN children from Ringshall visited the fire station at RAF Wattisham to learn about people who help others, in a visit arranged by their class teacher, Mrs Janet Ratcliffe. The children were shown the green fire engines, tried on helmets and helped the firemen put out a demonstration fire with several different types of extinguishers.

The Rev' Harry Chapman's retirement presentation at Ringshall School, October 1993

Scenes from the Christmas Fayre held at Ringshall School on Saturday 21 November 1998

Nobody sees the camera...

The arrival of Santa Claus

Mrs Sally Green, Headmistress, welcomes Santa Claus

Chloe and Emily Ford bid a final "goodbye" to Santa Claus

Gareth Roberts has a chat with Santa Claus

Ringshall School – Summer 1999

Ringshall School Fete – 19 June 1999

Elm Class

We danced at our summer fayre.
June 19th 1999

Years 3 and 4 doing the Numeracy Hour.
– *We are very good at mathematics*

Some characters and very clever children from Years 3 and 4

We all learn to swim at school.

– We like our old swimming pool. It is nearly 50 years old

Everyone at Ringshall School Summer 1999 except for Elm Class who were swimming

47

5
Historic Houses

Charles Hall

The following extract about the Manor of Charles Hall comes from "The Manors of Suffolk", Vol.2, by W. A. Copinger, MA, LLD, FSA, FRSA, (1908).

QUOTE: This was the Lordship of the Saxon Grim and of William de Burnoille under Roger Bigot at the time of the Domesday Survey.

In 1270 it was vested in Thomas Charles, a member of the Bentley family of this name, who had a grant of market and fair here at that date, and free warren in 1285. Amongst the Abbreviation of Pleas there is a finding in 1288 that Ranulph de la Wade de Rudgessale, William and Nicholas, his sons trespassed on the free warren of this Thomas Charles, at Ringshall, and the King had £11 for forfeiture in the said warren. In 1301 the manor was conveyed by deed poll from Sir William Charles to his son, Sir Edward Charles, Knt., who was succeeded in the lordship by his son and heir, William Charles. In 1339 William Charles, son of the last named William Charles, granted the reversion of the manor to Sir John de Stonore, Knt. The next we hear of the manor was that Henry Wentworth died seised of it in 1482, when it passed to his son and heir, Roger Wentworth. After vesting in one John Boxted it passed to Sir Richard Gresham, and on his death in 1548 went to his widow Isabella for life.

Charles Hall, Ringshall.
Photograph taken by Mr A Toomey of 3 Bakers Corner, Ringshall

She died in 1565, when the manor passed to Sir Richard's son, Sir Thomas Gresham, and from that time has passed in the same course as the main manor.

Charles Hall is a common farmhouse, with a chimney of early date and a moat. UNQUOTE

Now to the present "Charles Hall". This Suffolk farmhouse hasn't seen that many owners since the beginning of the nineteenth century. From 1811 to 1918 it was owned by the Rowley family of Holbecks, Hadleigh. From 1918 to 1946 it was in the ownership of Mr Herbert Gooding. He sold the property to Mr Leslie Chaplin in 1946, and it passed into the ownership of brothers Keith and Raymond Chaplin in 1975. Keith and his wife Rosemary now live there with their two children.

The entrance to "Charles Hall" as it is today – 29 June 1999

Ringshall House

Mr Luther Robinson arrived in Ringshall from Norfolk in 1940. He moved into Ringshall House, which is a Grade 2 listed building dating back to Tudor times (1485–1603), and has farmed here ever since.

He joined the small congregation at St Catherine's Church and became a church warden. His original intention was to hold this position for a fairly short time as he firmly believes that short tenures in public office are more advantageous to all concerned than overly long administrations.

Ringshall House Farm – A grade II listed farmhouse owned by Mr Luther Robinson

He ended up being warden for forty years.

The Reverend Price Jones is the first minister that Mr Robinson can remember, and he believes the church was without a clergyman for a few years, the services in the meantime being taken by a lay preacher.

A modern second farmhouse built in 1987 which is part of the farm

Having been without a rector for some time, the advent of the Reverend Price Jones was greeted by the villagers with pleasure. He came here as a young man in his mid twenties having been born in Wales of a farming family. He settled into community life very quickly and became very popular. He married a local girl, Miss Watson, from Laurel Farm, Hitcham. He stayed in Ringshall for twenty years before going to Horringer near Bury St Edmunds. He died in 1997. When the Reverend Price Jones left the area, he was followed by the Reverend Chapman who stayed for fifteen years and is now living in Wiltshire.

Mr Robinson is a firm believer that women should not be barred from high office and is pleased to see women entering the church.

Having spent decades nestling in the quiet countryside, the outbreak of the Second World War wreaked havoc on the church. Wattisham airfield was newly constructed and the flight path of the bombers was overhead. The tranquillity St Catherine's Church had always known was ended. The constant stream of planes throughout the war, and afterwards did much damage to the church. St Catherine's has needed much money for repairs, since the war particularly, and the community of Ringshall has always been willing to help raise the necessary funds. As in many small villages, the church is held in great affection. This doesn't mean the various ministers have had a "full house" for their sermons over the years. Apparently, even in the grim days of the 1939-1945 war, the congregation was very small, sometimes only eight people. Today the congregation is usually of a similar number. The church is also used by personnel at Wattisham. Children have been baptised here in its ancient font, and couples married here. In the churchyard lie the graves of British and Commonwealth airmen who have been killed, or died while serving on the Base during and since the war. The Church of St Catherine is never locked.

History of Ringshall House Farm

Formerly known as Hill House Farm, Great Bricett, but the house is now in the parish of Ringshall, so now known as Ringshall House.

The following information is taken from the title deeds ...

1795 — Farm part of a marriage settlement, settling land previously in the Bugg family of Stowmarket (only child and heir of William Bugg of Ringshall), on the marriage of Miss Mary Bugg to Mr John Stubbin of Higham, Suffolk.

1834 — Following death of Mrs Mary Stubbin (née Bugg), the farm was sold by her executor, Robert Partridge of Shelly Hall to Charles Partridge also of Shelly Hall.

1858 — Purchase of farm by Robert Makens of Ringshall, Suffolk from Charles Partridge.

1869 — Farm enfranchised by Robert Makens.

1871 — Conveyance by Robert Makens' executors to Walter Makens of Ringshall, Suffolk.

1913 — Bought by Maurice Wright of Whitton from the Makens family.

1932 — Acquired by William Hunt of Hill Farm, Needham Market.

1940 — Purchase by Luther Robinson of Hill House Farm, Ringshall from William Hunt.

1999 — Purchased by the Urshaw family from Luther Robinson.

The "Sitting Bull" – this photograph was taken in 1979 at Luther Robinson's farm

Ringshall Hall
Now the Home of Lesley and Mike Calame

Like so many of these distinctive, older houses, once inside the gate, visitors are very much aware of another time in our history, a more tranquil era.

Ringshall Hall is a picturesque and historic old manor house, Grade II listed, part brick, part stud and plaster built, with a lovely outlook over trees, lawn, and a large pond (Wire pond). The pond is now home to various species of ducks and geese also many grass snakes have been spied there. An air of quiet serenity is all prevailing.

The original property on this site was mentioned in the Domesday Book; the present house was built from the remains of the 18th century house that was somehow destroyed in 1788 (see historical facts at end of this text). However, many of the heavy, exposed timbers used in the beams and joists in the ceilings, walls, some of the large brick fireplaces, and oak panelling, were obviously retained from the former manor house which occupied the site in the 16th century. These timbers and beams are an excellent example of the carpentry of the period, 1530 to 1560.

One of the more famous residents of Ringshall Hall was Sir Thomas Gresham, who selected timber from the nearby woods for the construction of the Royal Exchange in 1565.

The house today stands in secluded grounds of approximately seven acres, with a large plantation of trees separating the site from St Catherine's Church. The

"What is on the menu today?" Lesley and Mike Calame in the grounds of their home, "Ringshall Hall"

area is certainly 'well timbered'. At one time Muckinger Wood was part of this estate, and was considered to be one of the most noted fox coverts in the district, covering 55.5 acres.

Once inside the oak front door, the visitor gets a good foretaste of things to come. The large entrance hall with its ancient fireplace, looked medieval. Two very large rooms lead off from the hall; one was probably the dining room, but apparently was used to store grain at one time (unbelievable!). It now houses a full size snooker table, which is proving very popular with friends and acquaintances.

Jo' and Mike Calame renovating fireplace in drawing room

The other large room would probably have been the drawing room. Did I spy an elegant chesterfield? How many people attended soirees in this room, I wonder? The men perhaps standing nonchalantly near the large brick fireplace, smoking their pipes; the women standing in groups exchanging gossip. Maybe the family dog would have lain nearby, having a well earned snooze!

A staircase, which is going to be restored leads to a landing with several spacious bedrooms. The first floor is being carefully renovated to blend in the old with the modern. The result should be spectacular!

The two, maybe three attic rooms (I lost count at this point), are being sensitively up-dated for modern day convenience; to the delight of Lesley and Mike's son, and two grandchildren who have designs on this upper storey.

Because the property is listed, all the restoration work has to be carefully carried out and inspected. From what I saw, this house is in very safe hands. Mike and Lesley know exactly what they are doing, and don't intend to take 'any short cuts' to make Ringshall Hall the house of their dreams.

At the beginning of their tenure of Ringshall Hall, and whilst they were abroad, their son and daughter discovered some old pieces of wooden framework dumped on one of the bedroom floors. Amazingly they had found the original panelling from one of the bedroom walls, which fitted in like the parts of a jigsaw puzzle, absolutely perfectly.

The large kitchen, with dark green Aga, is very comfortable, and has what was probably the large scullery leading off. Again, Lesley and Mike have skilfully blended in the ancient and modern, the result is delightfully cosy.

The intense renovation work has meant taking up floorboards in some rooms. Various small items have been discovered, such as sewing scissors, a 'finger bob' and an ivory comb. Under one floorboard were the words...

> "The owner of the Hall is mean
> with beer – Mr Sparrow (Bildeston) 1897"

Nothing of interest was found when the ponds were drained.

For Lesley and Mike the purchase of Ringshall Hall came about by chance. Mike was serving in the Royal Air Force in Germany and at that point in their lives, home was a modern neo-Georgian type house in Hampshire, when they were in England.

However, Mike had always dreamt of owning a property with quite a bit of land.....a fellow officer was busily going through sheaves of estate agents' brochures, looking for a home to buy back in 'dear old blighty'. Suddenly, Mike spied an interesting brochure sticking out of the waste paper basket. On closer inspection, his curiosity was aroused. He and Lesley decided to arrange a visit.

Reproduced by kind permission of Mr Ernie Thorpe. Ringshall Hall and grounds – photograph taken 1988

Driving through the main gate, Mike was entranced by the outlook over the large, wooded grounds, and the proximity of geese and ducks ambling contentedly across the lawns. It was magical. Turning to Lesley, he told her, "this is it, I want to live and retire here". At this point he hadn't even seen the house. Their minds firmly made up, the purchase was duly made. The Calame family had come to Suffolk.

Through her father, Lesley discovered her family, the Trussons, had Suffolk (Stowmarket area) connections, going back to the early 17th century. "No wonder I feel so at home here", she says cheerfully.

Their daughter Jo, and two grandchildren Alice and Katie, all live in Camberley, Surrey, Jo is a keen Marathon runner. Their son Andrew is a Serving Officer in the Royal Air Force, whilst serving as a Guard Commander on the Queens Colour Squadron he had the privilege of accepting the new Royal Air Force Colour from Her Majesty the Queen to mark the 75th Anniversary of the RAF. Andrew and his father, Mike, were one of the few father and son teams to see service in the Gulf war in 1990-1991. Mike's parents live in the old converted Tithe Barn, which is about 400 years old, and situated at the end of the curving driveway. When Mike and Lesley go away, his parents act as 'caretakers' looking after the house. Mike and Lesley's good friends Richard and Kathryn Martin from Creeting St Mary look after Tessa and Pep their two large black labradors.

Flight Lieutenant Andrew Calame of Ringshall Hall collecting the new RAF Colour from Her Majesty Queen Elizabeth II to mark the 75th Anniversary of The Royal Air Force. This ceremony took place on 1st April 1993

On finishing his formal education, Mike was an Aircraft Design Engineer for five years, he then joined the Royal Air Force where he flew fast jets and helicopters. He retired officially from the RAF on 31st October 1994, and his last tour of duty was as Commandant of the Royal Air Force Winter Survival School based in Oberammergau, Bavaria.

Nine and a half hours after his retirement he was offered the chance to do the same job, but this time as a civilian. He accepted before he even knew the terms of employment. He is again due to retire on 30th May, 1999 ......However!

Mike and Lesley have had the good luck to meet the descendants of some of the previous incumbents.

Mr and Mrs Hall from Scotland visited Ringshall Hall two years ago in order to see where their ancestor had lived (and died), in the 18th century (see historical facts at end of this text). They were thrilled when they discovered the grave of Elizabeth Bullock who lived in the Hall with her husband, John Watson, sometime in the 1730s. Elizabeth bore five children of whom three survived until adulthood, and went to live in America.

Mr and Mrs Hayward arrived from Perth, Australia, three years ago hoping to trace their ancestors. They too, were thrilled when they discovered Thomas Hayward had lived in the Hall. Thomas Hayward was born at Honnington, Suffolk on 1st September, 1832, and was the eldest of five children born to Squire and Mrs Hayward of Ringshall Hall (see historical facts at end of this text). Mrs Hayward was the daughter of Squire Canler.

William Hitchcock bought the farm for his son Rowland in 1925. Financial returns from farming were getting less, so the Long family decided to sell. The whole property was sold for ten pounds per acre. This included the farm, farmhouse, large tithe barn, set of farm buildings, and sixty acres of woodland.

'Rowley' Hitchcock engaged a very reliable man, George Worledge as head horseman. He would arrive for work every morning at 5 am to feed the horses, and bring his own breakfast with him. He lived at Battisford.

During the Second World War the house was requisitioned as a Mess for the Wattisham Base.

After the War the Dahl family lived in the Hall, and then a Swedish family called Hallmans resided there for a time. They carried out a lot of renovation work at the Hall.

With Mike's parents living at the entrance to the Hall, and very good neighbours, Sandy and Linda Bjornson, with their three lovely children, Freyja, Anna and Lief, living next door in their lovely barn conversion home, the Calames feel very happy in their 'retirement' home. Ringshall Hall is certainly in very capable hands. The next few years will undoubtedly see this dearly loved old manor house restored to its former glory.

PLAN *of the* RINGSHALL HALL ESTATE
SUFFOLK
1925

'REPRODUCED FROM THE 1925 ORDNANCE SURVEY MAP'.

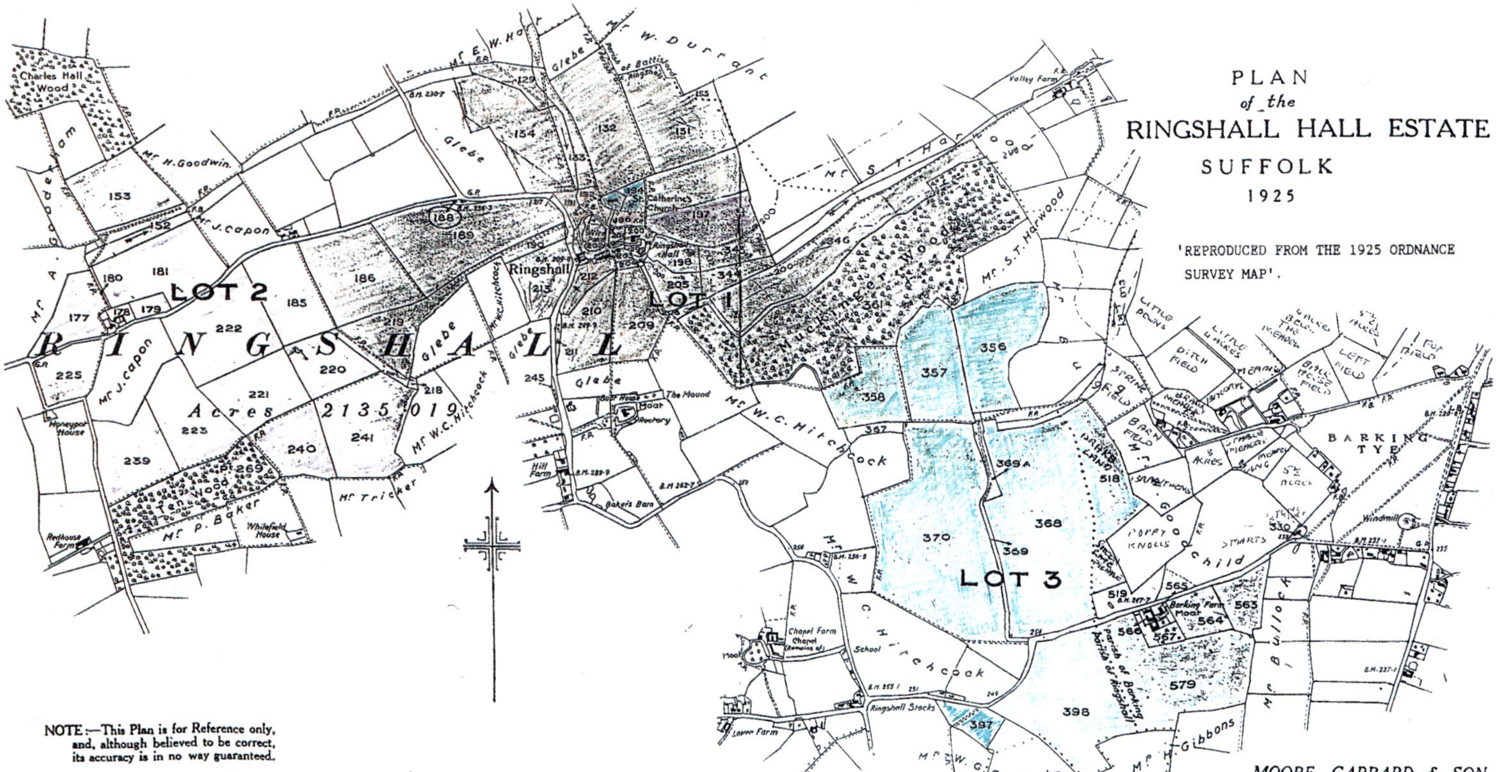

SCALE—6 INCHES TO A MILE.

NOTE:—This Plan is for Reference only, and, although believed to be correct, its accuracy is in no way guaranteed.

NOTE:—This Plan is based upon the Ordnance Survey Map, with the sanction of the Controller of H.M. Stationery Office.

MOORE, GARRARD & SON,
Auctioneers,
Hoxne, near Diss, and Eye.

THE following extracts are taken from a periodical entitled "East Anglian Miscellany". Subjects dealt with were history, genealogy, archaeology, folk-lore and literature, etc, relating to East Anglia. The texts mentioned here were written earlier this century, between 1901 and 1910.

Ringshall Hall

QUOTE: The Anglo-Saxon name is certainly very descriptive of the spot on which the remnants of this old Hall stands. Ringeshale being the "secluded spot or nook of Hring", and it is indeed a nook, for it is on low ground, backed by well timbered pastureland, and surrounded by little hills, on one of which to the north and quite close by is placed the church, (St Catherine). It was no doubt at one time perfectly enclosed by water, and it is not very difficult to trace the enclosure now though some of the moat has grown up, and other parts have been filled in. To the westward of the house is a large piece of water. Like a miniature lake, and 80 yards wide; from the corner thereof nearest to the church, running eastwards for about 100 yards, is a wide, dry ditch, filled up with rough undergrowth; southward of that extensive piece of water are situated the farm premises, and therefore that corner of the moat has been filled in; but southward of the Hall the moat exists in its original condition, with a small arm running to the back of the house, which doubtless was at one time only separated by a causeway, or it might be a postern bridge, from another arm which joined the aforesaid dry ditch on the north side. The house now faces west, and looks through some fine trees, and across that piece of water to the hills beyond; but I am inclined to think that originally it faced the south, and that what exists today is but one wing of the ancient structure. It is recorded by historians that in 1788 "the manor house was destroyed". I have heard a similar story so often, and found it untrue, that when I visit such a site it is with a doubt in my mind. Once inside Ringshall Hall that doubt was fully confirmed, for at the end of the building overlooking the southern moat is a very fine room, with one beam parallel with the moat, and two others crossing it, all well moulded and black with age. Upstairs again the floors are for the most part of very solid oak, but there is not a single detail anywhere worthy of record, and so, undoubtedly, when in 1788, the house was said to have been destroyed, two-thirds of it was pulled down, all the details carried away or sold, and the remainder adapted for a farmhouse. The ancient chimneys are all gone, but there is certainly a great deal in the appearance of the windows suggestive of the past. Those at the end of the building have three lights and a transome across, doubtless of the same shape and construction as when filled with leaded panes in the 16th century, and no one looking at the place today on this side of it from across the moat, would doubt for a moment but that they were gazing at the part of a house erected three hundred years ago.

The Gresham Family

Sir Richard Gresham was one of that goodly number of London merchants who further enriched themselves by the purchase of church property after the reformation. Some years previous to this he had made arrangements with Prior Castleton for the transfer to him of the Priory lands belonging to Hoxne, and in 1546 he had obtained from the same source the land in Ringshall connected also with Hoxne, and the chapel, with the site of the manors of Rawlins and Rockells; and now in 1548 he obtains the chief manor also. I do not suppose he ever resided in Ringshall. He was a son of John Gresham, of Holt in Norfolk, and was knighted in 1537, being Lord Mayor of London in that year. He married twice – first, Audrey, daughter of William Linne, of London, and second, a daughter of John Worsopp. On 10th February, 1548, he died and was buried at St Lawrence Jewry in London. He was succeeded by his eldest son, Sir John Gresham, born in 1518, and knighted in 1547 by the Duke of Somerset on Musselburgh Field. He married Francis daughter and heir of Sir Henry Thwaites, Kt., of Lownd in Yorkshire, by whom he had one daughter and heir, Elizabeth, wife of Sir Henry Neville, of Billingbeare, in Berkshire, and he died in 1560. He was succeeded by a brother, born in 1518, who was the celebrated Sir Thomas Gresham, Kt., the builder, in 1566, of the Royal Exchange. He was married about 1551 to Anne, the daughter of William Ferneley, of Creeting Hall, which lady was widow of William Reade of Beccles, but he was also a merchant in London. Sir Thomas Gresham, when in East Anglia resided chiefly at Intwood, near Norwich, but more often at Osterley Park, in Middlesex, now the fine seat of the Earl of Jersey; but he evidently retained a residence at Ringshall, fit for occupation when he needed it. A question then arises as to where that house was situated, and on which of his two manors. D. D. Davy has, in his collections at the British Museum, a long correspondence on the subject from Rev. C. F. Parker, rector of Ringshall in 1841, in which he gives the result of his investigations, as also a letter written by Sir Thomas Gresham in 1566, when a resident for a short while at Ringshall, and this correspondence is as follows:

"In a field adjoining that on which the chapel stood may be traced the foundation of a house to the length of 80 feet. It is surrounded by a moat; quantities of gravel have at different times been taken from the raised terrace on the north side. Beyond this last, which had a large pond at each angle, another moat encloses another piece of land, to which there was a bridge. Both on the side leading to Bildeston and on that to Ipswich, a hard road is found as far as the field has been ploughed, and this circumstance, and the size of the house, connected with the grant of the land to Sir Thomas Gresham, renders it probable that it is the spot from which Sir Thomas Gresham wrote his letter to Sir William Cecil."

The Letter to Sir William Cecil, dated 13th August, 1566

"Rt. Honble. Sir,

After my most humble commendations it maie like your honour to understand that at the XIII, of this present, I mette with my Lorde Keeper (Sir Nicholas Bacon, of Redgrave Hall, who married the sister of Lady Gresham) at Sir Clement Hetham's house (Sir Clement Heigham, of Barrow Hall), whereat his Lordship sealed the Queenes Laesties bonds and soe departed towards his house at Sainte Auburnes (St Albans), and being within XIIII mile of my house at Ringshall (whereat I make all my provision for my timber for the Burse). I was so bold as to starte to vewe the same, where I did receive letters from my servant Richard Clonghe, of the IIII of this presente, which accordinge to mie most bounde dewtie I have thought it good to send your honour that you may know what occurences passethe, and so tomorrow I intend to depart for London, whereat I trust to find in a redimness the 11. M1i which I promised to furnish the Queens Majestie bie exchange, and soe to make my repaire into Flanders with all the expedition that I can, for the accomplishment of Her Highness's instructions, and thus with my most humble commendations to the Erle of Leicester and the Erle of Ormond, with a carouse, I most humble take my leave of you. From my house at Ringshall in Suffolk, the thirteenth day of August, Anno 1556, at your honour's commandment, Thomas Gresham"

Lady Gresham's grandson was baptised at Ringshall Church, and there is the entry in the registers: "Mr Thomas Rede, the son of Mr William Rede and Garthie, his wife, baptised 28th July, 1586". The little boy here baptised, married Mildred, daughter of Thomas Cecil, Earl of Exeter, and died at Osterley without

Reproduced by kind permission of Mr Ernie Thorpe.
Ringshall Hall 'Wire' Pond – 1925

issue 3rd July, 1595, and was buried in Sir Thomas Gresham's vault at St Helen's, Bishopgate. Mr Parker continues: "As this boy was baptised at Ringshall one month before the letter of Sir Thomas Gresham was written, it would seem that Lady Gresham's son, Mr William Rede, lived in the house alluded to, for Sir Thomas, of course, could pass but little time there. The carriage of the timber can be proved by a document relating to a trial at Ipswich, and the claim of a Ringshall farmer. A lease also may be seen of lands in Ringshall from William Gresham, late of Westham, Kent, to Robert Southgate, whose name is in the register. There were then three houses in Ringshall, which may claim to have been the residence of Sir Thomas Gresham. (1) The Hall near the church, as being on the head manor, and having been a good house in the time of Charles I. Till this time I cannot find it mentioned, or that the Barkers had been resident during the forty years in which they held the manor. (2) Charles Hall, as being nearest to Battisford Tye, and some known lands of the Greshams, but I can discover nothing bearing marks of age besides the moat, the chimney, and one strong oak door with large nails on it, but this door is not in its original position. (3) House near the Free Chapel, as having stood on land that was given up to Sir Thomas Gresham's father by Prior Castleton in 1546. Also as being of a good size, with terraces, and moats, and having good hard roads towards Bildeston and Ipswich, before such were common in country parishes. No other good houses can be traced in Ringshall. The Hall, the house near the chapel, and the Parsonage standing between, and at about the same distance from each, had all of them fronts to the west, and all had moats. From my statements you will say that the Chapel-moated house could not have been on the Head Manor, or that of Charles; it must then be fixed at Rockells or Rawlins".

William Rede did reside in the house, and probably farmed the estate. He appears on the 1568 Subsidy List as "William Reade, Gent, £13 in Londes, paying 17s 4d". The names of the Southgate family also occur. "William Sowgate £15 in goodes, 12s 6d., and Robert Sowgate £3 in goodes, 2. 6d". Sir

Reproduced by kind permission of Mr Ernie Thorpe.
Ringshall Hall – 1948

Thomas Gresham died on November 21st, 1579, and William Gresham succeeded to this property and Battisford; he has been previously mentioned as granting the lease to Robert Southgate. I think he must have been a younger brother of Sir Thomas, for it could not possibly have been his nephew the owner of Titsey in Surrey, for he died the same year, nor the son of the latter, who was then but 13 years of age. Anyhow, in 1583 this William Gresham sold it to William Rowe and Thomas Byarde, who in 1587 sold it to John Barker of Ipswich, and thus it came into the hands of a family who not only owned it for a long period, but were probably answerable for a good deal, if not all the house, and were besides at some time residents therein. John Barker was the son of Robert Barker and his wife Miss Kinge, and the grandson of another Robert Barker and his wife, Anne, the daughter and co-heiress of a man named Bestney, of Cambridgeshire. He married Myllecent the daughter of John Bomart of Braband, and in 1609, he died and was buried in the church of St. Mary-le-Tower, Ipswich. His son, Sir Robert Barker, K.B., succeeded. He was of Grimston Hall, in Trimley. He was knighted in Newcastle in 1621-2, married twice; first Penelope, daughter of Sir John Tasburgh, of Flixton; and second, Miss Bateman, undoubtedly from one of the Elmhams. He was certainly a resident on this site when in 1640 he subscribed £2 6s to the ship money; and several children by Penelope, his wife, were baptised here. Margaret in 1629, Penelope in 1630, Francis in 1633, Katherine in 1636, Elizabeth in 1637, Robert in 1639 and Charles in 1642. Before 1655 he had sold the place to his younger brother, William Barker, a merchant of London, who had married Martha, daughter of William Turner of Highworth, County Wilts, widow of Daniel Williams, a merchant of London. Presumably, it is his house at Ringshall that is recorded in the Hearth Tax of 1674. "Alderman Barker, 14 Hearths", of which house, I feel sure, the present Hall is a portion. He was succeeded by a son, William Barker, who was also of Bocking Hall, Essex, created a baronet on 29th May, 1676. He married Elizabeth, daughter and sixteenth child of Sir Jerome Alexander, Kt., Judge of the Common Pleas in Ireland, and was succeeded by his eldest son, who became Sir William Barker, second baronet. He married Catherine Teresa, daughter and co-heir of Samuel Keck, of Middle Temple. Presumably, the family resided for a long time at Bocking Hall, but it is very evident from memorials still existing at Ringshall Church, that the second baronet and his wife resided and died in the parish. At the west end of the church, in the yard, stands a sarcophagus, of which the record in 1841 is this; "Of white marble, formerly very handsome and enclosed in iron palisades but the whole now in a state of dilapidation, some parts having been removed into the church". At the east end is this cut in marble, "Here lyeth the body of Dame Catherine Teresa Barker, wife of Sir William Barker, Bart., of Ringshall Hall, in this parish, eldest daughter of Samuel Keck, Esq., one of the Masters in the High Court of Chancery. She departed this life May 7th, 1736 in her 56th year. She left issue four sons, William, Samuel, Alexander and Robert, and four daughters, Elizabeth, Hannah, Martha and Grace. Her daughter Hannah

Barker departed this life March 2nd, 1741 in her 29th year." On the south side Sir William Barker was buried, but no memorial appears. Robert Barker, another son of the first Baronet, married another of the daughters and co-heirs of Samuel Keck. Sir William Barker the second Baronet, died at Ringshall, where he was buried on May 5th, 1746, ten years after the death of his wife, and he was succeeded by his eldest son, Sir William Barker, third Baronet, of Bocking Hall, and of Kilcooley Abbey in Ireland, who married in 1733, Mary, daughter of Valentine Quin, of Adaire, County Limerick.

In 1750, Sir William Barker sold this estate to Peter Lefebure, who died in 1753, when Elizabeth Lefebure, his widow, succeeded; but there is a doubt as to whether they were residents. In 1761 it was purchased by William Watson and Jonathan Watson, of Bury St Edmunds, the latter probably the son of the former, and it is he who came to reside at Ringshall Hall. "At the east end of the chancel, in the yard, a large space is enclosed in iron palisades. This is the burial place of the Watsons. There is an inscription in the church – "Near this place are deposited the remains of Mrs Elizabeth Watson, daughter of Josiah Bullock, of Faulkbourn Hall, Essex, wife of Jonathan Watson, of Bury St Edmunds, who died June 20th, 1763 in the 38th year of her age. Also on November 7th, 1803, Jonathan Watson, Esq., F.R.S. formerly J.P. and D.L. for the county, and Major of East Suffolk Militia, He was 84 years of age." Two of their children are also buried at Ringshall – George, on November 18th, 1766, and Ann on December 18th, 1766. There was also buried there, according to the registers "Christopher Watson, late of Westwood House, Horkesley, Essex, on 23rd June 1836, aged 84 years". "According to Davey's List of the Lords of this manor, Mr Jonathan Watson sold the whole property in 1783 to William Wollaston, of Finborough Hall, who was to hold his first court on 19th October, 1784 (in "Ipswich Journal", of August 12th, 1786, we read), "To be sold. The Manor of Ringshall with four freehold farms in Ringshall and one in Battisford, of the yearly rent of £400, with a large wood containing 50 acres." It is said that William Wollaston, of Finborough, 'destroyed the manor house in 1788' and no doubt about that time the greater portion was pulled down and the remainder converted into what it is today, a suitable farmhouse. About this time it became the property of the Adairs, of Flixton. Alexander Adair held a court on 22nd May, 1822, and since this time it has remained as part of the Flixton property, and was held by Sir Frederick Adair, Bart., when he died. The tenant of it, as given in White's Directory of 1855, was Thomas Hayward, and his name occurs again in the edition of 1885. In the year 1892 we find John Long as the tenant, which in 1908 is changed to Harry Long, who died there on August 14th, 1917 at the age of 52. UNQUOTE

....

*The above was compiled and written by **E. F. Botesdale**. It was obtained from **The Ipswich Record Office** by Mr Michael Poll of Ringshall.*

Lakeside Lodge

Once upon a time, on going through the main gates to 'Ringshall Hall', visitors would have seen an old dilapidated, thatched tithe barn, supposedly 400 years old, standing dejectedly to the left of the driveway. Years of neglect had taken their toll; and the interior was full of rapidly spreading ivy, old chairs, car parts, and was the resting place for old bits of rusting farm machinery. Spiders loved it!

Today it is a very different story. A charming cottage style home which has withstood the elements and the test of time. It has been completely remodelled and renovated, but still retains a rustic look reminiscent of old properties. A 'bench mark' (datum line) is still visible on one of the walls. To add extra dimension, a spacious sun lounge has been added, and this abuts onto what was probably the old cattle yard. This attractive room is obviously the 'hub of the home' as the views from windows across the 'Wire Pond' are spectacular. This pond is home to various species of ducks, and geese. I noticed their 'calling cards' on the grass.

The kitchen is fairly large and modern, with a very smart Rayburn cooker (somebody knows how to cook here). Leading through from the kitchen is a cosy lounge and as befits any well respecting country cottage, it has a woodburning stove with a pile of logs carefully piled in a basket beside the hearth. Above the fireplace is a large oak beam, probably four hundred years old, with a set of initials engraved into it. To complete this cosy home, there are

Marie Louise and Marcel Calame outside their home 'Lakeside Lodge' – 22 June 1999

two bedrooms, and a bathroom. Because of planning restrictions it was not possible to enlarge the bathroom window, and this remains an 'arrow slit'.

Throughout the property, specially made beams have been built in to good effect. Somehow there is a distinctly Tudor feel to the cottage. Looking through the casement windows to the plantation beyond, gives a feeling of timelessness. Surely Sir Thomas Gresham would have walked among the trees, perhaps pondering on how much timber to select for the Royal Exchange (1565).

I was invited to meet this amazing couple who are responsible for this remarkable transformation on a sunny June afternoon in 1999.

May I introduce you to ...

Marie Louise who was born in London in 1917, but spent her formative years in Italy. She returned to live in London just before the outbreak of the Second World War.

Marcel was born in Eastbourne in 1917, but when still very young, his parents went to live in France and Switzerland (he still speaks fluent French). The Calame family lived abroad for seven years before returning to these shores.

Marie Louise and Marcel married in 1940. Their only child, Mike was born, and they lived happily ever after, finally retiring and living in Bordon, Hampshire. They will be celebrating their 'Diamond' wedding on October 15th in the year 2000.

However, when their son Mike and his wife Lesley bought 'Ringshall Hall' they were keen for Marcel and Marie Louise to join them in Suffolk.

Marcel and his wife lived in 'Ringshall Hall' for the first ten months of their tenure in Suffolk, but once the decision was made to convert the old tithe barn, and the necessary papers signed; this energetic and enterprising couple set to work. Much younger people could well have been daunted by the prospect of this unusual transformation, but the Calames are made of stern stuff. With the help of experienced craftsmen, they set to work with eagerness and determination. Work started in April, 1996 and they moved in during the following August, with a few jobs still unfinished. They now have a cosy home they both love, and which their friends love to visit. It is called 'Lakeside Lodge'.

Ringshall Grange – David and Mary Gilmour

"No child could have wished for a happier home"
– Quote from the youngest of David Gilmour's six daughters.

Charles David Dalrymple Gilmour (known to family and friends always as David), comes from a military family with strong Scottish Presbyterian lineage. His father became a Colonel in the Black Watch and his mother was one of the famous Edwardian Gaiety Girls. Moving around the world from one army post to another, always living in rented properties, didn't suit the young David. He longed for a proper family home, a place to put down 'roots'. He was sent as a boarder to "Temple Grove" Preparatory School, Eastbourne (where Douglas Bader the famous world war two fighter ace, preceded him) and then to Eton.

An army career did not appeal to this quiet young man, and he became a Lloyds broker and then an Aviation Underwriter after the Second World War. Marriage and family life followed, but somehow he felt he was still looking for his 'roots'.

He first came to Suffolk in 1962, staying with friends in Earl Stonham. The quiet beauty of the surrounding countryside appealed to him, and he fell in love with the area, a love that endures to the present day. He was lucky enough to be sent details of "Ringshall Grange" through

Above: The Tudor wing – the Gilmour family settle into their new home – Summer 1965

Left: The Georgian and Tudor wings of the house – 1964

friends in Lloyds. It represented the perfect opportunity for the family to make the home they wanted.

The 16th century manor house stood within a medieval moat, the drive curving gracefully towards the front of the house, with well spaced trees standing sentry on either side. The garden was a wilderness, having suffered neglect from a succession of owners, but David could see before him the home of his dreams. This was where he would be able to close the front door, relax before a roaring log fire, knowing it belonged to him and nobody would be able to make him move unless he wanted to. On 1 April, 1964 he signed the necessary documents which gave him and his family ownership of this very special house.

David, his second wife Marianne, their two children, and her daughter by her first marriage, moved in, and in the ensuing years made this gracious house into a warm, welcoming home. He was very content despite having to travel daily to and from London. The years rolled by, gradually the garden was tamed, and the Gilmour family became integrated into the village of Ringshall. Then tragedy struck with the death of his beloved wife. It was a very sad time for the family. In due course, he met and married his present wife, Mary. She was brought up in Lincolnshire, but like her husband, feels a great affinity with the Suffolk countryside.

Mary and David are both very much aware of the historical value of their home and take their guardianship of "Ringshall Grange" seriously. Much research has

Would this game of Croquet perhaps have been played in the grounds of Ringshall Grange in Victorian times?

been done by the pair. One of the Gilmour daughters, now grown, recently assured them "that no child could have wished to have had a happier home". What a loving compliment to pay one's parents!

It is still very much a family home, with their daughters, their respective spouses, and numerous grandchildren (nine to date), still assembling for regular visits and holidays. With such a large, jolly family it is surely a certainty that the Gilmour clan will continue their gatherings for many years to come in the home in which their father, and grandfather, finally 'put down his roots'. Mary Gilmour particularly looks forward to the visits of their youngest granddaughter, Saskia, who is two.

'Monkey Puzzle' tree or Chile Pine at Ringshall Grange – 1948

Having met the latest incumbents of "Ringshall Grange", let us now view the house itself, and learn a little of its history.

The original house was built in the 16th century (circa 1580), in the reign of Elizabeth I, and resembled a typical Suffolk farm house of the Tudor era. Later a Georgian wing was added, although this part of the building was originally a separate entity. It was eventually joined to the older part of the house, and the large drawing room in the Georgian wing was divided, thus making two, much more comfortable rooms. In 1860 the Victorian owners added a further extension, particularly well matched to the existing Georgian wing. This extra dimension comprised a more modern kitchen and extra store room, also a bedroom and sitting room upstairs. Inevitably more passages also appeared.

A very graceful house, there is a distinct feeling of past grandeur on walking into the magnificent entrance hall. It has exceptionally elegant, high ceilinged rooms in the Georgian wing, and many older, historical features in the Tudor part. The original 16th century kitchen is no longer in use. Today's modern kitchen is light and airy with fitted cupboards and labour saving equipment. Staircases at the front and back of the halls lead to the bedrooms, some joined by inter-connecting passages. Gazing through the large sash windows I was very much aware of the historical aura of the medieval moat and gardens. What history this house has been through, the execution of Mary Queen of Scots – 8th February 1587, part of the glorious reign of Elizabeth I (1558–1603), and the Civil War between Cavalier and Roundhead which started in 1642 and saw the rise of Oliver

The house and medieval moat - 1996

Cromwell. The Georgian period was a time of expansion here, but also of bloodshed. The war of American Independence commenced on 4th July, 1776. Between 1760 and 1830 England was to pass from an agricultural to an industrial economy. The Great Exhibition of 1851 held in the Crystal Palace, Hyde Park, was a symbol of the Industrial Revolution. Great writers and poets were born, namely William Shakespeare (1564–1616), and Wordsworth, born in 1770. Jane Austin was only twenty-one when she wrote "Pride and Prejudice". If only buildings could talk...

It is thought "Ringshall Grange" went from private ownership and into the ownership of the Church at the beginning of the seventeenth century (c 1613).

In past centuries the clergy were held in high esteem, more so than today. During the eighteen-hundreds, and earlier, the local rectors, often being the only people in small communities educated to a high enough standard to teach, would hold lessons in their homes. A fairly large room would be set aside in "Ringshall Grange" (Rectory), it was probably the drawing room, before it was divided into the present two rooms. Cleric, or not, the cane would surely have been used for misdemeanours. Discipline then was as important as the three R's! Children were also taught good manners, both at home and in class.

Back to the twentieth century. This house has seen many changes and many different occupiers since 1910. It was requisitioned for the American Air Force during the Second World War (1939–1945) and was sold back into private ownership in 1944. Times were difficult for everyone after the war, and Mrs Howson who resided at "Ringshall Grange" between 1951 and 1960, rented out rooms, presumably for extra revenue.

David Gilmour's study is a snug room in the Tudor part of the house, and during my visit on a particularly cold April day in 1999, a log fire blazed cheerfully in the grate. A comfortable air pervades this room, giving it a cosy feeling. Apparently, the various Rectors over the ages, used this room to interview and talk to 'their flock'.

There is a much larger sitting room in the Georgian wing. Being on the first floor, this room has a good view of the grounds from the large windows. This is a retreat for Mary and her grandchildren – the latter regard it as 'their playroom'.

The original drawing room before the innovative alterations, would have been of mammoth proportions. It is difficult to envisage how people kept warm in such large rooms. Possibly the women with their more voluminous clothing had the advantage over the men!

Having been warmly entertained by Mary and David Gilmour, it was time to take my leave of "Ringshall Grange". Walking across to my car we noticed an unwelcome newly arrived Muscovy duck intent on leaving his 'mark' on the front lawn, much to the consternation of Mary. Looking back at the house, the pretty Georgian wing reminded me of the charming old rectory in Jane Austin's "Pride and Prejudice". I could almost see the quiet Mr Bennet, and the fidgety Mrs Bennet, whose main aim in life was to find rich suitors for her daughters. The scene was clearly set, the daughters would be playing croquet or lacrosse with friends on the lawn, and Elizabeth Bennet would undoubtedly be wishing the dashing Mr Darcy would appear.

The Georgian wing –
1999

It is certain the Gilmour family will continue to love and nurture this lovely old house for many years to come.

Other brief tenants of "The Grange" were Mr Rowland Hitchcock – 1934, 1935, 1936. Mr Ted Caley lived there as 'caretaker' until 1938, and was followed by Mr Charlie Howe, who resided there as 'caretaker' during the period 1940-1941. As previously mentioned it was then requisitioned for the American Air Force.

Without considerably more research it is not possible to construct a complete list of all the occupiers of The Grange, or, as it used to be called, The Rectory. However, the people who are known to have lived here include the following ...

William **Keble** M.A. B.D.	from 1613
George **Peppen** M.A.	from 1659 – son-in-law of William Keble
James **Peppen** M.A.	from 1689 – son-in-law of George Peppen
William **Peppen** M.A.	from 1707 – nephew of James Peppen
William **Peppen** B.A.	from 1744 – son of William Peppen
Charles **Parker**	1826
Edward **Hawkins**	1871
J F **Vincent-Fernie***	to 1944
Peter **Stainer**	to 1947
Brigadier L P **Twomey**	to 1951
Herbert F **Howson**	to 1960
Mrs V Q E **Turner**	to 1964
C D D **Gilmour**	Present owner

**Although the name J. F. Vincent Fernie appears on the title deeds, he never resided at "The Rectory".*

Round and About in Ringshall
Past and Present

The oak tree spreading its own welcome to Ringshall. Long may it do so! – 1999

Above left: The Old School House – now home to Helen Nunn and family

The "Old Post Office" – 1999

Above right: The Old School, Ringshall – 1999. Photograph taken by Mr A Toomey of 3 Bakers Corner, Ringshall

The new Village Hall – 1999.
Photograph taken by Mr A Toomey of 3 Bakers Corner, Ringshall

Hill House, Ringshall, present home of David and Rita Hitchcock.
Photograph taken by Mr A Toomey of 3 Bakers Corner, Ringshall

Demolition. This property was owned by the Last family and occupied by Mr and Mrs Cuthbert who subsequently moved to Needham Market – 1990

73

View from St Catherine's Church, showing the houses in "Coronation Glebe" in the distance – 1998

Looking across the fields to Wattisham Base – 29 June 1999

Looking towards Wattisham Airfield from St Catherine's Church – 1998

Looking towards "Coronation Glebe" and the Old Post Office – 1999.
Photograph – Andrew Toomey

The Rectories
Past and Present

The Old Rectory, Ringshall – built in 1949 and sold into private ownership in 1978 – 16th June, 1999

The New Rectory, Willisham – built in 1994. Home to the Rector, Kit Gray – 16th June, 1999

Lunch and Croquet Tournament at Chapel Farm, Ringshall – 20 June 1999

Below : Rita Hitchcock and her grandson check the score with David Secret

Below : Elizabeth Hitchcock concentrates under the watchful eye of her brother

Inset: The Champions! – Julie and Alistair Turnbull of Gosbeck with their two children, Victoria and James. This was the first time they had ever played croquet!

Left: William and Joan relaxing with a drink

76

"Coronation Glebe", Ringshall
Photographs by Julie Smith of Ringshall – 1999

Some of the houses in "South View" on the Offton Road, Ringshall
Photographs by Julie Smith of Ringshall – 1998

Some of the Newer Properties in the Village – 1998
Lower Farm Road, Ringshall

A view down Lower Farm Road, Ringshall – 1999. *Photograph taken by Mr A Toomey of 3 Bakers Corner, Ringshall*

Lower Farm Road, from the crossroads – 1998

Right: Julie Smith walking briskly along Lower Farm Road.
Is she late for a committee meeting? I wonder how late she was? – 1999

Above: Mr James (Jimmy) Wilden of 4 South View helping in the garden of Mrs Payne of Lower Farm Road, Ringshall – 5th May 1999

78

"Toad Hall" when lived in by Irene and Tony Hart – 1988. Now "Border Cottage", and occupied by Mr and Mrs Alliston

The back garden at "Chapelfields", now the home of Irene and Tony Hart – 1999

The old telephone box which stands on "Stocks Corner", Ringshall – 1999

Site of standpipe opposite school gates, from which the residents of Ringshall collected their water. The mains supply was not connected until April 1954

6
Chapel Farm

The Hitchcock Family

Before the Hitchcock family came to Ringshall, they resided in Bildeston, Suffolk.

In 1746 the name of Samuel Hitchcock, a fervent Baptist, appears as one of several signatories on an invitation sent to Joseph Palmer inviting him to become a Baptist minister.

On August 21st 1757, John Hitchcock was baptised. He was received into the fellowship on September 4th in the same year. It would appear that John Hitchcock was a man of strong principles, and not afraid 'to stand his ground' when necessary. The following gives some indication of his character ...

In 1759 Ephraim Ward was considered for baptism. An objection was raised by John Hitchcock, but was overruled by the rest of the church. In protest, John, Joseph Enefer and Samuel Cooper withdrew from the meeting.

On April 18th 1760 John Hitchcock was dismissed from the recently formed church at Woolverstone. Evidently, he had disagreed with the church on various matters and voiced his opinions strongly. He had accused them of being partial, of being wrong with regard to discipline, and administering baptism in private. However, Samuel Sowden, minister of the church at Woolverstone, sympathised with John Hitchcock, and in 1761 this church allowed him to go forth and preach the gospel.

In 1763 twenty-eight people formed the nucleus of a church at Wattisham and John Hitchcock was ordained as pastor. He subsequently built up a strong following.

There is mention of Samuel Sowden going to Nedging and baptising four people, afterwards 'administering the Lord's

Supper' to them in the house of Wyncoll Grimwood. Could this possibly be an ancestor of George Grimwood who worked so painstakingly for Ringshall Free Chapel for most of his life?

Once comfortably ensconced at "Chapel Farm", John Hitchcock held services in the old part of the house, until the congregation outstripped the accommodation. A small building was then erected at the farm entrance in 1790; this was the Parish Room, later to become the Village Hall on 2nd January 1979.

John Hitchcock was succeeded by his son, also named John, in 1800. He bought the land on which the old village hall was built in 1857 from Priscilla and Dinah Hitchcock (his sisters), for the sum of five-pounds. He was at this time still unmarried. Eventually John married Maria, but sadly within a few short years he died. After John's death, his wife remarried, and she and her second husband sold the land and chapel to Rev. Charles Parker for ninety-pounds. As Maria could neither read nor write, all her legal documents were signed with a cross, and all necessary names, etc, inserted by the solicitor.

William Cooper Hitchcock, grandfather of today's David and John, was the second son of seven boys and five girls born to Joseph Ennals Hitchcock, and his wife Fanny in the middle of the nineteenth century. Because of the dismal state of agriculture, the boys were apprenticed to various trades, other than farming. William Hitchcock, much to his dismay, was sent to a large drapery firm in London, and hated the experience. After a very short time, he returned home and worked on the farm, the life he loved.

William's wife Edith was the daughter of a nearby farmer, and one of a family of eleven children. She and William produced three children, Clement, Rowland and a daughter Phyllis who was to die at the young age of eighteen from an intestinal type of tuberculosis contracted from food. Her parents never really recovered from this loss.

The Hitchcock family in 1916 – from left, Phyllis (died 1924), William Hitchcock, Clement, Edith Hitchcock, and Rowland

When William and his wife Edith retired from farming, their elder son, Clement and his wife Jane (formerly Jane Baker from Gipping) with their small son Ben, moved into Chapel Farm. Two more sons, David and John were born later. Clement was to prove a very able farmer and astute businessman, and was to run this farm successfully for many years.

Clement as a boy was quite 'typical of the breed'. It appears he and his brother Rowland could be quite a handful at times. The following is a quote from Rowland Hitchcock's book "Rowley Recalls Farming, Fighting and Fun".

William & Edith Hitchcock with Rowley & Clement in the doorway holding Ben

"Like most children in those days, on the farm we always played at being horses. Unfortunately, being younger, I always seemed to be the horse and was driven; seldom the driver. The system changed a bit when mother bought loaf sugar in 1-cwt, or ½-cwt boxes. When emptied we made rabbit hutches with them, or sometimes fitted old perambulator wheels and shafts to make a cart. Having made a cart, my brother was quite happy to act as the horse, with me sitting in the cart and driving. Unfortunately, my brother always wanted to be a very high spirited horse. Our expeditions usually ended with him shying or rearing; eventually with the cart over-turning and throwing me out."

Clement Hitchcock served in the Grenadier Guards during the First World War, and although 'at home' during the Second World War, he did much for the war effort in Ringshall and the local areas, (see John Hitchcock's text entitled "No Pub – No blacksmith!"). For many years he was on the local Parish Council. He was quite a large man in stature, and his wife Jane, quite petite. She was however, a very dominant character, and worked hard both on the farm and in the village. She was a devoted member of St Catherine's Church for many years.

Many people remember Jane Hitchcock for her forthright manner. During the 1950s through to the 1970's, the villages of Ringshall, Gt. Bricett, Battisford and Barking sustained a thriving political group, namely the Ringshall and District

The young John Hitchcock at Chapel Farm with parents, Jane and Clement Hitchcock – circa 1939

Conservative Branch. This was successful mainly due to the enthusiasm of Jane Hitchcock. It has been said that meetings were always conducted in a very brisk, businesslike manner when Jane was 'in the Chair'. Although she had the ability to organise, she wasn't dictatorial.

Clement was badly injured in a car accident in 1963. This resulted in the amputation of a leg. He died at the age of eighty on March 25th, 1979. Jane Hitchcock, who was awarded the British Empire medal in 1982 for services to the community in the Stowmarket area, died quietly at Chapel Farm on 5th November, 1986.

Mrs Jane Hitchcock celebrates her British Empire Medal with Sir Joshua Rowley outside The Hall, Gt. Bricett – May 1982

Ben, the eldest of the Hitchcock boys, emigrated to Canada when quite a young man. In his early sixties, he had a serious accident and died from his injuries in June, 1990. He never married.

David married Rita Ward from Needham Market and went as a tenant farmer on a small farm at Mendlesham. After a while he transferred to a farm at Iken in Suffolk but when this farm changed hands, he and Rita sought pastures new in Gloucestershire, where he managed an 800 acre estate. After six years they moved to Oxfordshire, where David managed a 1,500 acre estate. He and Rita have two children, Susan and Nigel, and two

Ben Hitchcock with family pet dog, named Sheila. Ben gained a BSc at Wye College

Ben Hitchcock with his mother, Jane (from left), John and Elizabeth's three children, Ruth, Helen and Guy

A Walk In The Country Near Chapel Farm. Elizabeth with young son, Guy in the pushchair, having a 'well earned nap', and daughter Helen on the pony –1967

grandchildren, David and James. At the age of sixty-five, David retired and they returned to Ringshall, buying "Hill House", the property where his father was born in 1898.

John married Elizabeth Turnbull from Stonham Aspal on 2nd June, 1962 and they produced three children, Helen, Guy and Ruth. John took over Chapel Farm when his father died. Although farming 'is in his blood', he is very interested in engineering.

"The hand that rocks the cradle, rules the world". There is a lot of truth in that old saying, and it must be stressed that although this seems to be the story of the Hitchcock men, their lives might not have turned out so well without the stalwart support of their wives. Like conscientious partners everywhere, they brought up the children, ran the home, and when necessary acted as secretaries and accounts clerks.

Looking through the Nineteenth Century Censuses, it seems Chapel Farm held 110 acres in 1841 (employing 5 men and 1 boy) expanding to 129 acres in 1871 (employing 5 men and 2 boys). It is now a 400 acre farm.

In the present day of comparative economic prosperity, there are many harsh realities to face, and along the way hard decisions have to be made. Farmers today are as much prisoners of economic conditions as any other business-men. But even so, farming is a national institution without which the nation would not survive.

Top: Mr Clement Hitchcock and his wife Jane, attending the wedding of their son, John, to Elizabeth at Stonham Aspal Church on 2 June 1962

Above: Mr and Mrs John Hitchcock leaving Stonham Aspal Church after their marriage on 2 June, 1962

Below : David and Rita Hitchcock – July 1999

John and Elizabeth Hitchcock – 1999

Rowland Hitchcock

The following is the story of Rowland Hitchcock's birth, described by himself in his book published in 1984 under the title
"Rowley Recalls Farming, Fighting and Fun".

"February of that year was memorable for three people at least, my father, mother and myself, as in the first week, with hard frost and deep snow on the ground, I was born. When my arrival was thought to be imminent, some poor fellow was sent six miles on foot with a note for the doctor asking him to attend and, I suppose, greet me. However, all this took some hours and I could not wait for him, so by the time he had struggled in his horse and trap to our house I had already arrived, had a wash and brush up, a good meal, and was fast asleep. I do not remember all this happening, of course, but my mother would vouch for the truth of it".

So began the life of a very remarkable man. His mother, Edith, was the daughter of a nearby farmer, his father, William was at this time a tenant at Hill Farm, Ringshall, and he also farmed the adjoining Chapel Farm. There were two other children in the family, a brother, Clement, three and a half years old, and a younger sister Phyllis who would sadly die from tuberculosis at the age of eighteen.

Rowland's father was a keen sportsman, a very good shot and quite a good horseman. The horses he drove were all hunter types so that he could hunt them as well. The young Rowland was only four years old when he accompanied his father to a meeting of the Suffolk Stag Hounds. This obviously was the beginning of his life long love of horses and fox hunting.

In 1903 Rowley's father demolished the original Chapel Farm, built a new house, and moved the family in.

Rowland got up to the usual boyhood mischief with his older brother, and was very fond of his younger sister, becoming great buddies with her as they got older. She became rather a tomboy and joined Rowley in his hobby of sliding down straw stacks. With her long hair there were frequent noisy scenes when their mother combed her daughter's hair to remove the tangles and bits of straw. Another bit of mischief involved sticky fly paper. Rowley persuaded his

"Chapel Farm" as it was originally. Demolished in 1905

sister to climb onto the kitchen table, where above it was hanging a sticky fly paper which had a considerable number of dead flies sticking to it. Their mother had previously warned them about getting too near this fly trap. His sister managed to get her long tresses stuck in it, and the efforts of the two thoroughly alarmed children to disentangle the hair from the fly ridden paper proved a disaster. He mentions that the scene when their mother opened the door to see how her two cherubs were faring, was one he never forgot.

Thrashing a rick once in June at Ringshall, they found it had thousands of mice in it and the two boys had a wonderful day killing them. Lying under the rick they killed hundreds, but did not realise that some of the mice had crawled into the clothes and jackets. That evening, having hung up their jackets in the scullery, two very tired young boys went to bed. They were surprised to be awakened at about 10 pm by their father calling the cats. On going the rounds before going to bed, he had come across the mice running about the scullery. These, of course, had emerged from their clothing. Apparently nobody was particularly pleased about the incident in the morning.

In his book Rowley describes the George V Coronation celebrations in the village. A church service was held in the morning, in the afternoon there was a furrow-drawing competition, split up into three classes; ploughmen, non-ploughmen and ladies. This was followed by a high tea for all, in the barn at Lower Farm. All the children were given a coronation mug. This was followed by races, with classes for everyone. The highlight was a competition for catching a greasy pig, the pig being given by Rowley's father William Hitchcock. The following description of the race is in Rowley Hitchcock's own words from his book:

"I remember that father gave the pig, which was duly greased all over and let loose in a meadow. I have never seen anything like it. It must be remembered that women's skirts in those days were very long. They donned very old ones for this event, because of the grease on the pig. About 40 women set off in hot pursuit, several trod on their skirts before they got very far and fell flat on their faces. However, encouraged by their families, they were up immediately and

The Greasy Pigs race   By Lisa Cresswell, Stowmarket.

dashed off again. All the women seemed to be screaming and the pig was caught many times, but was so greasy that it easily got away and brought several more women down. The whole affair was quite extraordinary and at that tender age I stood wide-eyed to catch glimpses of a wide variety of bloomers in all shapes, sizes and colours. In the end the pig got tired and was finally captured by Mrs Bill Last. This lady had come from "foreign parts", probably a village a few miles away, as a teacher at the village school. She then married Bill Last, the mail van driver."

In her later years this lady ran the village shop and post office.

After the 1914-1918 war Rowland began working for his father who encouraged him to take part in field sports. He mentions going to the bank with his father in Stowmarket in the days when Barclays was Bevans Bank. As a young boy he was intrigued to see the gold being counted out and shovelled into bags. In those days customers always removed their hats when entering the bank, and of course, never smoked.

In 1925 at the beginning of the agricultural depression he bought his own farm, Ringshall Hall, and as a side line became interested in breaking and schooling young horses. He accepted a commission in the Territorial Army in 1926 and married in 1931, Norah, a qualified optician. An ancestor of Norah's by the name of Benjamin Jesty, a Dorset farmer, inoculated his family with cowpox and by so doing, saved them from smallpox.

In 1939 his Regiment, the 58th Medium Royal Artillery, was mustered and in 1940, as part of the British Expeditionary Force, he was rescued from drowning during the evacuation of Dunkirk by a very determined sailor who dragged him consistently to the surface when he was on the point of complete exhaustion. He went under three times, each time to be hauled up by this sailor, who accompanied his efforts with a few choice swear words. This sailor proved to be the late Lord Stanley of Alderley.

Rowland Hitchcock teaching his dog a few tricks

Promoted to Major, Rowland served in the successful North African campaign and was awarded the Military Cross, promoted Lieutenant Colonel and posted to the 166 (Newfoundland) Field Regiment, Royal Artillery. During the Italian campaign, which followed he was mentioned in dispatches and awarded the TD.

In 1945 after recovering from wounds sustained when the vehicle in which he was travelling was blown up, Rowland rejoined his wife who throughout the war had been running his business in Suffolk. Appointed Honorary Secretary to the Essex and Suffolk Hunt, Rowley became a Joint Master in 1957 and hunted hounds for ten years before retiring.

For forty years he lived with his wife at Layham Mill House.

Farming Before The First World War

The following chapter was obtained from the book by Rowland Hitchcock, entitled "Rowley Recalls Farming, Fighting and Fun". It has been reproduced here by kind permission of David and John Hitchcock who are nephews of the late Rowland. The book was published in 1984.

QUOTE: My father was a great believer in work and in the school holidays, at busy times, we had to do our share. At harvest time I spent many hours from the age of eight onwards riding the trace horse on the self binder when cutting corn, and a year later started carting the loads of corn home to the stack yard. It was all horses, as tractors had not yet arrived, and therefore great fun, as I enjoyed being with the horses.

Looking back it seems quite incredible to me that such great changes in farming methods and machinery could have taken place in my lifetime. I remember harvests before we had the self binder, a machine which has come and gone and is now a museum piece. My earliest memories of corn cutting are when it was done mainly by scythe, which was a great advance on the bagging hook. Then there was the horse clipper, drawn by a horse ridden by a lad. A man on a seat on the machine guided the wheat back onto a 'cradle' with a wooden rake which had its head set at an angle to its handle. In front of the cradle was a knife consisting of triangular sections, driven from a main wheel by means of a wooden connecting rod. This knife ran between 5 inch long steel fingers and cut the stalks of wheat as the machine was pulled

Pony & trap at "Chapel Farm" – Early 1900s

forward. The same system is now used on the present day combine harvester. One had to ensure that the knives were frequently sharpened, a blunt knife meant very hard work for the horse. The cradle was worked by the man with his right foot. When he reckoned he had sufficient wheat on the cradle to make a sheaf he raised his foot lever and pushed the bunch off the rake. This had then to be tied into a sheaf with a 'bind' of wheat stalks and thrown, say two yards, away from the standing corn to make room for the machine to make the next cut. When throwing the sheaf the tier grasped about six heads of corn and so withdrew the next bind from the sheaf, and followed onto the next one. It was necessary therefore when cutting with a clipper, that sufficient tiers were in action to keep the clipper busy, but I did take my turn at riding the horse.

The clipper was replaced by a Sail Machine, drawn by two horses; it had four sails, rather like windmill sails, but turning horizontally. This, like the clipper, had a section V knife driven from the main wheel and the sails swept the corn onto a 'bed'. They could be so adjusted that all the sails swept the straw off the bed and thus made a continuous swath, or were set so that alternate sails removed the straw, leaving neat bunches sufficient for a sheaf. These were swept away from the standing crop far enough so that the machine could follow round and cut the whole field.

In the case of wheat and oats the gang came in and tied it all up and then stood it up in shocks or stooks, but in the case of barley it was left in a swath and, when ready, raked into neat heaps for carting. This operation was called 'gavelling' and was frequently done by women, the object being to put a forkful on each heap for pitching. In those days it was the practice just before harvest began for a farmer to meet his men, or possibly the head man, who was usually the head horseman, and agree on a price for the harvest to what was known as 'see it in'. Seeing it in meant that a man would draw his normal weekly wage but no overtime pay, but would draw his bonus on the completion of harvest. If, as quite often happened, harvest was completed in a month, or under, the men considered themselves well paid. It is worth noting that, unlike today practically no harvesting was done on a Sunday. The state of the crop, good or poor, laid or standing, and acres per man, were all considered. There were generally about fifteen acres per man and the bonus varied between £4 and £5 per man, plus two bushels of malt for the harvest beer. The wage then was about 12s. per week for a labourer and 15s. or 16s. for a horseman.

It was a great sight to see twelve to fifteen men in one gang mowing barley, led by the head horseman who was 'lord' and in control. He kept an eagle eye open and cursed anyone who failed to cut his full stint. Mowing is a very skilled job; it was unlikely that a young man was considered a competent mower until he was at least twenty years of age. Setting the scythe to suit the individual was an art. It included adjusting the angle of the 'tacks' (handles). Sharpening too is a skilled operation; then using the darned thing! Only years of experience could bring perfection. These men worked from 6 am to 6 or 8 o'clock at night and perhaps walked a mile and often more to work, bringing with them their food for the day, which often consisted of a lump of fat pork and masses of wonderful homemade bread and a good onion. This was brought in a 'tommy bag' and packed with their bottles of home-brewed in a 'frail' basket and 'wholly' good it was too. A tommy bag was made of calico, about 10 ins x 7 ins with a draw string at one end. The frail basket was a woven rush basket about 18 ins x 15 ins with two braided rush handles and a leather top-latch looped through the handles and long enough to enable the basket to be carried over the shoulder.

In the light of the present day I think these men and their wives were the salt of the earth. They knew and took great interest in their jobs and were highly skilled. They took the greatest care of their hand tools, which they owned, and felt responsible for the maintenance of the farm implements.

I still marvel at the cheerfulness of these men. I think it was largely due to the fact that they worked more in gangs together than today. They had their lighter moments. I have seen elderly men, in heavy hob nailed boots, very rheumaticy, who, when the rabbits ran out of the corn, chased them like two year olds and really enjoyed it. All the rabbits caught in the harvest field were auctioned by the 'lord' at the finish of the cutting of each field. The proceeds were pooled and spent mainly on beer at the 'Harvest Horkey'.

Before the 'self binder' came into general use there was much more corn left in the fields and this no doubt was the reason for the introduction of the horse-rake. All the fields were raked and the rakings carted home. It was the custom when carting the corn to leave a 'policeman' in the fields. This was three sheaves bound together and left standing in the field to warn gleaners (women and children) that the field had not yet been raked and that they were not allowed to glean. I have known families to glean sufficient wheat to keep them in flour for most of the year.

Much of the corn was stacked in barns, thus the reason for the very high and wide barn doors, which allowed wagon loads of corn to be drawn in. The corn was stacked in the bays on either side of the 'middlestead'. The middlestead in the early days before the arrival of the threshing machine was used for threshing corn with a flail. This was a skilled job and unless very practised one could give oneself a really bad crack on the head. I saw this operation in England only for threshing beans for seed though I did use a flail a few times myself. In Africa in the last war I saw teams of eight, four either side of the 'bed' making a very good job of it. Each team hit the bed alternately, so timing was vital, and the Arabs were masters of the job.

In order to get as much corn as possible into the bays of the barn, it was quite usual to have a horse walking round to tread the straw as tightly as possible. I have often ridden the horse for this job. The difficulty was, having got up to the beams, the horse had to be got down. This was done by pushing it down onto a head of straw, men pushing from behind, and when the usually frightened animal started to slip down, the men who had pushed then held on to the horse's tail to steady it down.

Most of the corn, however, was placed in stacks in the stackyard. Building those was a skilful job, and the stacker, usually the head horseman, took great pride in building a good stack, as the men did in all their work. The keen men walked many miles, and later cycled, on Sundays to look at the workmanship, such as ploughing, drilling and stacking on neighbouring farms. A bad piece of work was reported in the pubs and the perpetrator heard a lot about it!

To denote that it was the last load of corn from the harvest, it was custom to place on top of the load a sizeable branch preferably from an ash tree. Why this was done and what history lay behind it, I know not; but it usually happened at 'beaver' time, that is about 4 pm. On this the last day of harvest all the men gathered in the stackyard and mother produced a large can of hot tea or coffee and newly baked currant buns. Father produced a bottle of gin, and while the celebration took place father paid out the bonus.

It was a jolly and sometimes hilarious affair, as the men usually brought extra beer as well.

One is apt to look back and glamourise, but I feel that these men, having worked extra hard from 6 am until dark most days for the last four or five weeks (but never on Sunday), felt a great sense of satisfaction and achievement as they sat, surrounded by neat and well built stacks of grain which they had produced and harvested, and sipped their coffee laced with gin.

I recall the dress of these men. They mostly wore corduroy trousers, a shirt

Farm worker. Early twentieth century (by Maureen Wills)

Farm worker's wife. Early twentieth century (by Maureen Wills)

and coloured 'neckerchief', or a striped, washable celluloid collar and no tie, heavy hob-nailed leather boots, probably made to measure, with a bowler or wide brimmed high crowned straw hat. The trousers were almost invariably tied with 'latches', leather or string, below the knee, and all wore a leather belt. The latter, when the wearer was on a specially heavy job, was pulled a hole or two tighter and a great support and comfort it was too.

The older of these men had very little schooling. Some of them had gone to night school at 1d per week and had learned to read and write, but otherwise had largely educated themselves. One of these, John Stockings, worked as a labourer, but he also had about five acres which he owned and farmed and he always had a sow or two, and some pigs fattening. He took a great interest in politics and was an ardent Tory. He wrote letters to various political leaders and was delighted when he received a reply saying that his letter had been received and was receiving attention. I cannot recall that he ever had a detailed reply. He was a man of squat figure, rather stout with a heavy moustache, married, with four or five children. He was a source of great amusement to me. He had a good sense of humour and related many anecdotes.

One day he said "I riled the missus last noight". I said "How was that?" He said "She cooked a beef steak and kidney puddin' for me tea. When she give me mine I say to her I say, 'Mum, this wat cher call stink don't it?' 'she say to me, she say, 'Why John thus beauful', and she was suffin' riled, so I say, 'thas wot I mean, thut stink luvly'." He had his mother living with him, very old, very large and fat, and one morning he said "A tidy job with mother last night". I said "Oh!, what was the trouble?" 'Well, we be hevin' our tea and presently the missus, she say, 'Where is Tabs?' (the cat), I said 'I ha'nt sin her since her cum in', so the missus went out and kept a-callin, Puss, Puss, Puss, so I say 'Leave her be, she'll cum when she's riddy'. Well, I never knew such a job, do you know, when mother got up off her chair, there lay poor Tabs flat as a bloody pancake and royut dead. I say to Mother, 'I say, dint you feel nothing when you sit down?' Mother say, 'Well I thout suffin fared sorft, but I never even felt a squiggle'."

John loved his home brewed beer and always brewed it from water from a pond which was filled by draining off the road. When it is remembered that although the roads were not tarred and there was no motor traffic, but that many horses used the road, also sheep and cattle, it will be realised that the water held a fair content of animal droppings. However, John, as did many others, preferred pond water to well water for brewing, as he said "The beer had a better flavour and more body". My father brewed beer as often as necessary; a large amount of beer was given away by the farmers. A bushel of malt produced about eighteen gallons of beer of reasonable strength; if only nine gallons it was potent. It was the custom among many farmers at this time to offer beer to any workmen arriving at the farm, as a tip. It was offered to any of our own workforce as an extra reward for some service rendered outside normal duty, and I believe much appreciated. A pint of mulled home-brewed on a cold night has I have no doubt warded off many a cold.

When harvesting the corn by machine, all the fields had one swath mown round with a scythe. Where poultry from adjoining cottages had strayed into the fields and trodden the corn down, making it difficult to mow, the men expected a drink from the poultry owners. My father used to laugh about the time when John Stockings mowed all round a field where six cottages adjoined and all the occupiers kept poultry. Father went to see how John was getting on and found him having finished mowing, leaning against a stile and obviously very tight, saying he could drink no more and could "put his fingers down his throat and feel the drink". Unfortunately he had been given beer at some houses and mead at others.

Brewing day was one of great activity and long hours. The large copper, having been scoured with wood ash and scrubbed scrupulously clean, was filled with water (in our case from the well!). The water was brought to boiling point and the malt put in. The boiling went on for some hours and then the hops were added and the whole boiled up again. Father always took out a quart jug-full before putting in the hops. This was known as 'sweet wort'. When cool it was very pleasant to drink, but soon went sour. After the boiling had gone on for some time the beer was ladelled into flat tubs and the malt and hops strained out. It was left to cool and then the yeast was put in. This started the beer 'working' after which it was left all night. By morning the tubs would be covered with a thick layer of yeast which was skimmed off with a 'flat' the same tool that was used for skimming the cream off milk. The beer was then ready to put in barrels. No one ever had to buy yeast; one simply went to someone else who had just brewed and begged a jug-full.

Once at Woodside my brother stepped backwards to avoid father who was carrying a kettle of boiling water, and fell into a tub of beer. Luckily it was only warm and no harm was done. I cannot remember that anyone complained that the beer had an unusual flavour. This brings to mind an occasion during harvest on a very hot day some years later. John Stockings was unloading a load of barley on to a stack which was getting rather high. Poor old John was sweating profusely, and the barley havels were sticking to his arms and face and chest. I was on the stack in the 'bully hole' and he looked pitifully up at me and said "Master, du you know, I'd loike tu stand in a tank of home-brewed right up to my chin and when I wanted a 'wet', I'd only hev to jist 'bop'.

Threshing the corn, one of my earliest memories, was quite a 'do'. The threshing tackle, consisting of a portable steam engine, threshing drum, and straw pitcher or elevator, was owned by a man who hired them out to farmers. He sent three men, an engine driver, a drum feeder and a corn stacker to work them. These machines were moved from farm to farm by horses. We would send horses to the next farm to bring the tackle to us. This usually involved four horses for the engine, three or four for the drum and two for the elevator. I have seen awful jobs for the horses in getting the tackle 'set' to thresh a stack, especially in wet weather. Having threshed what was required, the next client would send horses to haul the tackle away. This, of course, became much simplified when the traction engine came into being, as the traction engine hauled the rest of the tackle.

Many farmers used to keep a few stacks of wheat until just before the next harvest. The drawback to this was that mice and rats got into the stacks and did a great deal of damage. To overcome this, the stacks to be kept would be placed on 'ricks'. These consisted of iron legs, about two feet high, set on bricks with inverted metal cups on the top. A frame work of wood was built on the legs for stacks to stand on. All loose straw was trimmed off and the mice were unable to climb up the legs. This worked very well, but unless every care was taken mice would get in and breed very quickly. All farmworkers realised that it was a crime to leave anything leaning against a rick, even for one night, to allow access into the rick for mice and rats.

Threshing in my boyhood days holds many pleasant memories. The steam traction engine with a good driver who maintained it in good order was always of great interest and a source of amazement, especially the way it ran effortlessly hour after hour, driving the thresher. The Burrells, Ransomes, and the Garrett Engines, all Suffolk products, were very popular, likewise the Ransomes Threshing Machines.

Then there was the excitement of killing the mice and rats; we had good terriers who also enjoyed the fun. Some terriers ate all the mice they killed; then having got distended stomachs were violently sick and started all over again. On the other hand, some terriers ate none at all.

The workmen all had two pints of beer on threshing days, one at 11 am and one at 3.30 pm and I have many times drawn the beer from a barrel and taken it to the stackyard. It was interesting to hear the comments of the tackle men as they compared the qualities of the beer on the various farms on which they worked. Threshing by the Suffolk man, was always called 'froshin' and in Norfolk too, and many have heard of the man who said "I come from Swaffham, done three days froshin' fer northin', thas suffin' aint it?" UNQUOTE

No Pub – No Blacksmith!

Village life as I have seen it – by John Hitchcock

November 5th, 1934. My mother spent the early part of the evening watching the village firework display with my brothers, Ben and David. The excitement must have been too much for her, as she went into labour later that evening; and eventually produced the baby who was to complete the family. ME! Having already got two sons, I think they were probably hoping for a girl. There wasn't to be another baby born at Chapel Farm until my grandson William made his appearance sixty two years later.

My infancy was spent in and around Chapel Farm, an idyllic surrounding for three adventurous small boys. With my two older brothers we enjoyed family life on the farm immensely. I spent many hours with Walter ('Wick') Smith on a Fordson tractor, and one of us was usually sound asleep – and it wasn't 'Wick'.

Ben and David Hitchcock with Peggy Gooderham at "Chapel Farm" – circa 1934

'Wick' Smith served with my father in the Grenadier Guards during the First World War, and afterwards worked for the family at Vale Farm, Creeting (where father was the tenant farmer), and afterwards at Chapel Farm where they went to live in 1928 when my grandparents retired to "Fairview" (now Maple Cottage), Ringshall.

Eventually it was time for me to start my formal education at Barking Village School. My older brother, Ben was entrusted to take me on my first day. As soon as I entered the building, I decided it was better at home, and started to cry lustily, much to the consternation of the two teachers present. Miss Ablitt, from Needham Market, and Miss Barber the head teacher, in desperation, no doubt, decided it might quieten me down if I joined in morning prayers. Nothing would stop my loud sobs, I wanted to go home!

"Vale Farm", Creeting. Home to Clement and Jane Hitchcock before they moved to "Chapel Farm"

After a while I settled into the school routine, and Jack Johnson would become a fellow classmate. Most mornings I walked to school pulling my small wooden boat behind me (this was aptly named "Ark Royal"). Occasionally I managed to get a lift.

Boys will be boys! How many times my parents must have uttered those prophetic words. I was only seven when I nearly caused a serious catastrophe. Ted Coleman and I lit a fire in a chicken hut, unfortunately my father turned up unexpectedly. In panic, we quickly doused the flames by pouring water over them, and made a fast exit. However, we hadn't made a very good job of extinguishing the fire, and during the night the hut, which was covered in 'old man's beard' began to burn merrily. My father, who by now was fully alerted to the problem, ran and got water from the pond, and also called the local Home Guard. During the war years any fires, however small, were treated seriously and promptly as they could be a good 'give away' to the enemy. For once I was very keen to get to school the following day. Awkward questions could have proved embarrassing.

Ted Coleman working at Chapel Farm, circa 1961

The Second World War affected everyone in the country in one way, or another. Although very young at the time, certain memories remain clear. My father joined the A.R.P. (Air Raid Precautions) for the duration of the war.

Rationing came into force on 8 January 1940. Meat rationing began in March the same year. Families were issued with four-ounces of butter per week, and twelve-ounces of sugar per week. Some foods would remain rationed until 1954.

General goods (ironmongery, etc) were delivered regularly to local villages, usually on a Saturday, here, by Hopgoods of Stowmarket, and Swains of Needham Market (now Paul's Hardware). These old fashioned vans would be well loaded, and anything that couldn't be carried inside, could be found dangling perilously over the side attached by hooks to the vehicle.

Hopgoods (Stowmarket) Ltd, delivering to local villages – circa 1940s-1950s. (Produced by kind permission of Mr David Hopgood – 1999)

The winter of 1940-41 was very severe. Roads in the village were too slippery for the horse, so a Fordson tractor was used instead. The hard frosts caused the mud on the wheels of the tractor to freeze, so when the vehicle moved forward, the mudguards went with the wheels! My father had to use a blow lamp to free them.

Two types of shelters were issued by the War Department, Anderson shelters, and Morrison shelters.

We had a different type of shelter, and it didn't resemble either the Anderson or Morrison. It was obviously a Hitchcock prototype.

When the bombs started to fall, my father wasted no time in building an air raid shelter in the ditch, a third the way up Chapel Farm drive. It consisted of corrugated iron across the ditch, with soil on top. The banks were dug to make seats, and both ends of this refuge were open. If a bomb had dropped, I feel we would have been blown out like a shot from a cannon. Luckily, we never found out!

The Anderson shelter was designed to be dug six feet into the ground, with a curved roof and soil on top. It was made of heavy gauge corrugated steel.

The Morrison shelter (named after Herbert Morrison, Cabinet Minster in Winston Churchill's government), resembled a table with steel mesh sides. This type of shelter was designed for use in houses. Arthur Coleman, one of the local 'barbers' in my youth, possessed such a shelter, and I remember eyeing it with some interest every time I had my sixpenny haircut. It was difficult to imagine how Arthur, his wife and their large family, all managed to squeeze into the confines of such a shelter. They must have resembled sardines in a tin.

Families in Ringshall acted as 'host families' to a number of young evacuees from London during the early part of the war (probably 1940). These children, between the ages of six to fourteen, arrived here looking very dishevelled and frightened. To have been taken from their own homes and families and virtually dumped among strangers in alien countryside, must have been daunting, to say the least. On their first night in the village some slept on the floor in the Village Hall, and others at Chapel Farm. The majority of these youngsters had never experienced life outside London. The Suffolk countryside must have seemed strange indeed. As far as I am aware, once they returned home to their families, none of the evacuees ever returned to the village.

At the beginning of hostilities, Wattisham Base still had incomplete living quarters, and in the meantime my mother billeted some air force personnel at Chapel Farm. They came from New Zealand, South Africa and England – quite a mixed bunch. Sports, cars, dogs (one had a large St Bernard), and a number of girl friends, made life much more interesting for us youngsters. The St Bernard was quite agile considering its size, and would frequently jump into the moat on hot summer days, then straight into its owner's MG sports car (how RAF officers loved their MGs).

My father had a contract with Wattisham Base to clear kitchen waste to feed the pigs. Walter Keeble who lived in the "Old School House" at the time, with his wife Mabel and six children, was put in charge of this waste collection. He became a familiar sight along the lanes of Ringshall driving the four wheel tub cart, pulled by 'Gin' the Cob.

The War Department 'borrowed' Walter Keeble, together with tractor and rib rolls to go to airfields in Norfolk and Suffolk to keep the runways flat for the aircraft.

Walter always claimed he learnt how to speak German whilst a prisoner in the First World War. However, whatever words he remembered, wasn't sufficient to make the German prisoners of war in the area understand his lingo.

"Chapel Farm" Dairy van which was driven by Ronnie Smith

Between 1934 to 1945, Chapel Farm delivered milk and eggs, and butter and bread (made by my mother), to the local area. My father had to put a bore hole in at the farm to provide clean water for the milk round, and a stand pipe on Lower Farm Road for use by the village. During particularly bad winters deep snow drifts made it difficult to deliver.

I remember an amusing remark made by Mrs George Sayers of Gt. Bricett who regularly bought her eggs from the milk round because she reckoned she had a 'small swallow'.

My older brother David had frequently driven the vans round the farmyard. Father was therefore quite happy for him to help with the milk deliveries when necessary; although he wasn't legally old enough to drive on the road. On this particular day, he was delivering milk to Overhall Farm, Barking, and in his eagerness, forgot to turn the engine off or set the handbrake. When he turned round, he saw to his horror that the van was going ever faster down the hill ....ending up in a pond. Our father was NOT AMUSED!

1939 – Every able bodied person was keen to do something for the war effort. My mother organised a canteen in a wooden hut, inside the Air Base boundary. She did a roaring trade with the builders, etc, but was forced to leave when the air raids started. Undaunted, and determined as ever, she opened another canteen at the Pumpkin Garage, with stalwart support from Mrs Stockings, Miss Gooderham, and many other helpers. David and I would sometimes help to peel the potatoes.

1942-1943 – The 'Yanks' arrived at Wattisham Air Base and laid a hard surface runway. "Lightning" aircraft were brought in with wings removed so they could be transported along local roads. American engineers had to remove obstructing telegraph poles to facilitate their passage. Aircraft transporters were known as 'Queen Marys'.

The Americans were often described as "overpaid, oversexed, and over here". With their more sophisticated ways they were always very popular with local girls wherever they went. Most of these young men who fought so valiantly by our side were between the ages of seventeen and twenty one. It didn't take them long to fit into local communities, and become well liked and respected.

Once the war started in earnest, Wattisham Base and the surrounding areas experienced the might of the German bombers quite frequently. During the night, from Chapel Farm, we often saw the hangars burning; the flames would light up the sky, leaving an eerie glow. One particular bomb, meant for the Base, landed 'short of its target' and fell into a pond behind 'Nipper' Barton's house. This wooden structure had originally been used as a pigeon loft at Ringshall Hall before being moved to make a house, so the frame of the building was very light. The blast from the bomb blew the pond out, and the house moved sideways. There was no loss of life.

While ploughing in a nearby field in the nineteen-eighties, a large piece of shrapnel from this bomb came to the surface.

A meadow near the Rectory (now the Grange), was used by the Americans to erect approximately thirty six bell tents. These were used as temporary accommodation for other ranks. The officers lived in the Rectory.

Piece of shrapnel found in field of Chapel Farm. This came from the bomb, which landed just short of the pond behind 'Nipper' Barton's house on Ringshall Hall hill. Second World War, 1939–45

The Maintenance depot (vehicles and earth moving equipment), was at Ringshall Hall. Water was desperately needed so a water tower (at the Old Pump House) was requisitioned by the Air Ministry to supply water to the Air Base and Ringshall Hall. The American servicemen laid the pipes for the water supply by digging from Bakers Corner to Ringshall Hall, one Sunday.

The majority of Wattisham Base is in Ringshall. At the beginning of the war the government requisitioned several farms to build the runway; these included "Red House Farm" and "Rookery Farm". In 1950 further farms were requisitioned to enlarge the runway for jet aircraft. These included "Bradleys Farm" and "Box Tree Farm".

The Home Guard, familiarly known as 'Dad's Army' but initially called the Local Defence Volunteers, of L.D.V., was formed at the beginning of the war. 'Pill Boxes' were built in strategic positions around the Air Base and used as meeting points by the local Home Guard. This all important defence line went from Colchester, Sudbury, Lavenham, Bury St Edmunds and Mildenhall.

During the war years, the local countryside took on a very different look. Tank traps were constructed on roadways approaching the Air Base. These consisted of railway track dropped into slots on the roads, and on either side, six feet square concrete blocks were placed. Search lights were installed around the perimeter to illuminate enemy aircraft. Air raid sirens were placed in Needham Market and Wattisham Air Base, the 'alert' an oscillating sound, while the 'all clear' was transmitted on one note. These sounds became very familiar. Doodlebugs were very frightening. When the engine stopped, they glided silently to the ground.

Photograph of old Pill Box sited on Pump House land (1939-45 war). There was also a Water Tower on this land during the war years

We saw many American bombers returning with machine gun damage. During the invasion of Normandy in 1944, aircraft were taking off from all bases, dropping silver paper strips to jam German radar – code name 'WINDOW'. Occasionally, our countryside was littered with paper. Aircraft could be seen towing gliders to get more soldiers to France. The war in Europe was beginning to swing in our favour.

The clothing industry was quickly turned over to war production, and clothing was unobtainable without coupons issued by the government. Good material became almost non-existent. The U-Boat blockade stopped us getting anything from America. John Smith who worked and lived at Chapel Farm towards the end of the war, happened to miss the last bus home from Stowmarket. This necessitated a long walk in the rain. By the time he reached the farm, his shoes had fallen apart because of the poor quality of the material.

Cooper's buses ran from Stowmarket, via Battisford and Ringshall to Wattisham Base four times a day. These buses were ALWAYS full, and were owned by 'Poly Joe' who lived in Battisford, and driven by his brother, Amos.

The later war years saw Chapel Farm allocated a few Italian prisoners of war, and eventually German POWs. One of the latter was Ernst Gotscher who stayed on after the war, marrying a local girl. Tragically in the early nineteen-sixties, he and his wife were killed in a car accident.

Four Land Army girls, of various shapes and sizes, worked for a brief time at Chapel Farm during the war. They lived together in one of the farm cottages. Their outfits consisted of khaki corduroy breeches, a shirt, pullover, sometimes a tie, mackintosh, hat, also long socks, shoes and wellington boots.

My father, although not seeing active service during the Second World War, was very much involved with the local community in Ringshall and the surrounding area. Like so many others who stayed at home, he helped to keep 'the wheels turning'.

We will now leave the war years, and as it says in Alice in Wonderland…"talk of other things!"

The village school used to be at the top of Chapel Farm drive, and was run by Mrs Last, who also ran the Sunday School. Originally, the school was at "Stocks Corner" before being burnt down.

Arthur Coleman worked most of his life at Chapel Farm, as did his son, Ted. Jack Thorpe was quite a character and resided for most of his life in the village. Working in one of the fields one day, we were somewhat amused to see the spritely Jack Thorpe in hot pursuit of a hare. Round and round the field they went, three times in all, until eventually the hare met his match, and the conqueror returned to us triumphant, with the hare clutched firmly in his hand. The year was 1944. Jack's son John worked at Chapel Farm and still lives in Ringshall with his wife, Marion.

George Grimwood, another well known local character, was born with deformed feet. When topping sugar beet, he would tie wooden boxes to his feet to keep them dry.

I recall the following conscientious workforce employed at Chapel Farm over the years. My apologies to those I may have forgotten …

Sidney **Gibbons**	George **Hadley**	Jimmy **Wilden**
Harold **Last**	George and Clifford **Mudd**	Joe **Shave**
John **Norton**	Frank **Thorpe** (brother to John)	Sydney **Smith**
Ted **Caley**	Charles **Hadley**	Jack **Smith**
Jack **Johnson**	Ronnie **Stockings**	Ronnie **Smith**
Arthur **Sadd**	Fernando **Bersonetti** (Italian)	

More recent employees:
Jack **Brackenbury**   Andrew **Elmy**
Brian **Ruffles**   Graham **Stephenson**
Len **Le-Grice**   Stephen **Laffling**
Stephen **Laflin**   David **Gill**
Clive **Smith**

Charles Hadley who lived in Willisham, recalled 1920 as being a very dry year. After work he would walk along the footpath to Ringshall to get two buckets of water from a pond. Who says they 'were good old days?'

Up to the early nineteen-fifties, most people in the village were connected with agriculture. Not so today.

Chapel Farm employed between 8-15 people until the nineteen-eighties. There was a flock of 400 sheep until the early nineteen-sixties, 200 milking cows until the early nineteen-eighties, and 400 sows until the late nineteen-eighties. We are now in the nineteen-nineties, and how things have changed. There are now only two of us, and no livestock. The land endures, long after we are gone.

1970s – Wet feeding for pigs – amounts of food controlled by computer. Chapel Farm

I had my first motor car in 1943. It was an Austin Seven without a cylinder head, and was acquired from Ringshall Hall. With some help, and the efforts of 'Jack' the pony – with cart, we pulled the car to Chapel Farm orchard. On the hill I put it into gear, and to my amazement the pistons went up and down. I removed the engine and gear box, and we took it into Lower Farm Road. Well, boys being boys, we energetically pushed the car to the top of the hill, and then.... down we went at considerable speed. Ronnie Stockings lived in a cottage with a steep drive, and we frequently made use of this slope to get up speed. One evening we gave Jack Gibbons a ride (he couldn't have been thinking straight at the time), and such was our speed, we went too fast to drop him off at his house.

A few weeks later a hay stack caught fire at Chapel Farm and we needed the services of the local fire brigade. Two fire engines arrived and one of the firemen offered to buy my Austin Seven for the princely sum of five pounds. I accepted with alacrity. At about eleven o'clock that same evening one of the fire engines, with bell ringing loudly, towed the car away.

When the bus services were short of fuel, they used coal gas, contained in a trailer towed behind the bus. One memorable day, opposite the chapel, the trailer containing this combustible material caught fire, burning the nearby hedge, and causing us young ones much amusement.

In 1962 I married Elizabeth Turnbull from Stonham Aspal. We moved into "The Old Pump House", and are still happily living there today. This property was originally owned by Gipping R.D.C. (now Mid Suffolk), but as previously mentioned, was taken over by the Air Ministry during the Second World War.

The family consists of two daughters, Helen and Ruth, and a son, Guy, who farms with me at Chapel Farm, and lives there with his wife, Liz, and two small children, Katherine and William.

In 1962 irrigation was installed around the farm, using one of the two bore holes at "The Old Pump House".

My mother, Jane Hitchcock, was awarded the British Empire medal in 1982 for services to the community in the Stowmarket area.

Ruth, Guy, and Helen Hitchcock in the garden of their home, "The Old Pump House", Ringshall – 1969

A very vigorous lady, she ran a National Savings group during the war, and was a member of the W.R.V.S. Mother was also a founder member of the Barking and Ringshall Women's Institute, which inaugurated the bus service from Ipswich to Barking and Ringshall.

Farm Inventions at Suffolk Show, 1965. John Hitchcock with the Duchess of Kent

After full lives, my father Clement Hitchcock died on 25 March 1979, and my mother died on 5 November 1986.

At the Suffolk Show in 1965 I was introduced to the Duchess of Kent when she stopped to view the Farm Inventions stand, where I was exhibiting. In my eagerness to explain the rudiments of the various inventions, I forgot to remove my hat. Some gaffe!!

Quote from Farming Express, June 7th 1962

"Suffolk Farmer Lays on Miles of Irrigation Pipes"

Ten thousand yards of underground pipes carry water to all parts of Mr Clement Hitchcock's 350 acre Chapel Farm, at Ringshall.

Mr Hitchcock and his son John, have no more fears about a hot dry summer. They are insured against drought on a farm which is heavily stocked with 50 Friesian milkers and 50 followers; a flock of 400 Scottish Half-Bred ewes; 1,000 laying birds and 120 breeding sows.

Cropping is wheat, barley, oats, sugar beet and grass.

Last year 9,000,000 gallons of water were applied – 5 in. on 30 acres of sugar beet and 3 in. on 80 acres of grassland.

The result was an increase in yield of sugar beet from 14 to 20 tons an acre, 2,500 extra bales of hay, and much more grazing for the sheep and cattle.

"The equipment was new last year and we only experimented with it", says Mr John Hitchcock. "We still have a lot to learn and we can do much better. Irrigation will help us to increase production and lower costs. Even in the hottest summer we shall have no worries about grass for our heavy head of stock".

The Hitchcocks' scheme cost £7,000 for the underground asbestos cement pipes, 12 hydrants and a 3,500,000 gallon reservoir.

The work qualified for a 40 per cent Ministry grant which reduced the bill to £4,200.

They paid the full £1,000 for portable surface pipes. They have 1,200 ft of 5 in. mains and 1,400 ft of lateral piping.

The farm is 'dry' because it lies on high ground – a natural watershed. Water comes from a 700ft borehole on an acre of land bought for £3000 from the Air Ministry three years ago.

The plot included a cottage and two boreholes, each with pumping equipment installed in brick buildings.

Only one borehole is used at present. It has a submersible pump supplying 3,000 gallons of water an hour.

The irrigation requirement is 15,000 gallons an hour, so the water is stored in the reservoir excavated and built by contractors. Running costs for the first year were based on water for the 30 acre beet crop. They worked out at £24 an acre, including labour, interest on capital depreciation, and a pumping cost of 1s. for 3,000 gallons.

Five inches of water resulted in six more tons of beet to the acre. This made £36 in round figures – a profit of £12 through irrigation. Added to this was the extra grass. "We have been advised to use the water for potatoes", says Mr John Hitchcock. "But at the moment we have our hands full".

Irrigation is carried out on two acre plots. It starts on the grass in early spring and on beet when the leaves touch in the rows, about mid-June. Two men lay out the pipes on a plot in about three-quarters of an hour. They use a pipe trailer, made up in the farm workshop for £20. After the initial installation, one man can move the laterals in half an hour. As the farm is well drained, only 5/8 in. of water can be applied at one time. This takes about one hour and three-quarters.

There is a simple water requirement test for heavy clay soil. A sample is taken with a hand auger. If it sticks together like putty it has all the water it needs. But if it is dry and breaks up, the water is turned on. Another reservoir may be built to store water from the second borehole, which is 400 ft deep.

Irrigation is just part of an overall improvement plan for Chapel Farm. This will include automatic stock feeding, slatted floors for the sheep in winter and a new grain plant. "Outlay on irrigation has been very high. But a combine harvester which only works for four to six weeks a year, costs £2,500", says Mr Hitchcock. "We believe that we can use our irrigation plant for 14 to 16 weeks a year – and it is permanent". UNQUOTE

Sheep on slats during winter months to preserve grassland for spring – "Chapel Farm"

Funeral of Mr W. C. Hitchcock
This complete article from East Anglian Daily Times

Ringshall: At the funeral on Saturday, of Mr. William Cooper Hitchcock, the coffin was borne to the church on a farm cart drawn by the deceased's favourite cob. (E.A.D.T. photo)

A waggon drawn by his favourite pony Jock and driven by Mr A Coleman, an employee of twenty years standing, bore the coffin to church at the funeral in Ringshall on Saturday of Mr William Cooper Hitchcock, well known Ringshall farmer of "Fair View", Bricett who died on 7th June 1939. Mr Hitchcock had farmed "Chapel Farm", Ringshall for over 45 years. (Left to right in photo) 'Wick' Smith, Arthur Coleman (driving), Jack Thorpe and Walter Keeble.

The service at Ringshall Church was conducted by the Rev. J. F. Vincent-Fernie (Needham Market) and the singing of "Jesu, Lover of my Soul" and "Rock of Ages" was accompanied at the organ by Mr E. Caley.

Immediate mourners were: The widow, Mr and Mrs C. G. Hitchcock, Mr and Mrs R. W. Hitchcock (sons and daughters-in-law), Mr and Mrs Ernest Hitchcock (brother and sister-in-law), Messrs John and Joe Hitchcock (brothers), Mrs J. R. Osborne, Cambridge (sister), Mr and Mrs P. Ginn (nephew and niece), Mr and Mrs H. Jewers (brother-in-law and sister), the Misses Jewers (nieces), Mr Claude Hitchcock (nephew), Miss Edith Hitchcock, Mr Roger Hitchcock (cousin), Mr and Mrs J. Clover, and Mrs Hayward.

"Chapel Farm" in 1920

Ringshall As I Remember It From 1935–1997
By David Hitchcock

I have just returned to Ringshall having spent the last forty two years living in Gloucestershire and Oxfordshire. My retirement has brought me back to my home village and I now live in the house where my father was born in 1898. I am very happy to be residing at Hill House, Ringshall.

Let me share with you some of my memories of Ringshall.

I started school in September 1935. My brother Ben and I walked there and back every day accompanied by our mother. The second year was much easier as we were given bicycles and with one of the men who worked on our father's farm cycling along with us, there and back, we made the journey in comparative comfort. In those days there wasn't much traffic on the roads.

At the age of ten I started at the Stowmarket Grammar School. Once again my brother Ben and I reached our scholastic destination on our bikes. At the age of thirteen I began to help more on the farm when father had men away. Many weeks were spent milking the cows and going on the milk round. The more time I spent on the farm, the less attractive school became.

One morning when I was about fifteen years old, father got me out of bed early to go on the milk round as Ted was away sick. This meant me driving the van. Our father was quite happy to have me drive this vehicle as he knew we had been driving the vans around the farmyard. Everything went quite well for the first hour, until I arrived at Overhall Farm, Barking. Having carefully deposited the milk, I turned round and with horror saw the van disappearing into the horse pond. I hadn't turned the engine off or put the brake on. Hurrying to the local police station I telephoned my father, speaking with some care as Police Constable Barber stood at my shoulder and I didn't want him to know I had been driving the van. Luckily, I managed to convey the necessity for a lorry and a long rope to my father without the constabulary realising my plight.

In 1937 to allow for the easier transportation of the long steel girders from Needham station to what would soon become Wattisham aerodrome, Ringshall corner and Barking Lane corner were straightened out. These girders were about 180ft long.

Work went ahead at quite a pace and some of the men who had formerly been working on the local farms, left to work at the aerodrome. By 1938 work was advanced enough for the Royal Airforce personnel to commence moving in. I remember we lodged two RAF officers at the farm for six months while accommodation was made ready at the Base. Possibly, Pilot Officer Free, and Flying Officer Blake were the first of the RAF staff to move into the area. As they were Equipment Officers, they were responsible for fitting out all the barrack blocks, officers mess, and living quarters for the incoming airforce.

Two squadrons of aircraft arrived in early 1939. Namely, 106 Squadron and 110 Squadron. 110 was known as the "Hyderabad" squadron as it was founded by an Indian prince and all the officers were colonials. Some of the names remembered are: Flying Officer Hill from Canada, Flying Officer Wright from South Africa, Flying Officer Lightoller from New Zealand, and an Indian gentleman whose name I think was Flying Officer Ezehail. All these officers resided at Chapel Farm during 1939/40 at the start of the war.

The runways were nearly all grass and the aircraft spent a lot of time bogged down in heavy clay.

At this time the Local Defence Volunteers were formed from the men in the village. They used to meet and train in the Village Hall (remember "Dad's Army"). No weapons were issued to them, their 'uniform' merely consisted of armbands with the letters LDV on them. Luckily for us the enemy did not invade us at this time.

On 5 November 1940 a German aircraft dropped a bomb which fell beside "Nipper Barton's" house on Ringshall Hall hill. It came down in the pond behind the house and exploded. Fortunately as the pond was large and deep, the blast went straight up and left the house standing by the side of the crater. Nobody was killed, but Mrs Barton hurt her ankle. Not much return for a 500 lb bomb.

In 1942 the American army moved into Wattisham, not as a Bombing Unit, but as a Maintenance Unit. Their job was to travel to other airfields to build runways, etc. Tents were erected in the grounds of Ringshall Hall and in the Spring Pond meadow at the Glebe Farm. These tents housed several hundred black Americans. These were the first black people I had ever come into contact with and it was rather a shock. It appeared these black Americans had 'invited' about twenty women from Ipswich and set them up in camp in Muckinger Wood. I was under the impression they were there to do the washing and ironing for these Americans (I was only fourteen years old at the time). When we had to cart the harvest out of Wood Field, I remember our men were not too keen to go near the place.

During the war we had a little dog called Shrimp, and at the weekends we would hunt the hedges for rabbits. This little pastime kept us in pocket money. Alas we wouldn't get very rich at 'rabbiting' today as all the hedges have disappeared.

In 1940 a further area was added to the churchyard. St Catherine's Church was used by the Royal Air Force personnel from Wattisham aerodrome during the war years. About twenty men were killed during those dark days and some in later conflicts. These men, some from far countries, who fought for us, are now remembered in Ringshall churchyard.

The farm stopped using horses about 1946. We had our last foal born in 1942, which was subsequently sold at the Suffolk Horse Sale in Ipswich for ninety guineas (top price that year). We had one horse for yard work and two Welsh Cobbs for road work – carting swill, etc, from the aerodrome.

In June 1948 the local villages suffered a severe hail storm. Offton, Barking, Ringshall and Battisford took the full brunt of this storm, the hail stones were so big they killed ducks and chickens, broke glass in greenhouses, took leaves off trees, and destroyed the corn crops and sugar beet crops. Many farmers had no harvest that year, and I believe some farmers still insure against hail damage.

Farming changed in Ringshall with the advent of the first combine. Less men were needed, and sugar beet was being harvested by machine, tractors with loaders. More horse power and bigger ploughs also helped to speed the work up.

Back to the present day, and how things have changed in the village since my early days. We now have a new village hall with playing field and car park. A new school was built in 1949, which also takes children from the air base. Several new properties have been built in Lower Farm Road.

To have two reservoirs for water storage must be a great relief with the recent very hot summers. This helps the sugar beet. I also notice tower silos for grain storage, a welcome change from the everlasting 16 stone and 18 stone corn bags we had to handle. Some Suffolk barns are now being converted into attractive houses. The old Tithe Barn at Ringshall is a very good example of this sort of conversion. We now see old farm buildings being replaced by high steel buildings, which are much better for modern machines and corn storage.

Ringshall Prepares For Dark Days Ahead 1939-45

Although still a young boy in the late nineteen-thirties, I have vivid memories of people and events leading up to the Second World War. Village life continued, but many changes would take place in the ensuing years. Many goodbyes were said by local families to loved ones and friends. Due to the proximity of the aerodrome, many young people, all far from home, came into our lives. I think we made them welcome.

I remember clearly the years 1937-38 when Mr Frederick Thompson bought the cottage on the Barking Road and he also built a garage primarily to sell petrol. These premises were on the opposite side of the road to where the present garage now stands. This gentleman installed a large generator and manufactured his own electricity. It was said he had approximately one-hundred storage batteries in a shed which enabled him to operate the generator once a week. This source of electricity enabled him to work his petrol pumps and a thriving business ensued. Thus began Pumpkin Garage. Mr Thompson was quite ambitious, and proceeded to build a large shed, which he meant to convert into a 'Tea Room'. Unfortunately the war started and as he was in the Territorial Army, he was called up. At this time the only other garages which sold petrol in the area were at Needham Market and Bildeston.

During this time, 1936-37, Council houses were built on the side of South View for the occupation of agricultural workers. However, work had begun in earnest at Wattisham aerodrome and local young men decided work there was more attractive than toiling on the farms.

Mr Jolly was employed by Mr Hitchcock (my father), to deliver milk during this period. His area covered Ringshall, Barking, Willisham, Offton, Somersham and Bricett. Being quite an enterprising chap, he started a local Boy Scout Group. Twenty five local lads from the nearby villages joined and meetings were held at Ringshall school. The Group prospered until Mr Jolly decided to leave the employment of Chapel Farm, thereby making continuation of this Scout Group impossible. 'Open Day' at Wattisham Aerodrome in April 1939 was presided over by the Station Commander, Group Captain Gayford. Other personnel remembered are Flight Lieutenant Pretty (Adjutant); Pilot Officer Free and Pilot Officer Blake. The latter two officers were known as Equipment officers and these two airmen lived at Chapel Farm for several months. After the 'Open Day' at the aerodrome they moved into their allotted quarters on the Base.

My father had a contract with the War Department to clear all the swill from Wattisham Aerodrome during and after the war. He paid for it by the number of servicemen that were on the aerodrome, the price was based on per 1,000 men per week. The amount of swill was enough to keep approximately 500 pigs on a continuous throughput. Pigs in those days were sold when they weighed a hefty 12-14 stones. On one occasion swine fever broke out in the pig units and the swill had to be carted away and tipped onto the fields and ploughed in. This provided a great feeding ground for thousands of birds. Rooks, starlings and seagulls swooped down to devour voraciously. Swill was also collected from the American camps. Amazingly, this included oranges, grapefruit, packets of bread, breakfast cereals (all in perfect condition). Rich pickings indeed!! All the tons of swill, including many skins off bacon sides, were made into large heaps and when rotted down was spread as muck on the land.

My mother opened the Pumpkin Café during the war (about 1943). With the stalwart assistance of Mrs Stockings, Mrs Smith and Miss Phyllis Gooderham. They would cook eggs, sausages and chips for anybody who liked a meal out. The most eager customers were the young airmen from Wattisham, and later the American airmen. Customers were encouraged to sign the visitors book kept by my mother, and I am sure there were many interesting names amongst the entries. This little café closed its doors for the last time shortly after the war.

'The Water Tower' And 'The Pump House'

The Ministry of Defence bought approximately one acre of land from Mr C. Hitchcock to bore two wells to supply water to Wattisham aerodrome round about 1938. Being unable to supply large amounts of water, they were not a great success. However, when the last war started, wives and families of the Base personnel serving there were evacuated and so less water was required. Water was gravity fed to RAF Wattisham. A local farmer, Mr Ray Kemp, was also able to draw water from the line.

Sometime during 1954 the whole site and buildings were put up for sale and subsequently bought by Mr C. Hitchcock. He then had the reservoir constructed approximately one acre in area. The earth was dug out by dragline diggers making the depth of water 13 ft (4 metres) deep. An extensive system of underground 6 inch piping was laid to every part of Chapel Farm for irrigation. This system successfully watered all necessary crops. The reservoir today has a good supply of fish and is on hire to a local fishing club.

John Hitchcock and his wife Elizabeth turned the 'Pump House' into a fine family home and have continued to live there happily for the last thirty-seven years.

The "Old Pump House", home to Elizabeth and John Hitchcock – May 1999

Harvest time 1943 and the first Italian prisoners of war came to work at Chapel Farm. They came from a camp at Botesdale, arriving and leaving in a taxi. Their day started on the farm at 9 o'clock in the morning, and finished about 5 o'clock in the afternoon. Lunch and tea were supplied by

Mr Hitchcock, but the taxi driver spent most of the day in his vehicle sleeping. Perhaps it was the country air!

After the harvest, the same Italian prisoners of war actually lived on the farm for a time and had meals prepared by Mrs Hitchcock. The Hitchcocks had very mixed feelings about these Italians. The men were very agreeable and keen to learn our language, but it was difficult for the family completely to forget that Mr Hitchcock's brother, Rowland, was still in North Africa where several Italian Divisions were helping General Rommel in his fight against the British.

Altogether, we gave work to twelve Italian prisoners of war and then they were withdrawn and substituted by German prisoners of war. One of the Germans stayed on after the war, married an English girl and had two children. Unfortunately, some years later, their car was involved in a serious accident and both he and his wife were killed.

Ministry Of Defence Water Tower And Works, Pump House, Ringshall

By Mr George Green, 19 Little Hill, Gt Bricett
Formerly of The Pump House, Ringshall

The Works consisted of two Bore Holes, a Softener Plant and Storage Tower.

No. 1 Bore Hole: This was a submersible Electric Pump.
No. 2 Bore Hole: This Pump was belt-driven by a Rushton Hornsby Diesel Engine.

The Water Softener Plant was made up of a concrete tank filled with salt and water. The brine was then drawn off into a Holding Tank, which in turn passed through the softener tank, which was filled with clinker. As water was pumped from the bore holes it passed through the softener tank before going into a Storage Tank capable of holding 100,000 gallons. The tank was divided into two compartments each holding 50,000 gallons. Before going into the Storage Tanks, the water passed through a Chlorination plant, which contained a mixture of chlorine and sulphate of ammonia.

Water was gravity fed to RAF Wattisham. Local farmer, Mr Ray Kemp, was also able to draw water from the line.

Oxfordshire Farmer tells of Traumatic Accident Experience

The following event happened on 27 May 1993. Mr Hitchcock subsequently returned to Ringshall where he now lives.

QUOTE: A 63 year old Oxfordshire farmer, David Hitchcock of Broadwell Manor Farm, Broadwell, told of his recent traumatic accident experience at the Health and Safety Executive's (HSE's) Stoneleigh press conference.

Mr Hitchcock, who manages 1500 acres divided into arable, dairy and sheep, has worked in the industry all his life. He was silage making on the farm at the end of May and had brought the last load of grass with a tractor and trailer to the silage clamp before taking a break for lunch.

A colleague working on the clamp had already gone to eat. Mr Hitchcock put the tipping mechanism into operation and at first everything seemed to operate in the normal way. "Then suddenly the trailer jack-knifed lifting the rear wheels of the tractor into the air. I was tilted forward at an acute angle and then just as suddenly smashed back onto the ground with tremendous force. The full force of the impact jolted through my body and I hit my head."

Mr Hitchcock was horror-stricken when the tractor was lifted twice more and again violently smashed back to the ground. "I knew that I had been hurt quite badly although I remained conscious throughout the ordeal." By sounding the horn on the tractor he managed to alert his son who was working in a nearby field. It took ambulance men two hours to remove Mr Hitchcock from the tractor before he was taken to hospital.

Examination revealed that Mr Hitchcock had broken a vertebra in his back and had narrowly missed snapping his spinal cord, which would have crippled him for life. As it is he will spend the next few months in plaster requiring 24 hour nursing care from his wife Rita.

Of the accident he says: "I had never had any kind of incident in all the years I have farmed and have always been careful to keep machinery and equipment in good working condition. The experience I had was terrible and frightening. I think the accident occurred because the last load I brought in was heavier than normal due to the wet conditions, which could have unbalanced the machinery.

With hindsight a heavier tractor was needed to balance that particular load. Certainly all the staff on the farm are now more than aware that weight of a load must be carefully considered. I can only hope that my experience will serve as a warning to other farmers to be extra alert in wet conditions and ensure that the load carried is well within the machine's limit". UNQUOTE

The Next Generation
By Guy Hitchcock

My parents, John and Elizabeth Hitchcock produced three children, Helen, myself and my younger sister Ruth. I was born at the "Old Pump House", on 5 June 1965.

Like my father before me, I really enjoyed my childhood in the country, and was very fond of my paternal grandparents who owned "Chapel Farm". Whenever I had lunch with Granny and Granpa, treacle tart was invariably on the menu as they knew it was a particular favourite of mine. The farmhouse kitchen was Granny's domain. She was in charge! Whenever meals were served it was always my grandmother who seemed to be at everyone's 'beck and call'. It wasn't unusual to see her get up from the table several times during one meal to answer to the demands of her family. Bread was baked weekly, and the wholesome smell of freshly baked loaves, golden brown in colour, and so delicious to eat, is forever reminiscent of my boyhood.

Holiday times were usually spent at "Chapel Farm" which gave me a good grounding for my future work.

At the age of five I attended Ringshall Primary School. My Mother would pick me up at the end of the afternoon session, drop me off at "Chapel Farm", and then I would ride around with my father in his landrover. It was a very carefree time.

I was only six years old when I first learnt to drive a tractor. It was a small wheel horse tractor, which was redundant from the dairy enterprise. With this vehicle I was taught to back a four-wheel trailer. My apprenticeship had begun!

At the age of seven I was sent to Ipswich Prep' School. The regular car journeys were shared with Pat Oliver from "Moats Tye", whose son Jonathan also attended the school. Those days were not my happiest.

The summer of 1976 was very hot, the sun shone continuously from May onwards. But there was a price to pay! The moat at "Chapel Farm" dried up, well almost! There were a few luckless fish in one part of the moat, with a dribble of water. We put a plank across the mud and rescued the fish. When the digger cleared the mud out of the moat, we were amazed to find the area where the fish had been, went down to a depth of eight to ten feet. When all the mud had been cleared out, I was able to ride my scramble bike in the bottom of the moat.

In September, 1976 I went as a boarder to Cawston College in Norfolk. This school was in the heart of the countryside and I enjoyed my years there very much. The various outdoor activities appealed to me, especially the clay pigeon shooting. This part of my formal education finished in 1981. I was sorry to leave.

On leaving Cawston College, I had a year at home, working on the farm. In the autumn of 1982 I went to work on a farm in Oxfordshire. From there I went on to Brooksby Agricultural College in Leicestershire, where I completed a one year course.

Another year on the farm followed, and then it was back to Brooksby College to complete another year course. During my second year I met Liz who was on the same course.

Having left Brooksby Agricultural College at the age of twenty one, I went in for my Class 1 Heavy Goods Vehicle licence. Gaining this enabled me to help with the relief driving on the farm.

The autumn of 1987 was exceptionally wet and the crops were difficult to establish. Worse was to come! The hurricane which hit us on the night of 15 October caused unprecedented havoc in its wake. I remember clearly the sound of the roof tiles lifting and falling to the ground. From my bedroom window I could see the power lines flashing as they touched, lighting up the night sky. The following morning a sight of unbelievable devastation greeted us. Because of the previous wet weather, even large trees had been uprooted. Mighty oaks which had stood so majestically splendid for maybe four hundred years, or more, now lay toppled, their foliage bedraggled. On driving past "Ringshall Grange", I was saddened to see so many familiar trees torn from the ground, lying like gigantic matchsticks, higgledy-piggledy. I managed a glimmer of a smile, however, when I noticed the milk bottles left neatly in the driveway as the milkman was unable to reach the house. Business as usual!

The drive leading to "Ringshall Grange" after the hurricane of 15 October 1987. Note the three lonely milk bottles!

Everywhere were signs of chaos; greenhouses smashed, roofs ripped off buildings. It looked more like a war zone than a quiet part of East Anglia. It was horrifying to see such devastation. Those of us who experienced that night and the aftermath, will never forget it.

Because of the sudden fall in pig prices in 1988, we had to take the difficult decision to make a very loyal workforce redundant, and sell the pigs.

Romance was beckoning! Having constantly travelled for some time between Ringshall and Peterborough, Liz and I became engaged. The next two winters were spent renovating Chapel Farm house, which had remained empty since the death of my grandmother in 1986. In May, 1991 we were married and made "Chapel Farm" our home.

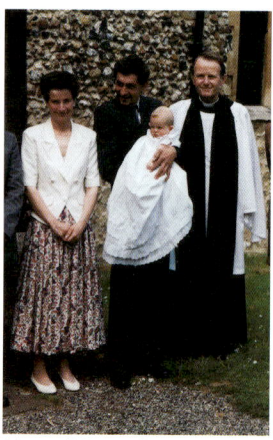

Liz and Guy Hitchcock at the christening of their daughter, Katherine on 8 May 1994. The Rev. Harry Chapman officiated

On the 5 November 1993 our daughter Katherine was born, sharing the same birthday as her grandpa (much to his delight). More family rejoicing when our son William was born in March 1996. He was the first baby to be born at "Chapel Farm" since the birth of my father. Katherine viewed the arrival of another baby rather suspiciously at first, but now they are the best of friends, and she clearly adores her small brother.

I wonder what the future holds for the latest generation of the Hitchcock family? Will William love farming as I did? What does the future hold for farmers in East Anglia in the next twenty years? A lot will depend on our closer ties to Europe. Today's farmers, as well as being aware of the vagaries of the British climate, have to be more aware of the economic situation than their predecessors. They have to be better educated, and able to deal with all the complications of modern living. Hopefully, I will be able to advise my son as my grandfather advised my father, and my father advised me.

The latest generation of the Hitchcock family at "Chapel Farm".
From left – Katherine, Liz, Guy, William and the family labrador called Badger

Ringshall Chapel
Compiled by Andrew Toomey

The remains of religious buildings are not uncommon in Suffolk. Nearly every parish has one and Ringshall is no exception. All that now remains of Ringshall chapel is some evidence of the floor and the scattered remains of the house that once stood by it. It is remembered mainly in the name of the farm on which it is to be found – Chapel Farm.

The site of Ringshall Chapel.
Photograph taken by Mr A Toomey of 3 Bakers Corner, Ringshall

In the twelfth century the Norman conquerors had settled into their new homes and begun to turn their thoughts to more spiritual matters. They probably were at an age where they could feel the next life beckoning and determined to do things that would make that life more comfortable! Some of the very rich landowners helped to found a monastery whilst the poorer ones would perhaps grant an annuity of some sort to a religious foundation. Those whose wealth was between the two helped to found small religious houses. These were a sort of monastery in miniature and became known as cells. They were tended by one or more monks and would also have provided a place of worship for the community. Ringshall chapel appears to fall into this category.

In the Domesday Survey there were five manors listed in Ringshall. The chapel was built in 1174 on the manor, which belonged to Richard de Rokele and Robert de Wyllakysham. They endowed it with '32 acres of land and two parts of all tithe corn and hay of the ancient demesne'. The tithes were then valued at 30 shillings per annum (£1-50p). The chapel belonged to the priory of Norwich and there are mentions of it in the Cathedral archives. Interestingly it is mentioned as a church in some of the records, indicating that it was a place of worship for the villagers. The earliest known record is the Papal Confirmation by Pope Alexander in 1176.

In 1294 the prior of Norwich settled the chapel of Ringshall on the religious establishment at Hoxne. The chapel was now, in effect, a satellite of Hoxne and all its revenue went there. The parish chaplain of Ringshall at the time was a man called Luke. He declared that the chapel was a free chapel belonging to the prior of Norwich and he assigned it to his cell of St Edmund at Hoxne. Nearly twenty years later the chaplain of the time, Robert Guer, had the whole of the income assigned to him for life. He agreed to keep the houses in repair and serve the chapel three times a week.

Documentation about the chapel is sparse. It is assumed that the building was abandoned at the time of the dissolution of the monasteries under King Henry the Eighth. We know that it was in ruins when a house was built on the site in the time of Sir Richard Gresham in the Sixteenth Century. Sir Richard's son, Thomas, was known to visit Ringshall. In fact by this time he owned all the manors in the parish. It was assumed that he stayed in Ringshall Hall on his visits but there is good evidence that he lived in the manor house built on the site of the chapel. It was Sir Thomas who took most of the oak trees from Ringshall to build his Royal Exchange in London.

When the chapel was closed, the people of Ringshall were not left without a place of worship. There is evidence that a parish church existed on the present site of St. Catherine's Church since the seventh century. After the Norman conquest this church belonged to the manor of Ringshall (now Ringshall Hall). The owner of the manor, William Bygod, confirmed his lands as gifts to the Priory of the Virgin St Mary and St Andrew's in Thetford. This gift started the existence of a small monastery on the grounds of the manor of Ringshall. It is possible that the parish church would have been rebuilt to serve this monastery. Certainly the present building does not give many clues to the pre-Norman church.

The dedication to St Catherine must have come after the time of the crusades as that saint was not known in the Western world before then. The tower of the church was remodelled about 1300 when an octagonal tower might have been added. The Parish register records that in 1804 the 'octagonal steeple was destroyed by a thunderbolt'. The tower was repaired and rebuilt square.

So many facts will never be known. Some because they occurred before things were written down and others because people never thought them worth recording. Perhaps, today, we can help future historians by recording things as they happen.

Sources

English Heritage
Lincoln Cathedral Library
Suffolk County Libraries and Heritage
Norfolk Record Office
Victoria History of the County of Suffolk
Monasticon Anglicanum (Dugdale)

Manors of Suffolk (Copinger)
Ringshall Parish Registers
Pocket Histories of Suffolk Parishes
The Domesday Book (Suffolk)
The Concise Oxford Dictionary of Place Names
The Hitchcock Family

The following text and photograph has been written and compiled by Mr Andrew Toomey, of 3, Bakers Corner, Ringshall.

Before the mains water arrived in Ringshall, villagers had to get their water from ponds or a well, if they were lucky enough to have one. In the 1930s the Hitchcock family of "Chapel Farm" sunk a borehole and erected a standpipe in the area shown on the photograph. This was for everybody to use. The local water is hard and it was brown coloured when first drawn. The colour would settle after it had stood for a while but people did not trust it.

The local councillor arranged for a standpipe to be erected opposite the school gates.

Site of Lower Farm Road standpipe

Saint Gilbert

Rumours have abounded for many years that St Gilbert may have established an Order in this part of Suffolk, namely in Ringshall. Chapel Farm features mainly in these stories as various monastic remains have been found in the grounds. No firm proof has so far been found of such an establishment.

7
The Farm Houses

Stoke Farm, Ringshall – A House Of Enchantment
By Mrs John Burt

Stoke Farm is believed to be six-hundred years old and today is the much loved home of Molly and John Burt. The farm is situated 10 feet (3 m) into the boundary of Ringshall. It hasn't got an illustrious past, but a very interesting one none-the-less. Let us now take a walk into history and see what we discover.

When they first came to Suffolk from Herefordshire, over thirty years ago, Molly and John Burt spent a long time house hunting. Molly was quite enchanted by the number of old farm houses which had ponds by their doors.

"It would be so nice," she told John wistfully, "if we could find a picturesque house with a pond, as well." That became her dream in the following weeks as they browsed through numerous leaflets and brochures from various estate agents. John Burt, an enthusiastic amateur cricketer, was keeping his fingers firmly crossed in the hope that their future home would be in a village which boasted a cricket team.

Much to their mutual pleasure they eventually found Stoke Farm, a very pretty house situated at the end of a long, straight driveway and approximately six-hundred years old. There was a much overgrown paddock, a few mature trees and, much to Molly's delight, the estate agent assured them there was indeed a pond, maybe two. Evidently, earlier in the Twentieth Century, there were four ponds in close proximity to the house. The existing ponds were temporarily obliterated as the previous owners had cut the grass a yard on either side of the drive but the rest was a wilderness.

Local people claim to have been told by past generations of the existence of a moat around the house, many years ago.

The property came with approximately three acres of land which would require much energy, love and care before it resembled the beautiful pastoral scene the family enjoy today.

One of the first jobs attempted by John Burt and eight year old son, Nigel, was to cut a path, with billhooks through the undergrowth. This was to enable Molly to see her precious pond more easily. However, disappointment awaited her! Where the water should have been was merely a marshy depression – a resting place for old rusting farm machinery and discarded bedsteads. There was no sign of water. John, always the optimist, promised his wife she would have her pond and with determination set to work to clear the debris. It took considerable time and effort but the result was a most attractive small lake that has been a constant source of delight to them both over the ensuing years.

Several varieties of birds frequent the pond. The heron and kingfisher are particular favourites. The former, a long necked, long legged wading bird gives a display well worth watching. Sporting in the shallow water, staring intently into the depths, the Heron will suddenly submerge its head and neck only to raise them almost instantly. A fish will be seen slithering down the bird's long throat. These antics will usually be repeated several times. To folk with 'ornamental' ponds full of various species of fish, the heron can be classed more as a nuisance.

The kingfisher is a beautiful bird and some of them are frequently seen perched on trees which are grouped round the pond. This colourful bird will gaze intently into the water looking for its prey. It doesn't usually have to wait long! Suddenly it will plunge into the pond, wings outstretched, then, quick as a flash, it will fly into the nearest tree with its prize – a nice slippery fish. As with the heron, the kingfisher will probably repeat this performance several times.

Molly has been known to sit quite still for three-quarters of an hour, watching the graceful antics of a kingfisher. Her appreciation and enjoyment of their 'small private lake' has never wavered.

Nigel Burt at the grand age of nine was mad on football. His parents decided a set of goal posts would make an ideal birthday present. In 1968 the paddock was mostly unkempt grass, ideal for rough and tumble football. Today, that same paddock, with its closely mown grass, is a most attractive feature of the grounds.

It didn't take long for the local children to descend en masse. To have a football pitch so close to their homes was indeed a treat. They would turn up every non schoolday, arriving very early in the morning, usually about 7 o'clock, and play until dusk, running themselves to a standstill.

Molly and John remember those times with nostalgia. A knock on the kitchen door would herald the arrival of these eager youngsters with a polite request to Mrs Burt for her son to 'come out to play football'. Nigel was NOT an early riser and his mother knew he was probably still curled up in bed, snoring happily, and blissfully unaware of the impatient delegation awaiting his arrival. Assuring the enthusiastic children that Nigel wouldn't be long, Mrs Burt would give them permission to commence their game.

The children's keenness never wavered. It was a delight to hear their joyous cries as they put heart and soul into their games. They quickly improved, called themselves Battisford United and would play against other youngsters from nearby villages. As they kicked the ball round the paddock they would chant the name of their beloved team over and over again. Did any of them dream of perhaps becoming a famous footballer one day?

Mr Don Haxell was one of many local people who derived great pleasure in watching these youngsters play football on the paddock at Stoke Farm. Apparently, when he was a young man, earlier this century, Battisford had a local football team. They played regularly on the paddock of this farm. John and Molly were delighted to know they were carrying on one of the village traditions.

Seeing those enthusiastic lads playing football in their paddock gave John and Molly a sense of security. Their son was safe and so were the other boys. They were never any trouble. In fact Molly only ever encountered one problem with Battisford United. They would get very thirsty whilst playing and twenty youngsters demanding cold drinks presented a slight hiccup. Not many homes boasted dishwashers in the nineteen-sixties and washing glasses or cups for all those lads was a daunting prospect. The problem was quickly solved by getting in a large quantity of ice pops. Everyone was happy!

Molly was very fortunate to inherit Mrs Haxell when they moved into the farm. She helped with the housework for several years and the family became very fond of her. Mrs Haxell had lived at Stoke Farm as a young bride during the Second World War. Her husband's family had owned the farm then and she had a fund of interesting tales to tell about the people who had lived and worked there during those times.

Garden parties were a regular feature when Molly and John first moved to Stoke Farm. It would be a gathering of friends and local people. Some of the latter

Stoke Farm, Ringshall – original house, 14th century

would have worked on the farm as young lads and the place held many memories for them. On one such occasion Molly was intrigued to see an elderly gentleman gazing intently at their back door. Noticing a somewhat bemused hostess, he said, "Just about there (pointing to the area near the door), was a hawthorn hedge, and that's where we turned the buckets for milking pails upside down to drain, after we had washed them out after the milking."

Nigel Burt had to do a project for school on an old house, and naturally he chose Stoke Farm as his subject. They got in touch with Mr Dickerson, who was born in 1903 and worked on the farm from 1912 and into the 1920s. He was an eager raconteur.

One of his first jobs as a lad of nine or ten was to sit at the end of the lane that led from the farm to the 'straight' road. In those days where the land joined this road there was a triangular piece of grass. On non school days it was his job to sit on this grass and 'drive' back any cows that strayed down the lane towards the road. Molly understood Mr Dickerson to say he was paid sixpence for this. Whether it was sixpence a day, or sixpence for the weekend, wasn't made clear.

The next story recounted by Mr Dickerson was very strange indeed, and concerned the Partridge family who resided at the farm earlier in the twentieth century. One night, Mrs Partridge was asleep in the back bedroom when she was suddenly awakened by a tremendous CRASH! The mirror on her dressing table had cracked from corner to corner with a terrific explosion. The following morning she learned that her son, who was living in "Pear Tree Cottage" at the time, had committed suicide during the night. As far as Molly is aware, the aforementioned incident was, and is to the present day, the strangest happening to take place on the farm.

Arthur Edward Partridge bought the property at public auction from Emily and Harold Paul for £950 in 1909. The daughter of Mr and Mrs Partridge married Mr Haxell and that is how the farm came to be in the hands of the Haxell family.

"Pear Tree Cottage" was situated to the side of the farm. A delightful property, it was rather crooked in appearance and resembled an illustration from the "Book of Fairy Tales" by the Brothers Grimm. When Mr Haxell and his bride moved into Stoke Farm, it is likely that Mr and Mrs Partridge went to live in this cottage. Such a move into a dwelling evoking such sad memories of their son's death, must have been very difficult.

Later on in his varied life, Mr Dickerson became one of the local barbers and would return regularly to Stoke Farm to cut the hair of the farm hands. The kitchen was always used for this 'operation'. With a steady hand (hopefully), and freshly sharpened tools (scissors, clippers and razors), the proceedings would begin. With Mr Dickerson snip-snipping, and general gossip in the background, a very convivial time was enjoyed by all. Such was the length and thickness of some of the hair, he claimed it took him half an hour to find the coat collar. Some coiffures today would be very similar.

How many of us, I wonder, have watched cricket matches from deckchairs in sunny weather, or maybe lying in the grass, and through pavilion windows when the weather has turned inclement. Even helped prepare the teas! To some, this very English game is part of the landscape and the life in which we are brought up. When the long vigil of winter is over, the cricket season begins. John Burt is an enthusiastic follower of cricket, and in Don Haxell he found a man equally interested in the game. They often sat in the lounge at Stoke Farm discussing the merits of various matches, both local and professional. Molly would sit in the corner by the large fireplace quite content to listen to the animated chatter of both men. Sometimes Don would pause in his conversation, and looking across at Molly, would declare soberly, "that's where my old grandma used to sit, just where you are right now". When she expressed pleasure in hearing this, he would add quickly, "aye and she died just where you are sitting too!"

Molly and John have resided in Stoke Farm for over thirty years but never cease to remind themselves that they are guests in this county. They are forever grateful for the friendly welcome that has been extended to them, and for the many warm friendships they have made. They are aware, also, that they are guests at Stoke Farm, one family in a long line of families that have inherited this farmhouse for six-hundred years, or more. Sometimes she thinks of the people who, in generations past, have stepped under the low lintel, probably weary after a hard day's plod in the fields, seeking shelter, sustenance and warmth from the old house.

One of the ponds near the house used to be called "The Tea Pond". This was so named because the water from it was used to make tea. No farm workers were allowed to dip their buckets into it. There was a well at this time in front of the house, but this was soft water and could only be used for washing. Unfortunately, as Stoke Farm is legally ten-feet into the parish of Ringshall, the inhabitants were not allowed to use the Battisford pump situated a few hundred yards up the road. They had to trudge the three miles to Ringshall, then with the precious water, the same distance home again.

Looking into the garden one evening in winter, Molly saw a breathtakingly beautiful sight. The moon cast a silvery path over the rippling waters of the pond, and long, intriguing shadows fell over the old naked trees in the paddock. In reflective mood, her thoughts turned once again to times past. How many lads, she mused, must have walked home to Stoke Farm late at night, perhaps after a convivial evening at the local ale house, with only the moon to guide them. Young people....and some not so young anymore have done a good deal of courting 'by the light of the silvery moon'.

Sometimes in the evening, Molly and John sit in the firelight watching the flames reflected in the old beams. Forever the romantic, Molly will try to 'will' back the ghosts of the many folk who have sat there before, wishing to see them, if only for a few brief moments, or perhaps to listen to their conversations.

Times past and times present blend into times future as Molly tries to imagine the other families, other generations, who will occupy this much beloved home in years to come. She wonders what they will look like and what aspirations they will have for the house. Will they learn to love the old building as she and John always have.

Since we cannot see their fates, can it hold them by the hand and send their souls through time and space to greet them. They will understand.

There is a poem which begins...

> "We must have beauty now and then,
> To feed the hungry souls of men".

Molly, a keen conservationist will understand those few words well. She says, "We have in this country many historical houses and glorious cathedrals of which we are justly proud, and rightly so! These are our inheritance; but we also have simple village churches where ordinary people like ourselves, have taken their seemingly insurmountable problems, or have given thanks for meagre triumphs. Suffolk is well endowed with old houses where these people would have lived. Old age and optimistic youth sharing this space. In these cottages new life has been conceived and born, bringing with it new hopes and new problems. In these walls people have aged and died. The very fabric of these buildings has been impregnated with the deep emotions of its inhabitants. These buildings are our inheritance and should be nurtured.

One dry summer the Burt family decided to clean out the other pond, removing the layers of mud and decaying vegetation. They were intrigued, on removing several cart loads from the pond, to find what appeared to be the remnants of a brick roadway. It led to the middle of the pond – and then finished abruptly. John puzzled for some time about this discovery. Where had the road come from, and where did it lead to? The mystery was at last solved. Evidently, in days gone by when a farmer had a good pond, he would build hard standing in the centre so that after a particularly mucky job, the horse could drag the cart right into the water. This made it easier for the men to wash both cart and horse.

Today we live in a very scientific age but when Stoke Farm was built, the world was very different. People had little, or no education, and tended to be very superstitious. Any unexplained illness, or bad luck was usually contributed to the work of witches. Clever, gifted people were often called witches, and some suffered terrible fates in the hands of these simple folk of yesteryear.

Many methods were used to keep witches away from their homes. One of the most popular ones was to plant a rowan tree near the house. In autumn this tree is usually covered with bright red berries. Witches hated the colour red. Another thing witches couldn't contend with was iron or water. It was quite common when building a cottage, to plant a bar of iron and a bottle of water close to the entrance of the property, usually over the lintel to the door. Another spot was under the hearthstone, presumably to stop witches entering from the chimney.

At Stoke Farm there is an alcove to the side of the fireplace and here there was a wooden cupboard. Some time ago, Molly and John decided to dismantle this cupboard and build a new one. On knocking the cupboard away, John discovered a false bottom. He tore out the wood, revealing the original hearthstone. Resting on it was a bar of iron and a little pot that had once contained urine, they suspect. This had, of course, dried up completely. The bar of iron was carefully put back into its hiding place. It must have been very effective as Molly and John have definitely seen no witches at Stoke Farm.

Battisford And District Cricket Club

By John Burt, Stoke Farm, Ringshall

Although the current Club was only founded in 1974 there have been cricket teams in Battisford and Combs in the years immediately following the Second World War. These teams folded largely because of the lack of a decent ground on which to play.

The present Battisford and District Cricket Club was formed after Combs had challenged Battisford to a game of cricket for a barrel of beer. Unfortunately – or fortunately, perhaps – the barrel of beer was broached and sampled before the game began – the result was that everyone had a marvellous time and no one knew, or cared, who had won the match.

However, enthusiasm was born – in Battisford at least, and Don Haxell and I decided to try to form a regular side. We had no proper ground but Don Haxell worked at Wattisham airfield at that time and he persuaded the authorities there to let us use their excellent ground for our first season. We only won one match – but that was enough; if we could win one we could win more – but where?

In 1975 the Club still played at Wattisham, but, during that year, the meadow behind the "Gardener's Arms" which had been farmed by the landlord, became available. Greene King, who owned the field, gladly allowed us to rent it from them – and Battisford Cricket Club had a home.

Of course to make a meadow into an acceptable cricket ground called for endless and voluntary hard work – and a great deal of money. We appealed to the Community Council and the local parish councils, and they all responded generously. One of the most generous responses came from Ringshall Parish Council, and in recognition of this we changed the name of the Club to Battisford and District Cricket Club.

Since those hectic days the Club has gone from strength to strength. We now own our own ground, and it is generally accepted as being one of the best village cricket grounds in Suffolk. Last season (1998) we gained promotion to the 1st Division of the Mick MacNeil League.

Could we have achieved all this without the generous help of Ringshall Parish Council? Probably, yes – but the struggle would have been much, much harder. Thank you Ringshall!

"The Boarded House" or "Chestnuts Farm House"

'On the flip of a coin'

This is a handsome timber framed house, originally built in the early nineteenth century. An impressive renovation and conversion has been carried out in the last seventeen years by Adrian and Graham Card, and their two wives, Carol and Alison, respectively.

In the bleak mid winter of 1999, but the house still looks lovely

It was early 1982 when the latest phase in the history of this unusual house began. Adrian and Carol decided it would be nice to leave Ipswich and head for the country. They wanted a property with a large garden. When they, with Graham and Alison, first saw "the Boarded House" it was quite dilapidated. It had been on the market for so long, the owners of the land on which the house stood, Mr and Mrs Jennings, had acquired planning consent to pull the house down with a view to building a bungalow on the land. Both families saw the potential for not one house, but TWO! It was a challenge, and with enthusiasm they laid their plans.

Barclays Bank lent them the necessary money. A tough time lay ahead as these four enterprising young people were to do ninety per cent of the work involved in the massive renovation, themselves. This house was formerly Grade II listed due to the construction of a 'hung' staircase, with galleried landings, plus pine beams to all walls, and sole plates. It has since been de-listed.

It is a 'balloon' construction of three floors with queen beams in the roof (one of two upright timbers between tie-beam and principal rafters of roof-truss). Today the footings have been re-laid where necessary to the original specification of eight courses of soft red bricks. The original house was most certainly NOT a good example of period architecture, seemingly built to a tight budget. The new owners discovered Roman numerals on all the wooden joists and beams, which might suggest it was built in kit form. All the rooms were of elegant proportions.

In its 'hey day' this house would have been run by servants. The Card family found bell mechanisms still in place when they purchased the property. The butler would probably have had his quarters on the second floor.

From "The Boarded House" To "Chestnuts Farm House"

A lot of work to be done!

Taking shape

What a transformation!

These photographs show exactly how "The Boarded House" was transformed from a rather sad looking property to the grand looking house of today. It is a very impressive conversion.

To make one house into two obviously presented problems, but with a lot of planning, two very attractive homes came into being; namely "Chestnuts Farm House, East!" And "Chestnuts Farm House, West". Inside, a central dividing wall was added, while the original spacious stairway was replaced by two separate stairways. The two chimney breasts remained, but the old chimney stacks were replaced. A remnant of the original wallpaper was discovered, date stamped 1807.

Believed to be members of the Tricker family who resided in "The Boarded House". Date possibly between 1850-1890

Next came the crucial question, who lived where? Ownership of their respective new homes was decided over a pint in "The Punch Bowl" Pub. Two polaroid photographs of the 'East and West' side were put into sealed envelopes. A coin was tossed, and the winner chose an envelope. Inside was the name of their future home. "We won our house fair and square", Adrian says proudly.

Today "Chestnuts Farm House", stands in pretty countryside on the northern outskirts of Ringshall. Entering through the large farm gate, the back of the house is approached by a wide shingle driveway, on which stands a quadruple garage. A path leads to a small enclosed courtyard, around which is a low brick wall. The gardens are an outstanding feature of the property, and extend to one and a half acres; mainly lawn interspersed with flower beds and shrubs. This has been a superbly refurbished house providing extensive accommodation.

Graham and Alison sought 'pastures new' in 1997 deciding to turn an old barn into their next home. They sold "Chestnuts Farm House, East" to David and Andrea McDonald, who now have a young son, Ewan.

Adrian, Carol and their young daughter, Terri Jayne, who is only five, still love living at "Chestnuts Farm House". Carol reckons it has a 'certain feeling'. Having looked around the outside of the house, and viewed their attractive garden, I would thoroughly endorse Carol's remark. Long may you all enjoy your lovely homes.

Right: The barn - before conversion and before Graham and Alison Card got their hands on it!

Left: They've done it again! – Barn conversion by Graham and Alison Card of Ringshall

Some of the people connected with "The Boarded House", were ....

1839 – Charles Grimwood (Owner)

– John Steadman (Farmer and occupier)

1885 – J. N. O. Tricker (Farmer and occupier)

The Waspe family lived in the house for a time, possibly until 1938. They were followed by the Gooderham family who moved there from their former home "Red House Farm", when it was demolished in 1938 to make way for No. 4 hangar. This family lived there until after the Second World War, and it is thought Mr Alfred Gooderham died there "approx 1945".

Adrian and Carol at the Christening of their daughter, Terri Jayne on 28th August, 1994 at St Catherine's Church, Ringshall

Terri Jayne at five years of age – 1999

Andrea and David McDonald with their young son, Ewan, of "Chestnuts Farm House, East"

1982 – Mr and Mrs Jennings sold to Adrian and Carol Card, and Graham and Alison Card

1997 – Graham and Alison Card sold "Chestnuts Farm House, East" to David and Andrea McDonald

Carol and Adrian are now having great fun trying to trace the history of their unique home. They are becoming familiar figures at the Ipswich Record Office.

Nayland Farm

"There will always be an England

Where there's a country lane

Wherever there's a cottage small;

Beside a field of grain"

From left: John Waspe standing with Sheila and Geoff Durrant outside their home, "Nayland Farm". John is third cousin to Geoff

Geoff Durrant is a Ringshall man, born and bred. His birthplace, "Nayland Farm", an early 16th century, Grade II listed farmhouse (probably built in the reign of James I), was rented by his grandparents, Mr and Mrs Moyes in 1909.

The lovely looking house stands proudly, still surrounded by countryside; although no longer a working farm. Geoff retired from farming in 1985 when he had a hip replacement operation.

Geoff, and his wife, Sheila are a very friendly and hospitable couple, and although never blessed with children of their own, have always been closely associated with the local youngsters in the Battisford Free Church. Both have taught in the Sunday school, and in addition, Sheila has been secretary of Battisford Women's Fellowship for the last forty years. Geoff has been a keen participant of the Battisford Free Church Band since the age of thirteen, and is proud to have played the cornet for fifty years.

All stories are best from the beginning, so here we go!

Geoff was born to Ruth and Walter Durrant who by this time were working Nayland Farm themselves. He was one of eight children, but sadly four died in infancy, leaving Geoff and three sisters, Kate, Winifred and Angeline. It was an idyllic childhood for the four youngsters. Being an arable and dairy farm there was always plenty to do, and see.

Ruth and Walter Durrant with one of their children

Walter Durrant (Geoff's father) holding one of his children. Early nineteen-twenties

When Geoff was about four years old he had a yen for a bit of adventure. In those days a pond situated quite near the house had a small 'island' in the middle. Access was gained by a rickety plank. The small boy had often thought it would be exciting to explore the 'island' in the middle of the pond. Maybe the tooth fairies lived there or perhaps he would find buried treasure! Geoff's imagination ran riot, and so with trepidation he began to cross the 'bridge'. It was like an assault course, with the plank bouncing and trembling with each step. Nevertheless, the little adventurer was determined to reach his goal. Geoff's antics were being watched by another, older playmate. Seeing the small boy balancing precariously on the plank, he moved swiftly to the side of the pond, giving the plank a quick shake, thereby tipping the helpless child into the water. Geoff was so frightened as he couldn't swim. The silly, mischievous lad, quickly realising the seriousness of the situation, dashed forward and pulled the soaking, gasping youngster out of the dirty water. By this time, probably hearing the commotion, his parents came running out. They were horrified to see their small offspring dripping wet and in a state of shock. He was immediately wrapped up warmly, given a nice hot bath and put to bed. He was to say afterwards that on being hauled to safety, he thought he had gone to heaven!

Geoff wasn't always the innocent party. In those days there was a working blacksmith's forge quite near the farmhouse. One Saturday morning, with

Walter Durrant (Geoff's father) using the grindstone

This photograph shows the grindstone and pump. Far left is the milk churn. Geoff's father is to forefront of the photograph

Earlier this century this was the front view of the farmhouse. This is now the side view

This is "Nayland Farm" in the early nineteen-twenties

nothing much to do, and 'idle hands make mischief', he and a friend wandered over to the forge. Before mechanisation a great deal more people than today were needed to run a successful farm, and before the machines took over, horses provided the motive power for many jobs. Hence the necessity of a good blacksmith. Knowing the forge would be closed until the following Monday morning, he surreptitiously checked that the coast was clear, before grabbing a hessian sack from the yard, and then proceeded gingerly to climb up the old wooden building. This was no easy feat clutching a brick and piece of tin as well as the sack. Once atop the roof, he stuffed the sack into the chimney, and secured the top with the aforementioned piece of tin, held on with the brick. What vandalism!! When the unsuspecting blacksmith lit his fire on the following Monday, the place was filled with smoke. He quickly climbed up the stack and removed the troublesome tin and brick, still not realising there was a sack crammed down the chimney. With his chimney still belching smoke, and by now probably muttering a few choice words, he managed to remove the vexatious object. In the meantime, Geoff disappeared. He didn't want to stay around in case the by now apoplectic blacksmith decided the culprit must live nearby.

Sheila grew up in Battisford and cannot imagine living anywhere else but in the Suffolk countryside. Her parents had three children, and she enjoyed a contented childhood with sister Enid and brother Fred. Her father spent all his working life in farming.

This is what home looked like when the Durrant children were young. "Nayland Farm" in the nineteen-twenties

At the age of five she started her education at Battisford Primary School and it was here that she first met the boy who was to become her husband, Geoff Durrant. Having spent six happy years at the local village school, Sheila was to

134

continue her education at the Area School in Needham Market. Geoff meanwhile went off to the Stowmarket Area School. (By this time he sported the nickname of 'Taters'). To enable youngsters to get to their respective schools more easily, bicycles were supplied by Suffolk Education Council. The country lanes must have been full of keen cyclists, panting in their eagerness to get to school!!

This photograph was taken in the nineteen-twenties. The cows look interested. The barn in the background has now been converted into a house by Alison & Graham Card

The Second World War had a profound effect on Geoff and Sheila, as it did on so many other youngsters of that era. Although most English villages still managed to maintain their air of tranquillity, general conversation was mostly about the battles raging on land, sea and in the air.

German bombers possibly used Battisford Straight Road as a marker en route for the Wattisham Air Base. At times, Geoff saw enemy aircraft heading towards the aerodrome. An Armstrong Whitworth Whitley (twin engine medium bomber) crashed in a local stackyard one day in 1941. There was one fatality. Their teacher took them and their classmates to view the wreckage. Somehow in those dark days of war, this didn't seem a morbid thing to do.

1941 seemed to be a critical year in the Second World War, shipping losses were rising all the time, and more and more U-boats were coming into service. The battleship 'Bismarck' was ready for sea in the spring of 1941.

In August 1941 at the Atlantic Charter meeting, the Americans agreed that American warships would in future be permitted to escort all the merchant ships, irrespective of nationality. At the same time, Canadian warships would be allowed to escort American ships.

Geoff Durrant with Patrick Murphy on a horse. Early nineteen-sixties

Throughout 1941 America was a neutral country under President Roosevelt. This was to change on Sunday 7 December 1941 with the Japanese bombing of Pearl Harbour.

Sheila experienced the shock of a bomb falling in the main street in Needham Market while she was in school. The bomb was seen to bounce over the school's boundary and into the playground before exploding. Windows and doors were shattered, the blast was heard for miles around. Pandemonium reigned, with children screaming, and terrified teachers trying to keep some semblance of calm. Staff and pupils swiftly left the damaged building and made for the air raid shelter positioned in the playing field behind the school.

Meanwhile, Mrs Barton, the mother of one of Sheila's friends heard the blast and had a premonition the local school had been hit. Fearful for the safety of her own daughter, she headed off towards the school in great haste. Reaching the scene of devastation she quickly located a harassed looking teacher who was doing a roll call of the pupils, and checking names against the register which was an up-to-date list of present pupils. Having ascertained her daughter was none the worse for wear, Mrs Barton waited patiently for news of Sheila. It was a long wait as Sheila's name was the last to be read out. Eventually a very relieved Mrs Barton and two very relieved girls, plus bikes, made their way home across the fields.

Because of the close proximity of Wattisham aerodrome, the wail of air raid sirens would often be heard. Most families built air raid shelters in their gardens. A large hole would be dug and sacks filled with sand or soil would be built up all around the dugout. On top was usually a corrugated roof, secured again with sandbags. There were no fatalities in the Ringshall area adjoining Battisford, and none in Battisford.

Sheila and Geoff's friendship blossomed in the ensuing years and in 1955 they were married at the Battisford Mission (now called the "Free Church" as the original building was badly damaged by fire). They took over the running of Nayland Farm, and have lived in the lovely old farmhouse ever since.

In past times the sacks came in various weights.

Oats	*12 stones = 1 Coomb*
Barley	*16 stones = 1 Coomb*
Wheat	*18 stones = 1 Coomb*
Beans	*19 stones = 1 Coomb*

The above information was supplied by Geoff Durrant of "Nayland Farm", Ringshall.

Mile End Farm, Ringshall

The history of Mile End Farm begins in 1600 when the house and farm were given to Sarah Hitchcock by the Baron of Wattisham (no trace of the aforementioned baron can be found).

Since the middle of the seventeenth century the history of this farm is uncertain. At the beginning of the twentieth century it was owned by Mr Herbert Emsden. He had a daughter, Millie who married and became Mrs Pipe. Unfortunately, Mr Pipe died during the Second World War, but the union produced a daughter named Joyce who now lives in Essex. Millie Pipe left Mile End Farm in 1971 to live near her daughter. It was then bought by John and Norrie Willis who lived there with their son Robert, an officer in the Merchant Navy. He left the Navy in 1975 after serving fifteen years, and started his own agricultural engineering business from the farm.

"Mile End Farm", Ringshall. Home to Sally and Robert Willis and family – 29th June, 1999

In 1979 Robert married Sally Taylor, and they took over Mile End Farm when John and Norrie moved to Stonham. After the death of John Willis in 1982, his wife moved to Old Newton to be near her daughter and son-in-law, Christine and Raymond Bullock.

Robert and Sally Willis continue to live happily at Mile End Farm, with their children Lucy and John. Their other daughter Amy, married on 15th May, 1999. Other contented inhabitants of the farm are an assortment of chickens, sheep, pigs, cats, and a beautiful Alsatian.

The Willis family and Seán. (From left) Seán, Amy, John, Lucy, Robert and Sally Willis

8
More Tales from the Farms

Memories of a Full Life and an Enjoyable Life
By Edward John Waspe

Edward John Waspe, hereafter to be known as John, was born at "Nine Elms Farm", Ringshall in 1914. The farm was owned by Mr Spencer Makens who had a great influence on his childhood and is remembered with affection by John Waspe. The family in those early days consisted of parents John and Rose Waspe, and sisters Joan and Mary. From "Nine Elms Farm", the family moved to "Newburgh Cottage", Battisford where his sister Mary still lives. The young John started work at "Woodlands Farm", Ringshall which was owned by his grandparents, and then worked for his father. All his formative years were spent in farming. His vivid description of the Tithe War in the years 1932-1934 which damaged relations between church and communities will be described later, in his own words.

When "Woodlands Farm" was eventually sold, John by now into his forties, decided that modern farming was not for him and a change of environment was necessary. It was quite a challenge, but with the indomitable spirit of the Waspe family that had stood them in good stead during the tithe war, he sauntered into Wattisham

"Nine Elms" farm in 1997. This is the house where John was born in 1914. Workmen were busy giving the house a good 'overhaul'. Miss Laurel Laflin (niece to John Waspe), carried on living in the house after the death of her parents, and until her own death on October 14th, 1998

aerodrome just before Christmas 1955 and presented himself for a medical. He passed with "flying" colours and the RAF personnel being satisfied that John Waspe was of sound mind and body, sent him off in the direction of the Officers Mess. From here he was duly despatched with the necessary cleaning materials to clean the public rooms. After a few weeks doing an assortment of menial jobs such as laying out the newspapers, etc, in the Mess he was asked to answer the telephone in the reception area. Although he viewed this latest job with some trepidation, he was soon to become Duty Receptionist. This entailed arranging accommodation for the officers, and generally running the Reception area. Not bad for a chap who had spent all his previous life in farming!

Memories of a day I spent at the weekly Thursday market day at Stowmarket in the early 1920s.

> *"To market, to market, to buy a plum bun,*
> *Home again, home again, market is done".*

I was about 6 or 7 years old when I remember that the Thursday market day at Stowmarket was a very special day of the week. That was the day when most of the farmers and their wives made the weekly trip into Stow, the wives to do their weekly shopping, and the men folk to attend the weekly market, to either sell their corn by taking their sample of corn in little packets into the corn exchange to offer or to get a price from the millers, or grain merchants, or to attend the auction of pigs, cattle and poultry to buy, or to sell their stock that had been transported earlier in the day. Also to meet in one of the market pubs to buy or sell or haggle over a deal, or just talk farming.

Thursday was quite a busy day on the roads in the early 1920s. Hardly any traffic on other days but on market day there would be quite a number of horse and cart, and farm waggons or tumbrels making their way to Stow, as this was the only means of transport except for one or two lorries (more about that later), most farmers made the journey by horse and cart; usually about the same time on a Thursday morning. If we were in the house at that time we knew who was passing without seeing who it was because we got familiar with the noise of the horse's trot, or the noise or sound of the cart wheels, this would betray the owner. If it was a heavy horse and cart coming along one would hear the heavy sound of the horse's feet clop clopping along, and the heavy dealer's cart would rattle over the rough granite or cobbled stones. More so if it had iron hard wheels. Then we would hear a little horse or pony trap coming along, the dainty patter of feet, and the cart wheels lined with rubber or leather, making very little noise over the rough roads, and we would immediately name the driver of the pony trap. As I look back over these past 70 years I remember those dear old faces as they sat in their carts.

The dear old gentleman with his bowler hat, a heavy fur lined jacket and waistcoat, a hard white collar, a heavy drooping moustache looking the real part of a typical Suffolk farmer. Beside him sitting his wife, wearing the same old Victorian bonnet and long black dress and blouse, buttoned up booties, looking so sedate.

Then another pair driving along this time a familiar trilby hat, and overcoat, his lady with a broad rimmed hat, held on by huge hat pins, always looking cheerful and a "hello" to everybody. As I lived at Nine Elms Farm, and later at Woodlands Farm on the Bildeston Stowmarket road there were a number of horse and carts passing by on their way to market.

Farmers and cattle and poultry dealers would come from Naughton, Nedging, Offton, Wattisham and Ringshall and Hitcham coming into Battisford, passing through Combs all going to Stowmarket. As far as I can remember there was just one car that was a familiar sight. This was a model T Ford a high built roof and bonnet and wooden spoked wheels driven by a Mr Gus Harvey.

The women of surrounding villages had to walk, or if lucky get a lift in one of the farmer's carts, not many had a bicycle in those days, and it was not often their men folk couldn't get along to market as they could not afford to lose a day's pay.

In those days no public transport as we know it. Now back to that lorry I mentioned earlier. The first lorry I remember in our area was owned by a Mr Joseph Cooper at the end of the Battisford straight road near to Bowl Corner. It was used to transport livestock to the weekly auction at Stow. To load pigs into this lorry was quite an operation. I remember seeing father and my uncles doing this whilst waiting for my grandfather getting ready to drive the horse and cart to Stow. In those days that lorry had no back board as today for the pigs etc to walk up. It had just an ordinary short back board and a gate tied above this to keep the stock in. The pigs or cattle had to be herded into the most convenient shed or barn for loading into the lorry, anything so that the pigs could be driven into the lorry. This was not always successful and there were times when pigs or calves had to be man handled. Grandfather did have a special loading gate or ramp made, as he often sent pigs to market by the farm waggon drawn by two lovely Suffolk horses.

I said there was no public transport in those days, well there was one means of transport in those early 1920s, Joe Cooper's pig lorry. The first passenger service for the village people of Battisford, Ringshall, Little Finborough and Combs. This same lorry that had transported livestock to market for auction had now been cleaned out of its straw and pig manure, some form of seating had been installed from stools etc for the passengers. There was still a smell of pigs but what did that matter they were getting a ride into Stow. Also a very bumpy ride over the granite stones and holes. I believe it had solid tyres. For the passengers to board the lorry was as nearly as much problem as we had loading livestock. The half back board had to be let down, and Joe Cooper would bring along a pair of steps for the passengers to climb up into the lorry, and a helping hand would be given by someone already in.

The inside of the lorry would almost be blacked out. There were no windows and the cover of some kind was tied completely over the front, back and sides. Quite often one would hear the question "Well how far have we got?", someone would answer "Now going past Combs butchers" or "Now going past the Live and Let Live" and so on. But it was better than walking. It was a very happy lot of passengers going to market in a pig lorry on a Thursday morning around about 11.30 am to arrive at the Dukes Head about 12 am. Out would come the steps or stool by Joe Cooper to assist the passengers to alight, all eager to get to the shops or to the market traders or the auction. Market day was now beginning.

Now to return to my trip to market with my grandparents in a dealer's cart, pulled along by "Billy Pony" the cart horse. The years I remember clearly are when I was 6 or 7, although I had travelled with them and with my parents from my earliest years. Now it must have been the school holidays that I went to market. "Billy Pony" for that was the name of the horse, had now been harnessed and strapped in the cart by my Uncle Charlie the youngest member of family of 15, and had been brought round to the farm house. "Grannie" would check to see that all was well, cart rugs, the huge cart umbrella, or any goods to be carried. Grandfather was restricted in his movement because of his arthritis, he always needed two sticks to assist him in walking, and it was with great difficulty that he climbed into the cart.

Now all seated and off we would start from Woodlands Farm, Ringshall, up the Mill Road, Battisford, round by the Punch Bowl corner, passing the Punch Bowl Inn, Little Finborough Church on the left, into Combs, and coming into the Combs Ford, and so into Stowmarket. The journey was often marked by cheerful greetings by my grandfather. He would shout out to anyone he saw working in the fields, "making a good job of that hedge," to another "don't fill that cart too high" someone hoeing "don't let the hoe get rusty" and so on. To the women folk he would make some remark, "made your beds", "got your washing dry yet?" and they would all return some remark. All knew Tubby Waspe for his jovial

Edw
Born at Nine Elms Farm

A Son

It's now eighty years ago that I was born,
My records tell me it was a Sunday morn
In the flaming month of June, to breathe the Suffolk air,
In that dear old country farmhouse, amid much love an

The weeks passed by when this new life became
A toddler in that farmhouse of Nine Elms fame
From room to room, from kitchen, stores and cellar
Was my playground for this bouncing little fellow.

The months passed by when I started to explore
The gardens and meadows; the orchards and much more
The trees and hedges, the flowers in full bloom;
All nature looked so beautiful around my farmhouse ho

The years slipped past and I was growing apace,
Into a fine lad, with a love for the open space.
For school chums to play with, for laughs and a game
Those days were the happiest, each day spent the same.

The years sped by and life brought its changes;
A *living* to be made for this growing teenager.
The *farm* and the field beckoned me on to toil,
To *plough* and to reap, I became a son of the soil.

E. Joh

character. To the road men, and we would pass 3 or 4 on our way, I remember so clearly he would shout out "all clear?" and he would get the same response from them "yes all clear". This all made the day going to market in the 1920s. The 5 miles to Stowmarket was quite an event for me. I enjoyed that journey so did grandmother as she too greeted friends and I know Grandfather enjoyed himself because his face would show it as he hailed everyone he saw on the journey. And the little Billy Pony trotted along carefully. He was going and taking us to market.

On Sunday 7 June 1914

The Soil

The years swiftly passed, and a man I became,
With muscle and brawn, all work came the same.
Swinging the scythe and reaping the corn,
Tiling the fields on the farm where I was born.

The years rolled on and the harvests came,
Each year I reaped of the golden grain.
Seed time and harvest, and cold and heat,
God's promise to man was both sure and complete.

The years come and go and great changes have come,
The fields I once ploughed are now all in one.
The trees I once climbed and the hedges explored
No longer hold beauty that I once adored.

Time marches on but the memories remain
When I reaped the corn and threshed the grain.
Cutting the clover, and cocking the hay,
From morning to evening, 'twas my life in that day.

And now I sit back in my armchair to rest
And talk of the times when life was at its best.
Seeing that old farmhouse as clear as the dawn;
Proudly I tell them, "That's the place where I was born".

1994

Now the arrival at the "Duke".

The "Dukes Head" was the terminal for a number of farmers, dealers, shoppers etc. Horses and carts would be arriving at frequent intervals during Thursday morning. The meeting of farmers etc was like a military reunion. Remember they had not met since last week. "Morning Tubby got any pigs down on the market?" or "got that wheat in?!" Another would say "How did your corn run?" referring to the threshing previous week. And so it went on. The women folk would be greeting one another, mostly concerning domestic news.

In the meantime the Ostler would be in attendance. "Billy Pony" would be unhitched from the cart, and led off to his appointed place in the stable, well looked after, fed and watered. Almost every pub in Stowmarket had its groom, or Ostler and stables to cater and care for the number of ponies, and horses, as many as 6 to 10 were accommodated in those days in each pub. It was like a garage is to us today.

Greetings and handshakes are now over and it was time for the women folk to get along to the shops and market traders, whilst the men folk would pop into "The Duke" for a "wet", although Grandfather did not drink alcohol, mostly a ginger beer also to carry on farm talk, or arrange a deal. Off I would go with grandma, and the first place of call she would make was a little tea room in Station Road kept by a Mrs Seaman.

There Grandma would unload her goodies, such as farm butter, eggs, cream or any other farm produce, which was a weekly order, and of course very appreciated by Mrs Seaman for her catering business. Mrs Seaman would be busy getting us a cup of tea, and bringing out her home made scones or rusks, and if not too busy serving any customers she and Grandma would be chatting away and relating the news of the week. I was more interested in going to market than the conversation going on in a tea room. Coming out of the tea room the next business was to go into the shops. First on the list was to order the week's groceries. Grandma would leave her order at one of the grocer's shops, quite a big order it was too, she still had 2 or 3 sons at home working on the farm, as well as 2 daughters to do the day's chores, milk to be separated, and cleaning all the utensils, food to be prepared for the family and countless other duties associated with running a busy farmhouse.

Well the groceries were ordered and paid for, and the goods would duly be sent up to "The Duke" by the messenger boys on the firm's trade cycle. Other shops were called in, The Chemist Shop on Market Corner, Wilsons or Stearns was a must. Often for some veterinary medicine for a horse or cow or for the family but the most necessary item was yeast. Friday or Saturday was bread making day. Many loaves had to be made for this family. Again they would have rather a long conversation as they were more than just customers, more like one of the family.

Another shop to visit was Wards Clothing Shop. Good old fashioned shop and just the sort for a working family. Corduroy jackets, trousers and good strong working shirts, ideal for the farming family. There would always be someone wanting some item of clothing. But all this was getting a bit boring for a 6 or 7 year old boy, I wanted to see the real market. So at last the shopping was completed, Grandma checking her shopping list. We were going on the market, this is what I had been waiting for.

Stowmarket square would be alive with its stall holders, hawkers, traders, cheapjacks as they were commonly called. Shouting at the tops of their voices to make themselves heard, trying to attract the attention of the crowd of onlookers. I remember only as if it was the other day. One hawker selling corncure, and what a lot of patter he made as he offered to cure a corn. He would invite an onlooker to remove the shoe and sock, and then apply the ointment on the corn, inviting them to come back next week and he would guarantee to remove the corn. Another I so remember would be selling a medicine to cure any cough or cold. "Anyone in my audience who has got a cough I will give you a dose of my coughcure" and he would offer a dose to anyone who cared to sample it. And some did I remember. Then another quack as they were often called offered his cure for eye trouble. It was said he could remove a cataract from the eye with his tongue. My father said he saw it being done. I never did and so it went on.

Crowds of people filled the Market Square on a Thursday, families and friends, farmers and cattle dealers all enjoying the goings on, laughing and talking among themselves, and also making some remark to all their "cure all". Then there was the attraction to the weekly auction. These made market day for Stowmarket. This was what market day was all about. Buying and selling cattle, pigs, sheep, goats etc, and not forgetting the poultry, ducks, rabbits and especially geese and turkeys at Christmas time. There were two large auctions going on at Stowmarket on market day. Woodwards in Station Road. Here were a great number of farmers dealers and ordinary folk congregating together to witness the selling of pigs and poultry. Gordon Woodward would be selling the pigs, of all sorts, sizes, a very fast auctioneer taking bids from the large crowd of dealers. I can still remember quite a number of those dealers, also the various signs they made in bidding. A finger lifted up, a raising of an eyebrow, one who stood quite a distance from the company of buyers and made a sign with his walking stick. I was young but I noticed some of their tricks.

I do not remember cattle being sold at Woodwards, these were sold at Knights cattle market in Crowe Street, but poultry, rabbits, ducks, geese and turkeys were sold in large numbers, especially at Christmas time. As far as I can remember the auction of poultry was carried out by a Mr Lister.

Knights' auction in Crowe Street was one of the main cattle auction markets in the country. Lots of cattle came from all over the country especially Irish cattle. It was a common sight on a Thursday to see the drovers driving these cattle from the station through the streets and market square to Knights. And often the process would be repeated after the auction, some being transported by train to various areas. Many of course would go to local farms, quite often driven along the road to the farms.

Then there was the auction of poultry, rabbits, ducks, geese, goats etc being sold in Crowe Street, just outside what was then Prestons clothes shop, now Dewhurst the butchers. There would be 2, 3 or 4 trolleys or trucks loaded up with cages to accommodate the poultry, rabbits etc, being pulled from Knights' sale yard, and lined up in Crowe Street as I have already mentioned outside Prestons. Again there would be a company of dealers, also many families seeking to buy a chicken or rabbit for the weekend meal. Shoppers too would stop and join in the auction, because it was next and joined the market traders and stalls and made a change from shopping. Straw, feathers and litter was scattered along the street into the market square but this was the weekly market, the weekly auction, the same company of people, so no one objected, it was the way of life in Stowmarket on Thursday the market day. The poultry market and auction now over, crates of hens, rabbits etc, now being loaded in the back of some dealer's cart or pushed home on a cycle or carried by hand – it was now time to think of returning to "The Duke". Grandmother would make her last call before home, and call in the Mayhews tea room for a cupper and a cake or bun for me, and then make our way to the Dukes Head at 3.30 to 4 pm.

Again the familiar faces would be arriving, again greetings would be shared, a pony would be harnessed ready for a cart. Joe Cooper's lorry would be awaiting to load up its passengers, the driver ready to be moving off to transport his passengers to the villages, for this same lorry would be returning to Stow to collect pigs or livestock bought at auction. The men folk were arriving at "The Duke" to have a drink and chat and discuss the market trade. Farmers mostly looking quite pleased with themselves having sold some farm produce. Our "Billy Pony" had now been put between the cart shafts by the Ostler, Grandma would be checking over her groceries etc, to see if everything had been delivered from the shops. And I would be taking my seat in the cart ready for the drive home. There was often a little waiting as Grandfather had "last words" with his farming friends, still talking or haggling over a "deal", or someone would come to the cart to have a last chat. But at last we were ready for home, but not quite, this was the time to buy supper, down Ipswich road we would go, over the market square, now already thinning. Traders, hawkers picking up the litter especially from around the poultry market, and Grandad would pull up outside Tick Wilding's fish shop near where the old post office used to be. More talking, more dealings. Grandad would buy a couple of rods of bloaters and load them into the back of his cart. There was a large family to feed when we got home. They were like us getting hungry, we had been to market all day. They had been working all day.

Now ready for home with a "see you next week Tich", "right ho Tubby", "come old fellow" to Billy Pony "let's get home". Off the little pony would go at a fast trot back up Ipswich road, past the Dukes Head, more "see you next week".

If it was summer time we had a joyful ride home. Again there would be greetings as we passed through villages such as "had a good day Tubby?" "Did they sell well?" and so it went on. If it was a dull, cold and wet journey home, we would pull the cart blanket around us, and sat under a huge umbrella that would cover the three of us up. The two cart lamps, one on either side with a candle for light would be lit not giving much light, but that did not matter very much because our Billy Pony did not need a guiding light to show him the way home, he had travelled this road every week for a number of years and he knew the way, and was as much anxious to get home as I was.

"Woodlands Farm" once owned by the grandparents of John Waspe and now owned by Mr & Mrs Kerridge

Home at last. I suppose it was 5.30 to 6.00 pm that we arrived home at Woodlands Farm. Grandfather would put his fingers in his mouth and let out a shrill whistle and Charlie would come to assist us out of the cart. Also to unhitch and unharness Billy Pony, lead him off to his stable to be fed and watered for the night. His weekly job was done. Grandma would be busy bringing in her purchases and busy preparing the bloaters for her family assisted by her daughters. By the time Grandfather got in the bloaters would be sizzling on the grill, a table all laid and furnished. The family seated around, and Grandfather would give his blessing and thanks for the food.

Sometimes I would stay for tea, usually I would be given the herring roes, no bones in these for a small boy. Or father or mother would come for me. I went home tired but happy. Grandfather and the rest of the family would be talking about the trade and dealing, and the general news of the day, who they had met and the subject of their conversation. Stowmarket had now returned to its normal peace and quiet. My day was done, tired but happy that I had been to market.

"Home again, home again, market is done".

John's vivid memories of The Tithe War (1932-34), which occurred here are recounted on the following pages.

The Tithe War as I saw it happen at Woodlands Farm, Ringshall, near Stowmarket, Suffolk in the years 1932-34. Woodlands Farm was owned by my grandmother and farmed by my father, John William Waspe and my uncle, Arthur Henry Waspe, the two executors for the family. I was in my late teens at that time and worked on the farm.

In the late 1920s and early 1930s agriculture suffered from the great financial depression. Prices for farm produce were very low. Wheat was fetching only about 10/- (top) to 15/- (75p) per comb of 18 stone, barley 15/- (75p) for 16 stone. Cattle and pigs and poultry often suffered heavy losses through fluctuating trade. Many farmers were going bankrupt every year. Tithe was a great burden to the farmer in those days. For Woodlands Farm, approximately 118 acres, the yearly charge was £50. This had to be paid to Kings College, Cambridge which was the tithe owner. Now this meant that the produce of a field of 10 acres of wheat or barley would just about pay the yearly tithe rent, without accounting for the labour on those fields or the cost of the seed sown at drilling time. Because of these financial hardships, farmers were withholding payment of the tithe and a tithe association was formed.

The Waspe tithe dispute started in 1932 when my father and uncle were summoned for non-payment of tithe, and they had to appear at Stowmarket Magistrates Court to be questioned by a young barrister from London who represented the Tithe or Church Commissioners. It all came about by a mix-up of names. The executors had received a demand for tithe which they had already paid. There were H A Waspe and H Waspe and H A Waspe Exors all paying tithe to Kings College, Cambridge. When the executors of H A Waspe received the demand, they just ignored it.

Arthur was called into the witness box. Arthur was a typical country man. He always gave thought before answering a question put to him and, the more educated the person he talked to, the more careful and cunning came the answer. The questions came fast from this young barrister, "Your name?" Arthur paused for a moment before he answered; "Your brother's name?" Again the pause; "Your mother's name?" Again there was a delay, then Arthur looked up at this barrister and said; "I really don't know, we always called her mother". This remark from Arthur caused much laughter in court. Arthur was often referred to as the man who did not know his mother's name. The next question was; "Are there any more Waspes in your area?" Arthur waited a moment, then a little smile came over his face, and he said; "Yes, hundreds and thousands of them".

This brought renewed laughter in court. The young barrister was really upset. "I don't mean insects" he said. The magistrate closed the case. It was all headline news in the local papers next day. The commissioners were trying to find out who were the rightful owners of Woodlands Farm. Arthur was not very helpful!

After the case was closed we heard no more until one day there descended on the farm a bailiff accompanied by police and a company called General Dealers, to impound all our farming implements that we had been using to cultivate the land. This was the first time we had met this company of General Dealers from London who were acting for the Tithe Commissioners in removing goods confiscated for non-payment of tithe to be carried off and sold. They rounded up our implements and stacked them in a large shed that was in the meadow; the drill, the horse rake, the harrows and cultivator. I was ploughing with our horseman when we had to take our horses off the plough for these men to cart it off into the shed. So we were denied of all our working tools to sow the seed and to cultivate the land. They were all ready to be carted away by this London company to an unknown destination. But kind farmers came to our aid and lent us a drill, ploughs, etc, to carry on the farm work. News soon spread around that the bailiffs had raided the farm with General Dealers. Farmers and farm workers came to give vocal support in jeering the raiders as we called them. However, the Waspes got to work. We were not letting this go off like this. Two or three of us went to this shed one night to render our tools useless and unsaleable. One wheel was taken off the drill, one wheel off the horse rake, the ploughs were stripped, etc, to be hidden away. Although the farm was searched by police, ditches searched and ponds dragged, the parts were never found. We were interrogated but no one knew anything.

This photograph was taken in 1933. The press wanted a picture of the Waspe family commencing the harvesting from the fields from which the bailiffs had withdrawn. The above shows the family with their neighbours

Well it went on for a week or two and then it all happened. One morning just as it was breaking daylight about 4.00 am, three or four lorries from these General Dealers descended on the farm to cart off our farming implements, accompanied by about 20 police officers. The alarm was given by a neighbour who lived opposite the farm, and my father and I rushed to the farm not fully dressed, joined by my two uncles. By this time the lorries were loading up our implements guarded by police. The four of us got to work and started to put obstacles in the path of the lorries as they had to come through the farmyard onto the road. There was a heap of faggots near the farm gate and I started to pile them against the gate but I was bundled away by the police. My father was also trying to obstruct the lorries: again the police were on hand. We were putting up a fight. Arthur felled one, I had a battle with one of these General Dealers, but we were outnumbered by the police and the raiders. Then I saw my uncle coming with a box of bees. He had got a veil on. I grabbed this box of bees off him and flung it amongst the police and these raiders. This worked marvellously. It soon cleared the police on the road, but by this time General Dealers had cut the chains on our farm gate and got out onto the road and away. If only we could have held them up another five minutes they would never have got away as help was arriving. So it was headline news next morning: "4 am raid on Suffolk farm by General Dealers and police to remove farming implements". This caused great anger amongst the farming community. That was round one of our battle with General Dealers. We carried on working and tilling the land with borrowed implements and it was with great joy that we reaped another harvest.

Now to 1933

Just before harvest in July 1933, one morning there arrived on the farm a bailiff accompanied by a number of police officers. We were expecting something like this to happen as we were still withholding payment for the tithe. The sale of farm implements did not raise enough money to pay the tithe rent owing. The corn was ready for harvesting and they had come to impound our crops of corn. On a farm the previous year they had attempted to remove four stacks of corn from Charles Weston of Elmsett. They had already taken things out of the house. Then one day this came to me, why not put notices in our corn fields to say these crops are sold? This I did, nailing a board onto a stake and placing it in the corn field. This really frustrated the bailiff and police. My father and uncle were approached to provide the evidence that the crops were sold. My father went to his seed merchant to see if they could help in any way. But the seed merchant had to point out to my father that they were only allowed to buy corn by the sample, not in the straw, nor standing corn. So we could not produce evidence of a sale. The bailiff then went on to impound a field of 10 acres of wheat and 7 acres of barley, ready for harvesting but uncut. Then the police put up a tent in one field with three police officers, all local police, and the bailiff to mount guard day and night. Word soon got round that 17 acres of standing corn was impounded for non-payment of tithe. The country roads leading to Woodlands Farm were alive with visitors. Farmers and farm workers came to support our stand, Woodlands Farm was again in the news. Ringshall was on the map and the daily newspapers took up the story. We were surrounded by newspaper reporters and press photographers and it was headline news. This went on for about 10 days but General Dealers had taken on more than they bargained for. The corn first of all had to be cut with a binder, no combines in those days. The sheaves had to be gathered up and stooked. Several lorries would have been needed to transport the corn. This would have taken a great deal of time and labour and, with growing opposition from the public, they had to withdraw. But the Waspes had been active, placing various obstacles in the standing corn, and I am certain there would have been many breakdowns trying to cut our corn.

We had a good relationship with the bailiff and the police, who were all local, and they sympathised with our protest in withholding payment of tithe. The tent in which they camped was approximately a quarter of a mile from the farm gate and all food and drinks had to be left at the farm gate to be collected by one of the police. We did not allow the tradesmen nor the public to come onto the farm. One day a tradesman was unloading his goods when I noticed he set a crate of beer near the farm gate. There were a number of people around including the press and reporters and photographers. I waited my time to walk up to that crate of beer and took two bottles of beer out. No one noticed. I slipped away with them and made my way round the yard, emptied the beer out and refilled the bottles with water from the horse pond. The water looked just like Cobbold's brown ale, which I had just emptied out. I returned to the farm gate and slipped these two bottles of water into the beer crate and slipped away. No one noticed. The next morning we all heard about it as the police investigated how they were supplied with water instead of beer. They had a laugh with us over it but I was the only one who knew what had happened. From that day all

"Woodlands Farm" with the large pond in the foreground. In 1933 during the Tithe War this was the horse pond, and it was into this water one memorable day, the young John Waspe decided to empty a few bottles of beer left in a crate at the farm gate. He then refilled the bottles with the pond water. Luckily the police had a sense of humour!

food and drinks had to be guarded all the time and a police escort up to the field. But as I have mentioned, General Dealers had taken on more than they could handle, and one day we noticed that the police had taken down the tent and the police and bailiff were withdrawing from the field. Word soon got around, the reporters were eager for a story and in all the daily newspapers the next day headline news, victory for the farmers. The newspaper reporters were anxious for us to have a celebration of the Waspe family, so they brought along some bottles of beer and with neighbouring farmers we went into the farm house for the celebration. They wanted this for their newspapers. Well, then we cut the corn, we carted it home to the stackyard and it was with great joy that we had reaped that which we had sown. So ended the tithe demonstration for the year 1933.

Now we go to 1934

We fully expected that something would bound to happen this year. We still owed tithe, and the Tithe Commissioners still wanted their money. There were other disputes and tithe demonstrations and farmers were still holding back their tithe. We, the Waspes, awaited the next move. The work on the farm went on as usual. With our borrowed tools we ploughed and planted, and another harvest came round. We cut the crops and stood the sheaves of corn in stooks, or shocks as we called them, all ready for carting to the stackyard and we just waited and wondered, will we be getting another visit. Sure enough, one morning the police and the bailiff descended on Woodlands Farm in just the same manner as the previous year. Ten acres of wheat ready to be carted to our stackyard was impounded as in the previous year. A tent was set up in this 10 acre field of wheat to be guarded by the bailiff and three police officers, the same officers as the previous year. As soon as the news leaked out the newspaper reporters and press and photographers descended on Woodlands Farm and a large number of public again filled the roads around Ringshall. Again the Waspes set to work trying to hinder these General Dealers from carrying our corn. We were fighting for survival, for our families, for our daily bread. How could we hinder?

It was decided to block all entrances from the field to the road by carting farmyard manure and piling it up in the gateways, leaving open the main access to the road, also hedge trimmings ready to be lighted at another entrance from the field. Now all the corn on this 10 acre field of wheat was ready to be carted. About 9 or 10 near rows of shocks of corn, the sheaves all neatly tied up with binder string. We decided to cut the string. Three of the Waspes went up to the field about 10 o'clock a rather damp and drizzling night, so maybe the police would remain in their tent. It was decided that one would take one row of shocks and one another and so on. Working as quietly as they could they crawled from one shock to another to cut the strings, 8 to 10 sheaves in a shock. Careful thought was given how to cut the string. If it was cut on the outside of the sheaves they would open up and soon be noticed, so it was decided to cut all the sheaves on the inside of the shocks. This was done and it went 3 or 4 days before anyone noticed all the string round the sheaves had been cut. This put the plans of the General Dealers back for a week. The police had to go on the carpet and all of us were questioned including our families. Nothing was given

"Woodlands Farm". The above photograph is of the gateway where the Waspe family tried to stop General Dealers

away. Well the operation of cutting the string was completed just before daybreak, including those that stood a few feet from the tent. We had to be on the alert as the police turned on a search light over the field every little while, but when we saw movement in the tent, we laid still and let is pass over. As I said, we were all questioned and even our wives and mothers, but they thought we were all in bed.

One day someone gave me a large rocket. One night about 12 o'clock I went up to a near field and tied the rocket to a gate post. I pointed the rocket so it should explode over the field well away from the police tent. I lighted the rocket and got well away from the field, a few seconds later it took off. Instead of exploding over the field as I had intended, it curled round and went off right over the top of the tent where the bailiff and police were in. Well that caused a panic. Next day we were all questioned and accused of firing a gun at the tent. Again no one admitted anything. But it was a terrific bang and they were frightened.

Then, after two weeks, on a Monday morning it all happened at Woodlands Farm, Ringshall. We fully expected it. On Sunday three of us went on a spying mission. One went to a certain police station, one to another town and we noticed there were police movements at the police station that morning. Scores of police arrived, sealing off all the roads to the farm and surrounding the field, escorting several lorries of General Dealers with a large number of men. No transport or cars were allowed near the farm, but it did not stop the public from getting on the farm, coming from across the fields, but all they could do was to shout and jeer the raiders. The field was surrounded by police to guard General Dealers. General Dealers' first job was to tie up all the sheaves that had been cut, this took at least 2 to 3 hours, then they had to load up the lorries and this took an hour or so. They were ready to move from the field through the farm yard and gate when the police noticed a smell of petrol coming from behind a brick wall near where the lorries were to pass. We found out afterwards that some member of the public had intended to set fire to the lorries by throwing petrol canisters as they passed through the farm yard, but none of the Waspes were engaged in this. So a change of plan was made to leave by a field entrance to the road. The farmyard manure from one gateway was removed. This took considerable time and that large pile of hedge trimmings at the road entrance failed to be ignited at the last moment. The police prevented anyone getting near. There were a few incidents as they approached the road. My aunt, Arthur's wife, laid down in front of the leading lorry. I was right beside her, but a burly policeman picked her up and threw her on one side. She was roughly handled. A farmer tried to stop the lorry and again the police came forward and he was treated rough. The lorries with our corn did eventually get away. Apart from my aunt and this farmer no one was hurt. This was the last demonstration by the Waspes. Questions were being asked in parliament as to how the burden of tithe could be released from the farmers. Also as to the way it was collected and used by Kings College and the church. The general public were surprised that our money went to help educate ministers for the church and to the college students, many of whom were sons of members of the House of Lords and Members of Parliament.

Mrs Waspe 'Goes To War'

The following extracts are from various newspapers dated August, 1933, chronicling the events involving the Waspe family of "Woodlands Farm", Ringshall during the tithe 'war'.

QUOTE: News Chronicle, Saturday, August 5th, 1933.

Tithe War in Widow's Cornfields – Bailiff Encamped with Wireless – College's offer to Mrs Waspe.

There was a new manoeuvre today in the tithe war which is being waged between farmers and tithe owners in this part of the country.

Farmers not only in Suffolk but throughout the whole of East Anglia are protesting against the payment of tithe, but the immediate trouble here concerns Woodlands Farm, owned by a 70 year old widow and her two sons.

They owed £50 tithe to King's College, Cambridge, and the court has seized a quantity of their farm tools, but as these only realised £2.10s., a bailiff has now seized two fields of corn.

Guarded by three policemen, the bailiff is encamped in a bell tent beside the ripening corn, complete with tinned food and wireless set.

The corn (17 acres in all) has today been advertised for sale by the court – "the purchaser to cut and remove".

But this morning the widow, Mrs Waspe, received an offer from King's College, Cambridge, that if she would make a token payment of £10 or £15 before the end of September, the College would remove the bailiff, take no further action this year, and negotiate with a view to some relief on a final settlement.

"I am not disposed to accept the offer", Mrs Waspe said today. "They have already taken farm machinery worth more to me than the £50 owing. Still I am in the hands of the Suffolk Tithe Payers' Association which is fighting my case.

Mr P. J. Butler, Secretary of the Tithe Payers Association, said: "My committee is meeting on Tuesday to consider whether the widow should accept the offer. It is extremely likely that we shall advise her not to".

If the corn is sold it will have to be cut by labour from outside the county. On barn doors and fences are posters protesting against tithes. On one gate is a sketch of a clergyman over the text: "and they covet fields, and take them by violence, so they oppress a man and his house". Slogans of protest are chalked on the roads for miles around. UNQUOTE

QUOTE: Daily Express – undated.

70 Policemen Guard Convoy of Tithe 'Raiders'

Seventy policemen surrounded Woodlands Farm, Ringshall, near Stowmarket today while men carried out a tithe 'raid'. The men were employed by General Dealers Ltd, a company which has carried out many similar operations. It has a paid-up capital of £2 owned by two solicitor's clerks.

The farmer, Mrs Waspe, a widow, who is helped by her five sons, had refused to pay tithe charges, and eight acres of cut wheat standing in a field had been impounded on account of arrears. For more than a fortnight policemen had kept night and day guard over the field. Today the 'raid' was carried out like a military manoeuvre.

Policemen arrived in coaches, dismounted, and at the word of command, rushed the farmyard. Behind them came seven lorries from which men jumped out and began to load the stacked wheat. When the men tried to gather the sheaves they found that the string had been cut, and they had to retie the wheat. The lorry convoy took five hours to load.

At the exit of the field it was found that the gateway had been blocked by an iron hurdle. When the obstacle was removed the journey was continued amid ironical cheers from the crowd. Each of the seven lorries was surrounded by police officers.

A woman, it is alleged, tried to throw herself in front of one of the loaded vehicles. She was picked up by a constable and carried to one side. A man was engaged in a brief tussle with the police. A clod of earth was thrown at one of the lorries as it was leaving the field. UNQUOTE

QUOTE: Daily Herald, August 10th, 1933.

Tithe Bailiffs Go Home – Cornfield Tents Packed Up – Mrs Waspe Will Mow Crops

The 'camping bailiff' tithe dispute at Woodlands Farm, Ringshall, ended dramatically this afternoon.

The two bailiffs and their bodyguard of policemen simply packed up their tents and walked away, leaving the 17 acres of growing corn by which they had lived 'in possession' since July 18th, to the 70 year old widow farmer, Mrs Hannah Waspe.

The senior bailiff told one of Mrs Waspe's sons that he had received orders to abandon the distraint. The victory was won by no display of force or by irresponsible speeches, but by a carefully planned course of persistent negotiation.

After taking legal advice about certain features of the distraint, Mr A. G. Mobbs, chairman of the Suffolk Tithe Payers' Association, communicated with Messrs Withers and Co, of London, the solicitors acting for Kings College, Cambridge, the tithe owners. Mr Mobbs told me the solicitors appeared amazed at the methods being used to collect the tithe, and they tried to get in touch with Mr J. M. Keynes, the Bursar of King's College.

By telephone and telegraph messages were sent to places up and down the country likely to be visited by him during his motoring holiday. I now learn that the distraint was abandoned because no tenders had been received for the corn. The farmers' boycott had been complete. Either Mr Keynes or another responsible official of the college then gave his consent to the withdrawal of the proceedings.

The unconditional ownership of her corn has reverted to Mrs Waspe, and harvesting will begin on Friday. It is thought unlikely that any further attempt will be made to distrain again on Mrs Waspe's property in the near future. Solicitors acting on behalf of the tithe payers in Suffolk have been trying to organise a peace conference with the representatives of all the Oxford and Cambridge colleges which own tithes.

It is thought in some quarters that today's move may have been a gesture of assent to this course, a clearing of the way to a better understanding.

When today they saw the bailiffs and the police striking their tents, the Blackshirts of the British Union of Fascists panicked completely. Dashing out into the road with shouts of "they are going to cut the corn" they began to throw bundles of brushwood, and a telegraph pole across the road leading to the farm. They then, with much shouting, assumed 'positions of defence'. Nothing happened and they were left high and dry with nothing to do. For hours afterwards they patrolled the roads and stood up in speeding motor cars waiting for the cheers that never came from the great crowds of people who had gathered. UNQUOTE

QUOTE: The Daily Mail, August 11th, 1933.

Iron Bars found in Wheatfield After Retreat of Bailiff

A remarkable discovery was made at the farm of Mrs Waspe, at Ringshall, today, after official intimation had been received from Mr C. W. Marshall, Registrar of Ipswich County Court, that by order of the judge, the wheat and barley seized at the farm for tithe, had been released. Iron bars and other obstacles were found in the field, and it is believed they were placed there by someone as a mark of sympathy for the Waspes, and to prevent unauthorised persons from gathering the crops. Throughout the day, men were searching the field for further obstructions, and Mr Arthur Waspe, who manages the farm for his mother, told me that he hoped to start harvesting tomorrow.

All Suffolk has today been rejoicing at the farmers' victory in the first battle of the tithe war. No one knows the real reason for the retreat of King's College, Cambridge, the owners of the tithe, but it is thought that the tithe owners are not likely to abandon all their claims. Indeed, it is anticipated that King's College will adopt other methods to secure the outstanding tithes on the Waspe's farm, and I am told that this morning other farmers in the Ringshall and Wattisham area, who are in arrears with their payments, have received formal notice to distrain in ten days.

In another part of the county the authorities have garnished the rent of cottage property to meet unpaid demands. This has occurred at Walsham-le-Willows, a village in the jurisdiction of Bury St Edmunds County Court. There Queen Anne's Bounty is the tithe owner on behalf of the church.

Mr John Grainger, of Walsham-le-Willows, owns in that parish 14 acres of tithe land. He is two years in arrears with his payments and owes £12. 15s. "That", said Mr Grainger "is something like 9s. an acre. That's not a tithe, it's a rent, and I cannot pay it. The result is that following a County Court order, a bailiff from Bury St Edmunds has been to the tenants of my two cottages on the land and told them to pay rent direct to the court".

Tithe Not to Blame – Bounty Chairman and the Real Remedy

Mr G Middleton, chairman of the Tithe Committee of Queen Anne's Bounty, which administers and collects the ecclesiastical tithe, in a letter to the Daily Mail, explains that it is only when the farmer is an owner-farmer that he pays tithe, and that an agricultural tenant is never called on to do so.

"Taking England as a whole", he says "the tithe does not represent much more than one-fiftieth part of the sale price of agricultural produce sold off lands subject to tithe, and it is normally only about five per cent of the total outgoings of the owner-farmer.

"The tithe agitators want an alteration of the law, but the owner-farmer, whose capital and credit have been vanishing as a result of the depression, would get less help as to tithe by any possible alteration of the law than he can get under the Bounty scheme for dealing with the problem. The real remedy is to make agriculture pay, and there can be no doubt that the position is being gradually improved".
UNQUOTE

One Man's Recollection of Life in Ringshall during the 1939-45 War

> *The last war, 1939-45 affected every man, woman and child living in this country. Men and women fought on land, sea and in the air. Others fought on the home front, the elderly helped to look after the young and did their bit to keep the country safe. Mothers were separated from their children when youngsters were sent away from battle scarred cities to safety in the countryside. But not all country areas were bathed in tranquillity. People living in and near RAF Wattisham experienced quite a few hair raising incidents.*
>
> ***The following is an account of some of these incidents experienced by John Waspe while working on the land during those terrible war years.***

Living close to RAF Wattisham, both before and after I married, I witnessed quite a number of German air attacks on the Station. In January 1941 Dorniers carried out raids on four successive Thursdays. These raids were made at approximately 12 noon on days of low cloud and poor visibility.

On this particular Thursday, three of us were working in a field about one mile from Wattisham aerodrome. The clouds were low, and it was a typically dull, misty winter day. Suddenly, I heard the unmistakable sound of a Dornier. By now I was quite familiar with the different types of German aircraft engines, and knew this particular uneven droning sound heralded a Dornier.

We all jumped speedily into the nearest ditch, and the plane flew so low the markings on the wings were clearly visible to us. No air raid warning was heard until the aircraft had passed over the Station. Crouching low in the ditch we were aware of absolute mayhem. Guns were firing from the ground, bullets flying all around us, and anti-aircraft shells bursting everywhere. The noise was deafening and by now we were feeling distinctly uncomfortable in the ditch. In fact we were scared stiff! Suddenly, the aircraft appeared and as promptly disappeared in the low cloud. Thinking it was all over, we climbed out of the ditch intending to make for home with all possible speed. Within a few short minutes the Dornier appeared again and resumed the attack. We again dived into the ditch and prayed we would all remain alive and intact. Again the aircraft disappeared into low cloud. After a short interval, we again climbed out of the ditch. No sooner had we started walking than the Dornier appeared again for a third attack. The three of us dived into yet another ditch, we were becoming somewhat expert in the "short run and jump". This third attack saw two bombs released from the Dornier, falling not too far from a nearby farmhouse and cottage. Fortunately, no damage was incurred. Two further bombs fell on the field behind us and the tractor I had been driving the previous day was covered in earth thrown up by the bombs, but was otherwise unscathed.

Although the Dornier passed over the airfield three times, unbelievably the gunners on the ground made no impact and the aircraft flew away intact. I don't think there were many casualties that day, but a number of aircraft were destroyed on the airfield.

Another Thursday and another incident. This time I was on the tractor ploughing on Mr Denny's farm when I was warned that the siren had sounded. Leaving my work I headed for appropriate cover. Again a Dornier flew out of the clouds, and once more the air was rent with machine gun and anti aircraft shells. It is doubtful that Wattisham scored a hit.

If working with a tractor we could always run for cover if enemy aircraft were spotted, but it was essential where horses were concerned that we stayed with the animal. At approximately 7.30 one morning when we were about to hitch our horses into the drill, suddenly, without warning, tracer bullets and shells started bursting all around us. The horses were terrified and it was with difficulty we managed to get them under control. That particular raid resulted in many casualties to RAF personnel.

On a great many occasions, the air gunners would turn their attention to civilians. My uncle was ploughing on the adjoining farm one day when he became aware of an approaching aircraft. The gunner aimed his fire at this solitary figure and my uncle dropped to the ground pretending he had been hit. He was very relieved when that little episode was over.

One of the most amazing happenings concerned a Heinkel bomber. Again we were on the farm when the siren sounded and this massive aircraft appeared overhead. Two bursts of gunfire were heard and then we saw a bomb released which fell close to a small cottage halfway up the hill near Ringshall Hall. The bomb fell in the pond close to the cottage in which lived Mrs Barton. Fortunately, the poor lady was unhurt but suffered severe shock. The actual cottage was shifted completely round on its foundations. The aircraft flew on dropping another bomb approximately a mile away. Even from such a distance we felt the blast.

There were a number of raids made during the early years of the war around Ringshall, Wattisham and Battisford by single German aircraft, and the final two incidents happened after I was married and living in Naughton. My wife and I were preparing to attend the Naughton Baptist Mission Hall when we heard the guns from Wattisham firing on three German bombers that were attacking the station. Several times the aircraft came over our house, almost at roof top height, and the German gunners were firing as they attacked. Nobody got to the service that evening and much damage was done to Wattisham aerodrome.

On the following Sunday when we attended chapel we could examine the aftermath of the attack at close quarters. A bullet had penetrated the Hall just under the eaves, passing into the main hall. A Bible lay on the reading desk and the bullet had entered the hard cover, but uncannily it had not reached "the work of God" itself.

John Waspe was at RAF Wattisham during the Cuban crisis involving Russia and America. The following is a brief outline of the events, which nearly resulted in the biggest catastrophe since the Second World War.

*F*idel Castro had assumed power in Cuba in January 1959 when he had overthrown the dictator Fulgencio Batista. He immediately set about nationalising many American firms (Cuba is only 90 miles away from America).

In April 1959 Castro made a friendly visit to Washington holding out the hand of friendship. By 2 September, 1960 the 'honeymoon' period was over. Storm clouds were gathering. Fidel Castro declared his allegiance to Russia.

The build up to the crisis began quickly. In May 1960 a Soviet missile shot down an American U2 spy plane. In January 1961, a few days before President Kennedy's inauguration, America broke off relations with Cuba.

On 15 August 1962 news of a build-up of Russian military personnel in Cuba, was reported to Washington.

On 29 August a U2 spy plane discovered eight missile sites that were only a week away from being operational.

While the world held its breath, Kennedy and Krushchev played a dangerous game of "brinkmanship". The tension mounted day by day.

On 16 October President Kennedy was informed that a U2 spy plane had discovered two nuclear missiles and six missile transporters south west of Havana.

President Kennedy announced a further 15,000 men were to be called up into the armed forces.

Russia cancelled all leave for its armed forces. The Russians now knew that if their ships did not turn back, the American navy would sink them. War clouds were gathering fast!

In the meantime, the world waited. Ordinary people everywhere felt helpless and scared. John Waspe was instructed by Flight Lieutenant Hayward to stay by the telephone as the tension world wide mounted. All his meals were brought to him.

The Officers' mess was deathly quiet, the atmosphere full of dread for the consequences that could lie ahead. Late in the evening of 27 October 1962 a deal was made which saved the world from the unthinkable Third World War. Kennedy wrote a letter to the Russian President stating he would agree to a non-invasion pact if the Russians would withdraw their missiles from Cuba.

On 28 October 1962 Krushchev announces over Radio Moscow that he has agreed to remove the missiles from Cuba.

At 6 pm on the evening of 28 October, John Waspe took the call saying the crisis was over. If Krushchev hadn't complied with President Kennedy's demands there surely would have been a nuclear war. How close the world came to Armageddon can be judged by the aforementioned. This was a momentous time in our history, and John Waspe was pleased he had a small part to play in keeping RAF Wattisham on the alert.

The 28 October 1962 was the longest day in his life and thankfully there were no more such tension filled times while he was there. John retired from RAF Wattisham at the age of sixty five.

To keep alive his interest in farming John used to travel to Bury market on Wednesday, and to Diss market on Friday. It was nice to meet old friends and make new ones. He and his wife took a great interest in period costumes and Victorian/Edwardian furniture. He now has a large number of these antiquities and displays them on occasions. These photographs show how impressive this collection is.

John Waspe and his wife with some of their exhibits of Victorian and Edwardian fashions

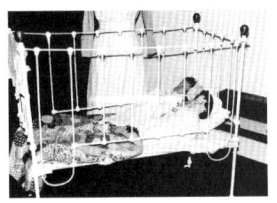

An Edwardian cot, and alongside an Edwardian nurse's uniform

John Waspe at the Sproughton Old Time Farming Rally – September 1994. John is "feeding" the machine which was owned by Mr Eagles. [The lady helping John in this photograph is Dr Fairweather of Bildeston]

Julie Smith (née Johnson)

Julie was born in Ringshall and the following gives a short résumé of her life in the village.

I was born at No.2 Coronation Glebe on the 18 April 1961 to Betty and Jack Johnson. Apart from my parents, the family consisted of my brother Robert and my maternal grandfather Jim Pettitt. My paternal grandparents, Ida and Jack Johnson, lived at No.6 Southview.

I thoroughly enjoyed my childhood in the village and spent many hours playing in the surrounding fields and woods with my brother and our friends.

Once the village had a post office and village shop, which was owned by Pam and Dennis Smith. I worked in the shop at weekends and enjoyed the experience immensely. It enabled me to get to know more people in the village, particularly Susan and David Habinson who owned the donkey farm at Broadview. Being very keen on horses, it didn't take me long to get involved in the exercising of their horse Rinney. As a child I always dreamed of owning my own horse one day but unfortunately the exorbitant cost of buying and keeping a horse made the reality unlikely.

Gathering in Coronation Glebe. From left: Betty Johnson and son Robert. Mr Pettitt (Betty's father), Josie Stone and Mike

I grew to love Rinney dearly and when Dennis Smith heard that her owners were thinking of parting with her, he immediately told me to go and fetch the horse and "he would make room somewhere on the farm". I walked her up the road on a leading rein and put her in the stable. We enjoyed many years of fun together. Occasionally, if she got the chance, she would trot along

The sun is shining and it is playtime in Coronation Glebe.
The children are: Steve and Mike Drury, and Julie and Robert Johnson

Dennis Smith on Rinney at Stocks Farm

the road to see if any of her old friends were in the paddock. Rinney was nineteen when I acquired her and she died in 1994 aged thirty two.

Pam and Dennis Smith had three children and during my time at the shop I grew to know the family very well. One particular weekend in the winter of 1979 when the snow was falling thick and fast I found it impossible to get home because of snow drifts. Having telephoned my parents to explain the situation I then settled myself in with the Smith family to await the thaw. The thaw was nearly a week in coming and in the meantime the village seemed to be preparing for a siege. As the weather worsened, someone took a tractor and trailer to a baker's in Ipswich and filled up with loaves of bread. News of the bread delivery soon got around, sending the local people hurrying to the shop. In no time at all the shelves were empty.

To get milk we all trudged across the snow covered field to John Hitchcock's farm (Chapel Farm) where fresh milk from the cows was collected in large churns. Clutching these we trudged back across the snow. Back at the shop we dispensed the milk into various bottles, jugs and anything else customers handed over.

Eventually I became engaged to one of Dennis and Pam's sons but unfortunately shortly afterwards Dennis died after an illness bravely fought. Pam then sold the shop and farmhouse and moved into the bungalow, which she and her husband had planned to live in on their retirement.

Children having fun in the straw fields.
Back row left to right: Simon Thorpe, Andrew Fovargue, Wayne Smith, Ricky Taylor. Front row left to right: Adam Holden, Lewis Poll, Philip Hall, Dale Smith, Maria Poll, Austin Poll

Reminiscences of Mrs Pam Smith of Stocks Farm, Ringshall

In 1954 I married Dennis Smith and moved to Lower Farm, Ringshall, which my husband had recently purchased.

It was split into two, we farmed all the land, and my mother-in-law lived with us. On the death of my mother-in-law, my husband's brother John Smith and his wife took over her part of the house. We subsequently bought the farm belonging to Mr & Mrs Jack Gibbons called Stocks Farm.

My nephew Derrick and his wife Pauline moved into our old home, we moved into Stocks Farm, thereby owning both properties. Mr & Mrs Gibbons had a bungalow built in 1963, which they called "The Mound".

The bungalow known as "Underwood" was built in 1962 for Mrs Goodchild and family, and is lived in today by David Secret and family.

Mrs Violet Gibbons, wife of Jack Gibbons photographed outside Ringshall Church when she was a guest at a wedding held there

When John Smith and his family moved from Lower Farm, we pulled the old farm house down brick by brick and I helped to clean all the bricks, which we subsequently sold. The site was then sold and four properties erected. These properties are called "Mews Cottage", "Teasel Cottage", "Poppies", and "Field View".

When we first moved to Ringshall, Lower Farm Road was called Bildeston Road. This was altered as there was already a Bildeston Road on the other side of the village. In those far off days there was only Stocks Farm and Lower Farm along that side of the road, all the other properties have been built since the nineteen sixties.

In 1954 water was not laid on in the village and to get water was quite a performance. It entailed going to the old fashioned pump opposite the school. We then had to hook the pail onto the chain, turn the handle, and down went the pail. Reverse the handle and up came the water. Nobody wasted water then, it was too far to go for the next bucketful. By the end of April 1954 we were connected to the mains supply.

In 1965 we experienced a serious fire in a piggery at the back of the barn. This resulted in a new barn being built.

A rather colourful character nicknamed "Hally" lived in the cottage where now stands "Stocks House"; and he sold cigarettes and sweets from his living room. Around the corner was the local post office run by Mrs Last. She retired from business in 1971 and my husband and I took it over. To enable us to cope with this new venture we had to build an extension to Stocks Farm. We opened for business on "Decimal Day", 15 February 1971. We had to extend yet again as we needed extra space. Sadly in 1980 my husband Dennis died and I sold the same year and moved into my present bungalow. I now assist my son in the running of the family business.

At the end of Lower Farm Road stands two properties, namely "Toad Hall" and "Broad View Farm" (in Great Bricett). Originally "Toad Hall" was called "Border Cottage" and was in fact two houses.

• *Since the above article was completed, changes have taken place at "Toad Hall". Irene and Tony Hart now reside at "Chapelfields", Lower Farm Road, Ringshall. John and Penny Alliston moved into "Toad Hall", and have subsequently changed the name back to its original "Border Cottage".*

Pamela Smith proudly showing her Community Safety Award

The words are:
This is to Certify that
PAMELA SMITH
Was awarded this certificate
By Mid-Suffolk Crime Prevention Panel
In recognition of Her outstanding contribution to Community Safety

Pam Smith lives in this bungalow in Lower Farm Road

The 'Life' and 'Death' of "Lower Farm"

"Lower Farm" was formerly occupied by the mother of Dennis Smith. When he married his wife, Pam, the house was made into two separate homes. When Dennis Smith's mother died, his brother John moved in with his wife. When Dennis and Pam moved, their nephew Derrick and his wife, Pauline moved in.

"Lower Farm" illustration by Daphne Gadsden

The site was then sold and four properties erected, namely "Mews Cottage", "Teasel Cottage", "Poppies", and "Field View".

Fred and Emma Poll – Howes Farm, Ringshall. (Date unknown)

Mr Fred Poll at Chapel Farm, Ringshall – 1924

Extract taken from **"East Anglian Daily Times"** January 28th, 1961

Sunday School Awards at Ringshall

Ringshall Sunday School party was held at the Parish Room on Saturday. Unfortunately seven scholars were ill and unable to attend. After tea, given by Mrs E. Last, the superintendent, assisted by the Rev and Mrs H. Price Jones, an enjoyable time was spent in party games.

Prizes for attendance were presented by Mrs Last to the following: Girls: Rita Cuthbert (50 Sundays Attended), Lynette Jones (48), Anne Boswell (48), Anita Bersenetti (48). Boys: Timothy Jones (48), Thomas Wilden (48), Stephen Wilden (48), Adrian Boswell (47).

The rector thanked Mrs Last for her regularity in attending Sunday School every Sunday and mentioned also that for 62 years she had been an unfailing and loyal worshipper at Ringshall Parish Church.

To express their appreciation the children gave her a rousing three cheers and left with a packet of sweets and an orange each as well as a present.

Clifford Last of Ringshall.
Second World War – 1939-45

Sunday School tea in the old School Room, circa 1960

Bottom left:
Richard Gibbons,
Brian Gibbons,
Derek Quinton,
Michael Johnson,
Heather Scott,
Pauline Gibbons,
Philip Gibbons.

Bottom right:
Maureen Wilden,
Jill Johnson,
Robert Wilden,
Maisie Steward,
Wendy Gibbons,
Joan Johnson.

Top left: Rev. Price Jones

Top right: Mrs May Last

6th July, 1991

Mr Cecil 'Twist' Cooper was born at "Plantation House", Battisford on 6th June, 1914. He died aged eighty-one, on 3rd June 1996. He married in 1940. His wife, Winifred 'Winnie' (née Churchill) was born on 14th June 1920 in Wiltshire. She died aged seventy-eight, on 6th January 1999.

Cecil resided at "The Boundary", Lower Farm Road, from early 1948. He kept a smallholding all his life. The family consisted of son Richard, who lives at "Walnut Tree Cottage", with his wife, Elaine and daughter, Katie; and a daughter, Ursula who lives in Needham Market.

Above: Gwen and Leonard Le Grice of "Gardeners Rest", Lower Farm Road, Ringshall – 1998

The following photographs are of members of the Thorpe family of Ringshall

Jack Thorpe (John's father) recuperating in hospital having fallen off a sugar beet lorry and breaking his hip. He certainly seemed to enjoy his stay – circa 1965

Jack Thorpe surrounded by family. From left, John and Marian with Jenny and Shirley (front). John's sister Joan with her husband, Bill. Brother Frank with wife, Ann

Grandad Wright (John's grandfather) – circa 1938

Right: Grandfather Wright with grandchildren Joan, Frank and John. Circa 1938

Left: John's mother, centre, with on right, daughter Joan and on left, Joan's daughter Doreen – circa 1950

Frank Thorpe (John's brother) – circa 1947

169

John's sister Joan with her husband, Bill – circa 1980

Marion and John Thorpe celebrating their Ruby wedding in the village hall on June 10th, 1996

"Knit In" For Ringshall Church Funds – Rev Brian Short Officiates – 1977

Here we are again! Wattisham Base Christmas lunch – 1992

Senior Citizen's Christmas Lunch at Wattisham Base – 1988

170

Elaine and Richard Cooper – 1998

Richard Cooper with his daughter, Katie – 1998

Mr and Mrs Joe Payne of "Inter Vivos", Lower Farm Road, Ringshall – 1984

Mr and Mrs Wilson of "April Lodge", Lower Farm Road, Ringshall – 1995

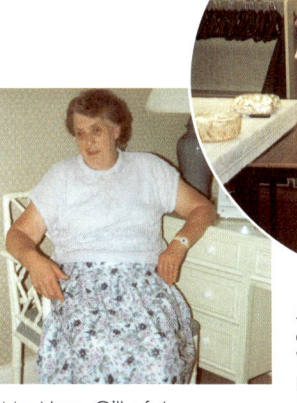

Mrs Nora Gill of 4 Coronation Glebe, Ringshall – 9th August 1992

Jack and Betty Johnson celebrating their Ruby Wedding Anniversary in Ringshall Village Hall – 15th June, 1997

Mrs Higgins of Lower Farm Road, Ringshall – 4th July 1999

Ringshall Village Hall Management Committee – 14th June, 1999. (From left) John Wills, David Upson, Alison Roberts, Mandy Taylor, Angela Green, Liz Hitchcock, Elizabeth Hitchcock and Maureen Wills. (Absent) Nora Gill, Julie Smith, Jack Johnson and Rosabel Peck

Left: David Upson with wife Rebecca and son Dominic; the couple now have a second son, Toby. David is the chairman of the Village Hall Management Committee. He is a native of Essex and was educated at King's Cathedral School, Ely. For three years he was a chorister at Ely Cathedral. Rebecca and David were married at Stisted near Braintree and subsequently bought the fruit farm in 1988 from which products are distributed in the UK and abroad

Above: Mandy Taylor at Blenheim Palace - 1999. Mandy lives in Lower Farm Road and is an active member of the Village Hall Management Committee

Ringshall Parish Council - 25th June 1999. From left: Liz Hitchcock, Helen Nunn, Nigel Last, David Secret, Sally Willis, John Hitchcock and Carol Card

(From left) Kirsty, Angela, Roy and Claire Green. Not a football in sight!

Mary and David Gilmour in the grounds of their home "The Grange", Ringshall. Naturally their dog who is called Bentley, didn't want to be left out! 28th June 1999

(From left) Oliver, Zoe and Ian Hale of "Rose Cottage", Lower Farm Road, Ringshall – 4th July 1999

Above: Barry Warren has lived in the area all his life. When he was fourteen his grandmother gave him a transistor radio. This started an interest in radio which has always been with him. Barry is a keen radio amateur and has talked to other enthusiasts all over the world. He has even listened to Australia's Flying Doctor!

He builds and maintains his own equipment by buying Government surplus stock. In 1972 he received a card from King Hussein of Jordan who was also a radio amateur. The card confirmed their conversation. Barry is pictured here by his satellite dish aerial

Photograph and written text by Andrew Toomey – 1999

Andrew Toomey out and about in the countryside – 1999

Left: Jan and David Ford with their children, Chloe and Emily outside their home "Skylark", Lower Farm Road – June 1999

Below: In the room to the right of the front door, after many hours of hard, and sometimes difficult labour, this book was born. Long may it live! – 2000

The author Maureen Wills and her husband John outside their home "Highfield House", Lower Farm Road – June 1999

WPC Diane Porter, local Community Police Officer – 1999

174

Around The World In ....

Some interesting facts about Olive and Don Forsbrook

Olive and Don Forsbrook love cycling. They cycle between six and seven thousand miles a year. Olive is the oldest competitive female cyclist in Suffolk. They own eighteen bikes, and her husband, Don, will often jump on one of the bikes and do a 100 mile trial. A gentle bike ride means 30 miles or so, pedalling at 12 or 13 mph. The average speed for most of us being 6 or 7 mph. They usually do a regular 100 miles a week in the saddle. "We do get a bit tired after that" says Olive cheerfully.

They regularly compete in events of 10 miles, 25 miles, 50 miles and 100 miles Time Trials. Usually they take part in forty, or more, events in a year. Shopping is done in Ipswich every week – on the bike. Don clearly intends to go on cycling as long as he can. He feels it keeps him more alert.

Holidays are spent abroad every year – on their bikes, of course! They cycle from Ringshall to Harwich, take the ferry to the Hoek-van-Holland, or Hamburg, and will then take two weeks heading in the general direction of Luxembourg cycling in and out of various countries and enjoying every minute of it.

Action Replay! – Olive and Don Forsbrook in action – 1997

Ringshall Carpet Bowls Club 2000. (Back row, left to right) Richard Cooper, Joe Hammond, Don Haxell, Russel Tyte, Tony Hart, Irene Hart, Cyril Mitchell. (Front row, left to right) Nora Dickman, Noreen Seaman, Laurie Seaman. Missing are: Maureen and John Wills, Mick Bridger, Mavis and Roger Bliss

Celebrating 50th Anniversary of the end of the Second World War, May 8th 1995. 'And a good time was had by all!'

Jack Johnson "clowning" around at the old Village Hall

John Waspe standing in the grounds of his grandparent's old home, Woodlands Farm, Ringshall. With him is the present owner, Mrs Kerridge, whose husband John owns Kerridges Garage in Needham Market – October 1998

(From left) John Waspe, Sheila Durrant and Geoff Durrant – 16th October, 1998

Vintage tractor display at Ringshall Church

An evening of Whist at the Village Hall

Inset: Marion and Jean making the tea

Christina and Michael Poll with their children (from left) Austen, Maria and Lewis. Taken in their garden – 4th July 1999

Above: The Thorpe family (back row from left) Scott (15 years), Caroline (Mum), Shaun (13 years), Stephen (17 years) and Simon (19 years); (front row from left) Samuel (10 years), Suzanne (6 years) and Sarah (8 years). Missing from photograph, Sophie (12 years), Samantha (22 years) and father – 1999

Scenes From The Ringshall Village Fete Held on Saturday 18 July 1998

Owners and pets getting ready for the pet show

John Waspe with his display of Victorian/Edwardian antiquities. David and John Hitchcock seem very interested. All the paintings on the walls were done by the pupils of Ringshall Primary School. Their originality, and clever use of colours greatly added to the overall effect

The Following photographs were taken at 'Mile End' Farm on Saturday 16th May, 1998

This enjoyable pig roast was hosted by Sally & Robert Willis

(From left) Dale Smith, Betty Johnson and Rosabel Peck helping at Pantomime, 1999

Wayne Smith (right) of Ringshall and friend Chris competing in Norfolk and Suffolk junior motor cycle grass track – 1998

Dale Smith (right) with his friend Richard competing in Norfolk & Suffolk junior motor cycle grass track – 1998

9
When Ringshall had a Village Shop

Jack Johnson remembers

The Village Shop – Circa 1920–1930

Ringshall once had a small village shop which was situated in Lower Farm Road near the junction with Stowmarket Road. This was run by a lady called Alice Hall, who lived in a cottage adjoining the shop with her husband Frank. He ran a retail coal and coke business, amongst other things. Mrs Hall was born locally and had gone to London in service as a young woman and, while there, had become a very good cook. Frank was born in a very large house in Kimbolton where his mother was a cook and although he never saw his father, he always understood he was a man of some standing. On leaving school he started work in stables at Newmarket where he learned to ride and execute the duties of a groom and stableman. On the death of his mother he went to London where he got a job as a coachman and met Alice.

This photograph is of Hally when he was eighty seven years old. It was taken outside his old shop in 1950. The young lady with him is Jill Johnson, aged five years. She is now Mrs Jill Cresswell, co proprietor of "Johns Tours" of Combs

Alice and Frank Hall decided to come to Ringshall and bring up their daughter in the quiet Suffolk village. Apart from having friends and relations in the village Alice thought there would be less chance of her husband getting up to mischief in such an environment. Little did she know! Frank or "Hally" as he was to become known, was quite a character. Alice ran the shop and her husband acquired a pony and cart and started a retail fish business. He drove to Stowmarket and bought fish and retailed it around the countryside. He then started a retail coal and coke round, buying the coal in Needham Market and retailing it around the countryside. Apparently he also had a very tuneful bass voice and an entertaining falsetto and would often be heard singing popular songs or hymns. He was often seen driving the length of Needham Market singing hymns at the top of his voice, outside the homes of well known church goers. He also had rather a rich vocabulary at times!

After a few colourful years, his business ventures failed possibly due to competition from retailers of coal with lorries who undercut him and also the death of his two horses, which due to financial difficulties he could not afford to replace.

When his business ventures failed he went to work for "Rowley" Hitchcock and as he was a lover of horses and a first class stableman he became a much valued strapper and cleaner of saddlery.

Frank was a real old rascal of a character. If he could "stir" somebody up, he would, and the following is a typical story concerning this extraordinary man.

My friends and I were in Hally's house one evening when the Reverend Price-Jones came up the path. "Good evening Mr Hall," began the reverend. "Hang on a minute matey", replied Hally, "could you go back and close the gate?" Mr Price-Jones duly obliged and on his return Hally said "thanks matey, it all helps to keep the flies out. Now what can I do for you vicar?" Mr Price-Jones, looking slightly bemused, replied that he had brought some things from the harvest festival. "Well matey" answered Hally promptly, "you can take them round to Mrs Last, she will flog 'em in her shop no doubt". The Reverend Price-Jones beat a hasty retreat obviously feeling somewhat perplexed by his encounter with Mr Frank Hall.

Another eccentricity concerned his mode of shop keeping. If someone came into his shop wanting several items, he would fetch one, then ask them again before fetching a second item. He would repeat this performance as many as twenty times. It was a very bewildered customer that eventually left the premises, leaving Hally having a good chuckle.

He would pick up the coal from Needham Market making various deliveries on the way home. He laughed about the time he overloaded the cart at Needham Market, got thoroughly drunk in the "Waggon and Horses", and subsequently proceeded home to Ringshall. On approaching the Blacksmith's Hill at Barking, the horse came to an abrupt stop, waking Hally up in the process. He hurriedly set the brake to stop the conveyance rolling back, and then waited for some assistance in pushing the lot up the hill. On reaching the top he thanked his helpers and then drove on, still with a sack of coal on his back! He had completely forgotten in his "happy state" that he had carried one sack up the hill to lighten the load.

During his "Post Office" days, he used to deliver telegrams around the area on an old bike. One afternoon he had a telegram for Ringshall House (farmed by Mr Luther Robinson). On approaching Southview a cat ran into Frank's wheel and he and his bike finished up in Stumpy Gooderham's pond. Some say the telegram never did get delivered.

Mr Hall outside his shop. Is the cat going to have a bath?

Frank Hall was a scallywag about whom all those who knew him would have fond memories. Nobody would forget such a character who was so full of mischief. He died in 1954 aged 91.

Mr George Grimwood – Born 13th April, 1878

George Grimwood was a farmworker, and also Minister of the Ringshall Chapel. He lived in a semi-detached cottage on the Bildeston Road and latterly in the middle dwelling of a group of cottages in Lower Farm Road.

The local people always knew George by the nickname of "Hatton". He was born with club feet and they never grew beyond his babyhood days. He always had to have special shoes made and during the years of manhood he would mend the shoes himself, stuffing them with sheep's wool for comfort. Unable to sleep in a prone position he would frequently sit in a large armchair, resting his chin on his hand and walking stick, thus sleeping in an upright position.

Hatton worked for many years at Ringshall Hall when it was farmed by "Rowley" Hitchcock (later to become Master of the Suffolk Hunt). In George's later years he would follow the threshing engines around the farms, working the "chaff" part of the threshing process. This was generally known as the dirtiest job of threshing. As one farm finished, "Hatton" would move to the next and continue this job hopping for some time until all the stacks in the area were threshed. During this period, "Hatton" would never wash. He would turn up morning after morning to man the chaff box with the previous day's dirt and havels still in his ears and clothing. "No sense in washing 'em off", he would say with satisfaction in his voice "I shall only be 'darbed' up again".

The poor old fellow used to 'stamp the silage' as it was blown into the Bin at Chapel Farm. The grass was cut and chopped then blown into the Bin. The process was completed by pouring liquid molasses and black treacle over it. "Hatton" used to be covered in this unsightly mess, but he was always happy in his work.

"Hatton" ran the Ringshall Chapel with a lady named Miss Barbara Goodchild. The Sunday School was well attended and therefore very successful.

Every year a presentation was held at the Chapel when books, etc were handed out to the various children in recognition of achievement and attendance. The ensuing tea party was described by "Hatton" as a 'bun fight'. Much fun was had by all at this annual event.

Mr George Grimwood and friend at Felixstowe. He would have been well into his eighties when this photograph was taken. He died in 1965

Barbara and George would also organise a sports day. This event was held during the long summer holidays on the meadow opposite the Chapel. This meadow belonged to "Lower Farm" and was known locally as the 'Chapel' meadow. It was used mainly as grazing for cattle, and occasionally the horses and pony belonging to Mr Gibbons would share this pasture.

The children of the village, of which I was one in those days, keenly anticipated 'Chapel' sports day. There wasn't much entertainment then, and "Hatton" dreamed up some wonderful events to keep us interested throughout the day. Everyone was awarded a Mars bar at the end of each race. It must have cost the dear chap a fortune to put this event on. All the children were very grateful.

In 1965 George Grimwood was taken ill and had to go into hospital where he died. He was in his late eighties.

Stocks Farm

Before and during the 1939-45 world war, Stocks Farm was farmed by a gentleman named Tom Gibbons. He also owned Lower Farm and Rickyard Farm.

Tom was quite a rotund fellow and his trademark was a bowler hat. In fact, so fond was he of this mode of headgear that he was never seen without it. He regularly attended the market at Stowmarket, driving there in his pony and trap, and with a few gins inside him, relied on the pony to get him safely home again.

When Tom died, his son Jack took over the farms and ran them with the able assistance of his brother-in-law, Jim Game. Jim was one of Suffolk's finest heavy horsemen and looked after six Suffolk breeds. He would prepare the horses for the various shows, and this took a great deal of time and diligence. Jim won many prizes for different owners at the Suffolk, Norfolk and the Royal Show. Apart from his expertise with the "shires", he was also the local barber and executed a very proficient "short back and sides" for 3d.

John Thorpe who still lives in Ringshall, was another stalwart workman in the time of Jack Gibbons. He was Jack's first tractor driver when these machines were introduced on farms after the Second World War. John continued to work for Jack until the farms were sold to Mr Dennis Smith. Upon the sale of the farms, Jack and his wife Violet retired to their

The photographs below were taken just after the war (1939-45) when Stocks Farm was still mainly "horse powered". The Suffolk wagon pictures, shown loading wheat sheaves, were taken during the harvest

The lady in this photograph is Mrs Ida Johnson with young son, Michael

Mr John Thorpe (holding "Blossom"), Michael and big brother Jack (Johnson) on top of the load

Jim Game (wearing trilby), John Thorpe, and Jack Gibbons on load

bungalow built in the Rickyard farmyard and called "The Mound". From here they continued to enjoy their whist evenings and would cheerfully travel from village to village to take part.

Mr Dennis Smith farmed Stocks Farm until his untimely death at the age of fifty. During his time in the village, Dennis did a lot of work for the community. He was a prominent member of the Parish Council, and put much effort in keeping the old village hall in a state of good repair. He was one of the founder members of the "Village Hall Management Committee", and it was his ambition to see the erection of a modern village hall. It was Dennis, along with other Parish Council members, who was involved in the final decision to build the new village hall. This is the attractive building standing in Lower Farm Road, and which we are all lucky enough to be able to use. Not many villages can boast such a beautiful, well designed and spacious hall. It must be added that this venture would never have been possible without the generosity of John Hitchcock. The playing field is leased to the village from John on a ninety-nine year lease for an annual "peppercorn" rent. Sadly, Dennis never saw the finished building, but he will always be remembered with affection in the village of Ringshall.

Stocks Farm is still farmed by Dennis's widow Pamela and her son. This son and his wife Julie and their sons, Wayne and Dale live in a modern bungalow called "Justeleevin" on the site of the old "Lower Farm" buildings.

We will now go back to another era when Suffolk still boasted large flocks of sheep. In those days, many farmers would bring their sheep to Stocks Farm for "sheep dipping". A sheep dip was built in the lower part of the farm where the stream runs from Wattisham airfield through to Offton, Somersham and on to the Gipping. The sheep dip is still there to this present day. Flocks from all over the county were brought to be treated. After dipping the sheep would be turned into the meadows abutting the stream. These meadows were known locally as the "Dripping" meadows, and it was here that the sheep were dried off before being driven back to their respective farms. These facilities were still being used up to the outbreak of the Second World War.

Stocks Farm Slaughter House

This establishment existed at the back of the farmyard near a large pond, from which water was drawn for use in the slaughterhouse. The slaughter of animals ceased on these premises roughly about the same time as the demise of the sheep dipping.

"Pumpkin" Garage

The Garage was started by a gentleman called Freddie Thompson. Freddie was a first class cricketer in his prime and played county cricket for Northamptonshire. The original business was situated opposite the new garage on the old road next to a quaint little cottage. A modern house has been built on the old garage site.

The original timber building was erected on site by Jack Johnson Senior, Freddie Thompson and Mr Jacques. The building was purchased from the Ministry of Defence, and was originally one of many sited in the meadows at Ringshall Hall for the use of an army battalion and American GI's.

Whilst the building was in course of erection (1948) the area was hit by the worst hail storm in living memory. The hailstones took days to melt away and some were as big as golf balls. In the meantime this freak storm destroyed crops of wheat, barley, beans and peas. Freddie, Jack and Mr Jacques had to shelter beneath a section of the building and couldn't hear themselves speak above the noise of the storm. Remembering our dog was still out in our garden somewhere, and probably scared stiff, I made a dash for home. I was almost knocked out by the ferocity of the storm before I managed to get myself and the dog safely indoors.

After a few years, the "Pumpkin" Garage was bought by Mr Jack Gray (of Wolves Farm, Hadleigh) and moved to the present site. It now trades as "Anglian Motors". The bungalow standing next door to the present Garage was originally built for the use of the Garage manager.

Extract from local paper – East Anglian Daily Times, Summer 1947

'Golf Ball' Ice In Storm – Crops Are Blitzed

SUFFOLK FARMERS were out in their fields until darkness fell last night trying to assess the damage and to think out ways and means of salvaging what remains after the widespread devastation caused by the ice-stock which blitzed thousands of acres of corn and other growing produce on Wednesday night.

Damage will run into many thousands of pounds, and reports of the violent effect of the freak storm on wheat, oats, barley, sugar beet, beans, peas and other vegetables continued to arrive throughout the day.

Last night 24 hours after the storm had cleaved its way Northward through a five mile wide belt of the rick corn area on the East and West, Suffolk border villages were still finding traces of jagged lumps of ice and hailstones "the size of golf balls".

Work was still going on yesterday pumping water from flooded premises after a heavy storm which struck the Midlands and Home Counties with tropical intensity during Wednesday night.

Beginning in the Semer district, the storm's track is estimated to have covered an area of something like 60,000 acres as it travelled towards Norfolk.

Following an inspection of his area, Mr H J F Wood, secretary of the Ipswich branch of the NFU will today make a report to the Suffolk NFU for submission to the London headquarters of the organisation.

So heavy was the ice that it smashed windows of houses and cottages, damaged thatched roofs and greenhouses. It battered to death numbers of chickens, ducks and geese. The noise of the ice, with the severe electrical storm, terrified animals on the farms and in the meadows.

Several buildings were hit by lightning.

Acres of wheat, barley and oats, as well as private gardens, were wrecked. Fruit trees were stripped and windows smashed at Barking. Villagers said that while the "whirlwind" of hailstones, the size of small apples, lasted, they hid in their cellars.

At the police station the hailstones, which broke 28 panes of glass whirled into a front room and smashed the glass of a bookcase against the wall opposite the window.

An East Anglian Times reporter who toured part of the affected zone around Offton, Nedging, Naughton, Great Bricett and Bildeston, saw field after field of damaged crops.

Many fields contained corn, which was due to be harvested in one or two weeks.

Acres of wheat, barley, oats, sugar beet, beans, peas and potatoes had the appearance of having been slashed by a giant whip. Much of the corn, stripped of its kernels, was left a total loss. Orchards were damaged, and cottage gardens and allotments, with small but valuable plots of vegetables, also suffered severe damage.

Villagers of Nedging Tye told of an "alarming experience" as the storm swept over the district, suddenly turning the Summer evening sky from sunshine to a total blackout.

Mr A J Pratt of Tye Farm, said: "When the electrical storm was moving away we heard a distant roar which got louder and louder as the ice storm approached. It lasted from between 20–30 minutes. Afterwards there was a white carpet all round."

Mr Pratt, who farms 285 acres, estimated last night that 80 of his 97 acres of barley had been affected, and about three-quarters lost.

"It was a promising crop. It had escaped the barley disease," he said. "We farmers have done everything we can to produce the crops this year, which is so vital, and now, on the edge of the harvest, they have gone. It is the last straw."

Walking round his land at Cooper's Farm, Nedging, was Mr B G Preston. He said 14 acres of wheat, 10 of barley, as well as a quantity of oats and peas had "all gone".

"It seems as though the corn has been threshed overnight," he said.

He described hailstones, which fell on his farm, as resembling pebbles an inch and a half in diameter.

The "Old School House" – Mr & Mrs Walter Keeble

A house sees many families, many characters, come and go during its lifetime (if only bricks and mortar could speak, what tales they could tell). Mr and Mrs Walter Keeble lived in the "Old School House" for many years and the following is a short résumé of those times.

Walter worked for Chapel Farm before and after the last war (1939-1945). I believe he finished farm work in the late nineteen fifties and was latterly employed by the builders who constructed the Brookfield Estate at Bildeston. He remained with this firm until he officially retired but being a hardworking man, as all the 'old boys' of his day were, he continued work as a gardener at Ringshall Hall.

During the war years one of Walter's jobs at Chapel Farm was collecting the swill from the cookhouses at the camps in the area. This was later processed and made into pig feed. In those days he had a four-wheel horse-drawn dray pulled by a Cobb horse. Onto this conveyance he would place the bins of swill. At some time during the day Walter's cart would pull up outside his house and he would be seen to retrieve strings of sausages, chicken portions and various morsels of food which would then be transferred to his own table. His wife Mabel was always delighted with these free offerings, "They ain't nuthin' wrong a thut", Walter would say defensively. "Blast, they only chucked it away ter day". In spite of Walter's 'little sideline' tactics, his sterling efforts carting the swill, meant that many fine 'porkers' went to market from Chapel Farm.

Walter Keeble – early 1960s

Mabel Keeble was a very extrovert lady who loved taking part in social evenings held at the local village hall. She would entertain with gusto, and her monologues would be lengthy and very funny. One of her favourite pieces was called 'Our Albert', made famous by Stanley Holloway.

Walter was an ARP warden during the war. He and another ARP warden, Syd Wilden, took their duties very seriously. One of their responsibilities was to ensure the blackout was strictly observed. They undertook all their tasks during this worrying period in our history with vigour and common sense, thus helping to ensure that the village of Ringshall was kept as safe as was possible.

"Sonny" Palmer
2 Coronation Glebe

Sonny Palmer was one of the first residents to the "Glebe". He and his family lived at No. 2 (at this present time it is home to Jack and Betty Johnson). The Palmer family lived in this house for about six years before moving to the thatched cottage opposite the new rectory at the top of Ringshall Hall hill.

Sonny Palmer was one of Suffolk's finest ploughmen and would enter ploughing competitions all over East Anglia. He could 'draw a furrow' with the best and won many of these contests. Not content with his prowess with the horse-drawn ploughs, with the onset of tractors he proceeded to exhibit his customary expertise with these new machines too.

He worked for many years at Ringshall Hall farm. On his retirement he would do odd jobs around the grounds, mostly producing excellent vegetables from the gardens and greenhouse. Sonny was an expert gardener and local people reckoned he 'knew a thing or two' about the growing of plants and vegetables. In general terms he was 'green fingered'.

For the main story concerning this lively character we must go back to his days as a tractor driver at Ringshall Hall farm. It was during this period that Mr Dahl took over the farming at the Hall. Sonny had a tendency to agree with everything that was said. "Yes, that's right", seemed to be his favourite mode of reply. Mr Dahl, who was a Scandinavian, found this particular employee rather difficult to understand.

One day when Sonny was ploughing the field leading to "Muckinger Wood", Mr Dahl waved him down and gave him instructions to plough the field on the hill next. "Yes, that's right", replied Sonny. Mr Dahl then mentioned that he wanted to try out the new chap recently employed by him. "Yes, that's right", replied Sonny again.

Mr Dahl then told Sonny to let him know when he had finished ploughing the field. "Yes, that's right", said Sonny. Sonny finished ploughing the field, refuelled the tractor, re-set the plough and left the machinery parked in Hill field ready for the following day. He then told Mr Dahl all was in readiness for the new chap to start the following day. The next day dawned and Sonny was told to 'muck the pigs out' by Mr Dahl. The new chap was then taken to Hill field, and commenced ploughing under the watchful eyes of Mr Dahl. Man and tractor set off downhill and on reaching the bottom he lifted the plough, turned round and tried to turn back up the field to no avail; the tractor just started to spin. Mr Dahl made his way down the field to see what the problem was. "I don't know", the poor hapless chap replied, "I think we'll have to slip back up and plough down hill". Although Mr Dahl agreed he realised it would take twice as long to plough the field. Deciding expert advice was needed he decided to seek out Sonny, but told the new chap to carry on in the meantime.

Sonny was found in the piggery. "The damned tractor won't pull uphill", said the exasperated boss. "Yes, that's right", replied Sonny, "I think I better go to plough and you put the new chap mucking out". Mr Dahl readily agreed and told Sonny to send the new chap to take over in the piggery. "Yes, that's right", replied Sonny.

Sonny gave the new chap his revised instructions, watched him until he was out of sight, then reset the plough and carried on ploughing uphill. Up and down he went leaving the land perfectly turned over. When Mr Dahl entered the field later on he was somewhat puzzled. Waving Sonny down he commented on the excellent job he was doing. "Yes, that's right", was the cheerful reply and Sonny continued on his way with rather a smug expression on his face.

Coronation Glebe

The row of houses known as "Coronation Glebe", were built on land owned by the church and was therefore known as 'glebe land'.

The Parish Council and the Reverend Price Jones were primarily responsible for gaining planning permission from the Suffolk Council. The houses were constructed by Sadlers of Ipswich, known to be one of the premier building firms at that time. As the properties were built in the coronation year of our present Queen Elizabeth, they were aptly named "Coronation Glebe".

Ringshall Church. Rosemary Gills from 4 Coronation Glebe, Ringshall. Julie Johnson (now Julie Smith), is the small bridesmaid, second right

Jack Johnson of Coronation Glebe. Through photographs he introduces us to family, friends and interesting happenings so far in his life

Young Jack Johnson in pram with his favourite teddy bear (1936)

Members of the Wilden, Johnson families – 1949-1950. (Left back) Robert Wilden, Jill Johnson, Michael Johnson (middle), Campbell Wilden.
Robert is son of Felix and Vicky Wilden. Jill now wife of John Cresswell (John's Tours Coaches). Michael now lives in Ardleigh, Essex. Campbell is son of Peggy Wilden

Jack Johnson, Estate Carpenter and Joiner of 6 South View, Ringshall. Father stands nonchalantly beside son Jack's first car, 1933 Singer saloon (Le Mans Overdrive)

Jack Johnson is shown with the Suffolk mare "Katie". He was at that time on leave from the Royal Air Force. This photograph was taken just before the retirement of Mr Jack Gibbons and the sale of the farms

Inset: (Left) Mickey Johnson (9 yrs) with Jack Johnson and Suffolk mare "Katie"

Betty Johnson with baby

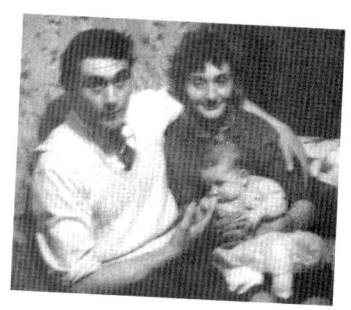

Betty and Jack Johnson in 1961 with daughter, Julie

Ringshall Corner

The most famous 'corner' in Ringshall must surely be where the telephone box now stands. During the eighteenth century and before, the village 'stocks' stood there and no doubt many an interested glance took note of the latest incumbent. Wrong doers were certainly punished in those days and I'm sure not many people fancied a second humiliating sojourn in the stocks.

From about 1945 to 1952 the 'Free' Church from Battisford would assemble for 'open air' services. The congregation was led by "Poly" Joe Cooper. He owned Cooper's Coaches of Combs.

Speeders Beware! This is what could happen to you. Julie Smith putting on a brave face

Mrs Battle and her daughters (from Battisford). Everyone was gathered at the last fete held in the field adjacent to "The Grange" – 1964

Jack Johnson's van in heavy snow. Hope he wasn't in it! – 22nd February, 1979

10
Tooting and Hull meet Ringshall

Felix and Vi' Wilden (née Coleman)
This Man Can Trace His 'Roots'

The Wilden family have lived in Ringshall for many generations. The original home for this branch of the family was "Fair View" (now called Maple Cottage), Offton Road, Ringshall; this property was in the family for approximately two hundred years. This house now belongs to Nicholas Webb and his family, and from here Mr Webb runs an antiques business.

Rose and Sidney Wilden had eight children, Denis, Bessie, Ida, Mary, Felix, Sidney, Dorothy and Peggy. Felix born in 1918, was named after his father's sister's son who was tragically killed in the 1914-1918 war.

His grandfather, James Glover Wilden (born 31 March 1834 and died 30 March 1906), was a local shoemaker, and one of his regular customers was Mr William Hitchcock who would order and pay for shoes for his farm workers. It must have been useful having a 'cobbler' in the family.

The young Felix started his schooldays at Barking school in the early nineteen-twenties. His elder sisters, Mary and Ida accompanied him there. He was only four years old when his serious education began. In those days the school had two rooms which contained three classes. The teachers were Mrs Earthey, Mrs Potter and Mrs Haylock (Head teacher). He would leave home at 8.30 in the morning, and lessons commenced at 9 o'clock. Any pupils who were late without a good excuse were punished. Bad behaviour was quickly quelled with the cane. Nobody relished that!

This photograph was taken at Barking School, circa 1923: (Left to right)
Top row, Billy Welham, Ada Largent, Miclian Lambert, Ella Cooper, ?, ?, Tommy Laflin.
2nd row, Tip Pearl, ?, Mary Wilden, Ida Wilden, Ena Pearl, ?, Bessie Wilden
Bottom, Frank Grimwood, Ena Thorpe, Doris Bugg, ?

A memorable occasion occurred when a monoplane was sighted flying from the Ipswich direction and going towards Stowmarket. All the pupils were allowed into the playground to view this aircraft, and local people gathered on Barking Tye to get a good sighting.

Another treat for the pupils in those days was to watch the hunt gather outside the "Barking Fox" where some of the riders enjoyed a 'stirrup cup' before setting off. Members of the hunt looked magnificent in their hunting pink, and the public would invariably gather to watch this spectacular sight.

During 'break' hot Horlicks was given to the lucky pupils who could afford the one-penny charge.

In the nineteen-twenties there were two wells on Barking Tye. One was situated on the edge of the Tye near to where the garage stands today, and the other well was in the middle of the Tye. From this latter well the boys, on reaching the grand age of nine or ten, were allowed to 'draw' water for school use. Occasionally a particularly frisky horse would chase the boys making their task slightly trickier.

Felix left Barking school and continued his education at a school in Needham Market. To enable pupils to get to this establishment more easily, the local council supplied bicycles. He left school at thirteen years of age.

They do say that cats have 'nine lives', and so has Felix Wilden. 'Accident prone' is a very apt description. From normal childhood scrapes he went onto more serious misadventures, and these have continued for most of his life.

With such a large family to feed, Mrs Sidney Wilden shopped in bulk. Her bread order alone consisted of eighteen loaves per week. For this mammoth purchase she placed her order regularly with the local baker, Danks Howe at Great Bricett. His bread was freshly oven baked and was delicious. On this particular day, son Felix was asked to collect two loaves on his bike. Cycling merrily homewards, with two loaves firmly ensconced in a basket perched over his handlebars, he suddenly became aware of the sound of a motorised vehicle approaching. This was a butcher's van owned by Mr Emsden and driven by Basil Jarvis. These old vehicles had solid tyres and open cabs. Brick Kiln hill in those days consisted of a rough granite surface, treacherously uneven for motorised vehicles, and absolutely hated by cyclists. Suddenly the van swerved towards the young boy, and Felix with no room to get out of the way hit the motorised vehicle and somehow contrived to end up in the cab with the driver. This man was undoubtedly horrified at Felix's acrobatic arrival in his cab. The scars from the lacerations caused by going through the windscreen are still visible on his face today. Two very surprised and worried people immediately on the scene were Mr Grimwood (nicknamed 'Hatton' by the locals), and Mrs Barton who organised Felix's swift removal to hospital in 'Titch' Taylor's car. Mr Taylor was the local village parson at the time. The chauffeur was Mr Frank Elmer.

At the age of twenty, Felix like so many other young men of the time, was called up into the Forces. For youngsters living in country areas who had never been away from their villages before it was a daunting prospect. A much coarser world awaited these innocents. Loud voiced drill sergeants would yell such inane orders as "come on, speed it up, you haven't got all day" as they jogged laboriously round the parade ground. Their time would be taken up with lectures, drills, exercises and inoculations. Home comforts would seem a long way off. However, this particular young man bade farewell to his family and

Seconds later, the young Felix Wilden ended up in the cab with the driver! I wonder if the bread was still edible?

friends and went jauntily off to do his duty for 'King and Country'. The next few years would change his view of life completely, not just because of the war, and he would become more resilient and wiser in the ways of the world.

The reality of war was very different to anything these young people had previously imagined. Some would return home; some would not. His training took Felix all over the country, Arborfield Garrison, near Wokingham, Surrey, Newcastle and Scotland. Whilst at North Shields, Newcastle an ENSA concert took place with Gracie Fields on the bill. As Felix was the proud possessor of a smart blue suit (made at Burtons and costing fifty shillings), he was chosen to hand 'our Gracie' a cup of tea.

Home on one of his precious 'leaves', tragedy struck the family. The local school had an outbreak of diphtheria and meningitis. His sister's only child caught diphtheria and died. The family was heartbroken. Felix began to feel unwell, the doctor was summoned, and the young soldier found himself ensconced in the Ipswich Isolation hospital. His misery was compounded by the realisation that his mother was also infected with the virus. She was isolated in the women's ward.

Once more fit and well, Felix went home and awaited instructions from the War Office. Eleven months later he was still waiting! Although he was kept active and fit working on the local farms, he wanted to get back to his Battalion, so with no directive from the army forthcoming, he decided to use his own initiative to rejoin his regiment.

Travelling was not easy during wartime, and for a hard-up soldier it was even more difficult. He eventually made it to the Garrison and approached a fellow member of the armed forces outside the gates enjoying a leisurely cigarette. This was 1940 and deserters were harshly dealt with in the Services. Felix was most certainly not a deserter, but couldn't seem to get this languid fellow puffing his cigarette to understand his predicament. He cheerfully told Felix he would probably be shot as a deserter, or put in the 'Glass House'. Neither solution was very appealing. Luckily he did manage to rejoin his Unit without undue fuss. In fact, due to a clerical mix-up he was given 'back pay' for the duration of his absence due to illness.

The war dragged on and Felix found himself on Tilbury Docks ready to embark on a liberty ship (American built transport), en route for Normandy. With a fervent dislike of heights, the act of climbing down the rope ladders on disembarkation filled Felix with horror. With so many men clambering down in quick succession, the thought of getting his hands squashed to a pulp by large army boots, gave him the courage to 'grit his teeth' and climb down as quickly as possible. The serious business of fighting had begun. He went through

This photograph shows a German cross. I believe these crosses were given to German mothers by the Government to celebrate the birth of three children, or more. On the back of this particular cross, the inscription reads: Quote "16th Dezember, 1938" Unquote. Underneath is Hitler's signature. Note the German spelling of December

Felix found this medal in an abandoned house somewhere in Europe towards the end of the war when the German armies were retreating

Arnhem and saw the terrible destruction in the aftermath of the battle for the bridge over the River Rhine, when so many British men lost their lives, then through the Ardennes and eventually finished up in Hamburg.

The war years were not all gloomy for Felix. In 1943 he married Vi' Coleman who originally came from Tooting, London. They met when both were serving in the army. In 1945 their son Robert was born, and in 1947 their daughter Maureen was born. They are delighted to be celebrating their fifty-fifth wedding anniversary this year (1998). The Wilden 'family tree' continues to bloom.

I asked Vi' how she had managed to settle in the country so well having spent much of her early life in London. It must be remembered that when she first came to Ringshall life here was a lot less sophisticated than today. Water came from a well situated opposite the Primary School gates and had to be scooped up in buckets. Not many people had cars so it was necessary to walk everywhere. Getting to the doctor's surgery at Needham Market was quite a test of endurance, particularly if parents had children 'in tow'. It was all so very different then but her answer was simple. She came because she loved her husband, and where Felix is that is home to Vi' Wilden.

The Wilden Clan. From left: Eddy, Vi', Dot, Margie, Mary, Jenny, Annabel, Peggy, Felix, Rob, Sid, George

Recollections of deliverymen who went from village to village selling their wares during the nineteen-twenties.

Mr Kitten — Baker
Mr Purr — Clothier
Mr Catton — ?
Mr Blizzard — Butcher
Mr Hopgood — General salesman selling candles, pegs, frying pans, paraffin and odds and ends. The name of HOPGOOD is now very well known in Stowmarket and the surrounding areas for their top quality furniture store. Good service is still 'second nature' to this family.

Hopgood & Son, Stowmarket delivering to local villages. Circa 1920s -1930s. (Produced by kind permission of Mr David Hopgood)

Most deliveries were made by horse drawn vehicles in those days and the horses became as familiar with the customers as did the delivery men.

Felix takes a rest. Is it time for a cup of tea? June, 1998

Vi' inspects the vegetables. Bet she won't find a weed! June, 1998

Nephew 'Jackie' Johnson. At age two years

The wedding of Robert Wilden to Jenny which took place at Combs Church on July 4th, 1970. Felix and Vi' Wilden standing to far left of the bridal couple

The wedding of Maureen Wilden to Godfrey Edwards on 15th May 1965. Mr Price-Jones officiated and the wedding took place at Ringshall Church

This young lad with the cheeky grin is Felix Wilden. The photograph was taken while he was still at school

Once Upon A Time ....

The summer of 1925 was long and hot, and the autumn came in with a blaze of colour. Felix Wilden was seven years old and remembers one incident of that particular autumn still very clearly.

It started like many other days and Mrs Wilden had plenty to do with a large, boisterous family to look after. Sensing her two younger sons were feeling rather bored, and perhaps fearing mischief afoot she decided to allow them to leave the confines of the garden and take a stroll along the lane, which ran past their cottage. With his mother's admonishment to take care of four year old Sidney, still ringing in his ears, Felix and his brother ambled slowly along Offton Road.

Hands in pockets, kicking a few stones, and maybe chatting about their latest conker collection, they made their way towards Ringshall House, which then was owned by Mr Robert Makens who resided there with his sister, Kate. Mr Makens was of rather formidable appearance and usually made his presence known by appearing in his carriage, which was driven by Mr Barton, (nicknamed 'Buskins', presumably because of his shiny buskins).

In those days, Ringshall House sported a large white painted gate, which led from the lane into the apple orchard. Leaning casually on the gate, the small boys looked longingly at the scrumptious fruit. Felix made a quick decision "Would you like an apple?" he asked Sydney. "Yes, please" replied the youngster, eyes shining at the prospect of such a prize. The trees looked temptingly climbable, and in a trice Felix was over the gate and into the branches with his young sibling looking on admiringly.

'Scrumping' was fun. This was something Felix hadn't done before, but he knew boys who had! Suddenly, his concentration was punctuated by a loud bellow and Mr Barton appeared in the orchard. He was furious, and poor Felix nearly fell out of the tree, such was his terror. It was all too much for little Sidney, who took one look at the highly agitated, fearsome looking man and decided to run home as fast as he could leaving his hapless brother to 'face the music' alone. Felix was dragged unceremoniously off the tree and with Mr Barton's hand *firmly clenched round his shirt collar, he was marched into the house to face Kate Makens. This was quite an ordeal for the small boy, but Miss Makens, undeterred by his nervousness, wasted no time in telling him what she thought of naughty boys who tried to steal her apples. After a stern lecture, the thoroughly frightened child was sent home!*

Once safely back home, Felix decided the less his parents knew of his escapade, the better. Both boys decided 'discretion was the better part of valour'. However, unfortunately for them, Miss Kate Makens had other ideas. Using a basket of apples as her excuse for calling, she informed Mr and Mrs Wilden that their young son, Felix, had been caught 'red handed' scrumping apples from her orchard. Rose and Sidney were appalled, and felt obliged to apologise profusely for their errant offspring. The day ended with a woeful Felix being administered a sharp slap on the back of his legs by an exasperated father.

Felix never went 'scrumping' again, nor did he view Miss Kate Makens with much favour after that either.

Material supplied for the above story by Mr Felix Wilden – 1998

The Story of Janet Shann (née Smith)

Janet was born on 1 May 1955 at Lower Farm, Ringshall to Pamela and Dennis Smith. Two brothers followed, Steven and Neil.

Life for the three Smith children was secure and happy. Janet can remember when Lower Farm Road was mainly bounded by fields, and not too many people around. She recalls with affection Mr George Grimwood, who lived in a cottage further down the road. He loved to lean on his garden gate and would chat endlessly to the local children. He was a man who had a special affinity with young people. Summer picnics were great fun. Their mother would prepare the food and the children would hasten off to find their father on the combine and once settled in a comfortable spot, would attack their food with relish while watching Dennis at work. The country lanes were mostly devoid of traffic and that meant lovely leisurely cycle rides with friend Jenny Thorpe and sometimes Mum would come along. In those summer days the sun always seemed to be shining.

At the age of five Janet started her formal education. Ringshall Primary School was still a fairly new building at that time and didn't have any additional classrooms, or a swimming pool. Today's pupils are so lucky to have such a pool. Living so near to the school, Janet was able to walk home for lunch, and this made a welcome break. Her childhood in the village was happy and contented, and boredom was unknown. Laughter was never in short supply in the Smith family home, and even some of the dramas had their lighter side.

Many years ago, Stocks Farm had a fine old wooden barn, and this building usually housed a number of pigs. When Janet was thirteen there was a serious fire at the barn. The Fire Brigade was hastily summoned but the firemen had great difficulty in controlling the squealing pigs, who kept running back into the barn in their panic. Pandemonium reigned, with the Smith family, firemen and pigs running in all different directions, and the smoke getting thicker and thicker. If it hadn't been so serious, it would have made a hilarious scene in a comedy film. The building burnt for four hours. A strong new metal barn was erected in its place.

Another slight 'mishap' suffered by the Smith family, and once more involving a fire, took place in Janet's mother's bedroom. This time it was a chimney fire and once again along came the now all too familiar men from the local fire brigade.

It was 1961 and Janet's mother was learning to drive. Most novice drivers find their first few lessons frustrating and a bit daunting. Although having regular lessons with a local driving school, Pam decided to bolster her confidence by having a few extra lessons. Family friend Roger Buxton was willing to help, and on a fine summer evening they optimistically set off in Pam's Austin A35 along Lower Farm Road, heading towards RAF Wattisham. All went well until Roger decided to test Pam's reversing skills. The intention was to reverse from Lower Farm Road into Carters Lane. So far, so good! Suddenly Pam realised the handbrake wasn't where she thought it was. Panic ensued. The car seemed instantly to develop a will of its own and headed with a sudden burst of speed

Really Pam! This was meant to be a driving lesson

towards the nearest verge. Next minute, the hapless driver, and helpless passenger found themselves upturned in a ditch, with the driver's door facing skywards. With difficulty, the two heaved themselves out, no time for dignity, just relief to be alive and on solid ground. An added humiliation for Pam was the appearance of her instructor, driving past just as she clambered unceremoniously out of her upturned vehicle. Roger, having made sure all his limbs were still in working order, trudged back to Lower Farm where Dennis quickly organised a tractor to pull the car out of the ditch. What he said to his wife will NEVER be repeated, and certainly not in this book.

Janet's parents enjoyed their family, thereby giving their children a secure, happy home. Her father, Dennis, was a gentle man who would always help anyone. He loved children and was in his element helping to organise parties and outings, etc. Later on he would relish his role as grandfather.

Her mother always took a great interest in the farm during her husband's lifetime. Janet can remember Pam going sugar-beet hoeing (singling out), many times. In fact she would 'turn her hand' to almost anything.

Ringshall local Post Office when owned by Dennis and Pamela Smith – circa 1975

And so Janet's childhood passed, and she became a young woman. When she left school she helped her parents in the local shop which they now owned as well as the farm. It was whilst serving in the shop that Janet met her future husband, a young man from RAF Wattisham. She was just nineteen. They married on 14 August 1976 at Barking Church when she was twenty-one. The reception was held at The Swan, Needham Market.

Preparations for any wedding involve careful planning and organisation, and it becomes more complicated when the bride decides the only way to ensure her wedding cake is 'that bit more special' is to make it herself. Janet enthusiastically set about gathering together all the ingredients. The two baking tins for the top two tiers were easily obtained, but unfortunately nobody could help supply the larger tin for the bottom tier. Both she and her mother 'scurried around like two squirrels looking for nuts'. They tried every suitable shop in Ipswich, Norwich and local villages. Even the RAF Wattisham couldn't help. There didn't seem to be any answer to their predicament!! Suddenly, their good neighbour John Hitchcock came to the rescue. He made the exact size tin out of a piece of metal.

Janet with her mother, Pamela outside Barking Church – 14th August, 1976

The wedding cake

Janet with her father, Dennis outside Barking Church

Janet was able to produce her masterpiece as planned. (The photograph shows what a splendid job she made of it). Gwen Le Grice has still got that 'special' cake tin.

Janet and her husband started their married life in a caravan parked behind her parents' shop, and then in a mobile home. Their elder son, David was born while they were living there in 1978. His birth was not without drama and excitement.

June 3, 1978 dawned clear and bright, and the expectant mother was fully involved in the local preparations to celebrate the Queen's Jubilee. The baby wasn't due until the 22 June and Janet felt absolutely fine. That afternoon she energetically took part in a children's sports event held in her parent's barn. In the evening a barn dance was held and the whole family thoroughly enjoyed themselves. The partying went on until midnight. As the last guests disappeared, Janet and her family set to work to wash the glasses and cutlery, etc, and generally to clear the debris. With most of the cleaning done, she went home for a well earned rest. The farm was quiet, not many things stir at 3 o'clock in the morning, but things were beginning to stir unexpectedly in Janet's home. She wasn't going to get that well earned rest! Prolonged discomfort, and subsequent pains made her realise the baby was going to arrive earlier than planned. On hearing that Janet's 'labour' had started, the family were galvanised into action trying to organise the young mother's swift removal to hospital. It quickly became apparent that the only available car belonged to her brother, and this particular vehicle was laden with the left-over food from the previous evening. Bread, sausage rolls, salad foods and cakes - all horribly squashed together. The

Janet arrives at Ipswich Hospital for the birth of David. Hope nobody looked inside the car!

intention was to give some lucky pigs a treat! Janet was in no position to be choosey, so allowed herself to be bundled into the car, and in this unceremonious manner she arrived at Ipswich Hospital in the early hours of the morning. David was born at 2.10 pm on 4 June 1978.

In 1979 the Shann family moved to their present home, 2 South View, Ringshall. It was here on 27 June 1981 that their second son, Colin was born.

David and Colin have both enjoyed a carefree existence in the village, in close proximity to other members of their mother's family. Their uncle now runs the farm, and the two boys are frequent visitors, having the added bonus of a doting grandmother still living on the premises. Sadly their grandfather died a few years ago. David is an apprentice mechanic in a local garage, and Colin is an apprentice cabinet maker in a very well known and respected firm.

To celebrate the Queen's Jubilee in June 1978 the Parish Council presented all the village children with a specially inscribed mug.

To celebrate the marriage of Prince Charles to Lady Diana Spencer on 29 July 1981, the Parish Council presented all the village children with a specially minted crown piece.

Fun in the Snow

Colin and David Shann relishing the snow scene outside their grandmother's farm

The snow was so high at this time local people walked on hedges

Before "Meadowlands" was built this pretty scene was part of Pam Smith's garden before they added the shop premises – circa 1964

Colin being taught to ride – circa 1984

206

11
Recollections and Changing Times

It started with Duke William of Normandy who became William I of England - William the Conqueror.

> *Le Gris ou Gris prit part à la Conquète de L'Angleterre en 1066 Génelogie de la maison d'Erard le Gris avec ses cinq fils suivit la bunniere de Roger de Montgomerie, depuis Comte de Shrewsbury.*

The above tells us the name **Le Grice** (Le Gris), is of Norman origin and was first heard of in this country after the Norman conquest of 1066. It then tells us that Le Gris, with his five sons, were followers of Roger de Montgomerie, subsequently Count of Shrewsbury. The name Le Gris was Anglicised in 1754.

It isn't possible to go back to the Norman invasion of 1066 here, but on reading through the Le Grice 'family tree' I realise it is worth remembering the changes that took place in this country under William the Conqueror.

The Domesday Survey was decided upon while William was in Gloucester in December 1085 (the year before his death). It was a very clever idea and was carried out quickly and thoroughly by royal officers who were sent into nearly every corner of the land to discover the exact wealth of England, and thereby its customs and much additional information.

The whole country was radically altered by the Norman conquest. Great stone castles were built to enforce William's rule. The Tower of London is a reminder of such structures. The old aristocracy was swept away; we see from the Domesday Survey, 20 per cent of the land was owned by the King, 25 per cent by the Church, 50 per cent by the Norman barons and only the remaining 5 per cent by Anglo-Saxons. French became the official language. The Normans brought England into the mainstream of Europe, and it was from the fusion of Norman and Anglo-Saxon that the English nation started to emerge.

William I died in battle while fighting for the disputed Vexin territory (land between France and Normandy). He was thrown from his horse and died six weeks later on 9 September 1086 at Rouen. He was buried in Caen. As history clearly shows, he was a man of great character, intelligence and resourcefulness. One of the greatest generals the world has ever known.

By Emily Ford – 1997

We will start with the immediate family of Leonard Le Grice, namely his parents Wilfred and Mercy and sister, Daphne.

The parents of Wilfred Le Grice farmed at Brick House Farm, Naughton during the nineteen-twenties, and possibly until the last war (1939-45). He was born into a strong Baptist family, his father, Frederick was one of eleven children born to Charles Le Grice and Francis Clarke of Cotton, Suffolk. Frederick Le Grice would occasionally conduct services at Ringshall Chapel. The family at this time consisted of mother, father, son Charles (who was to die young), Mildred (known affectionately as Millie), Wilfred, Gladys, Thomas (who would eventually manage the farm) and Joyce.

During the week the young Le Grices would attend the local school in Naughton; and on Sunday they would attend Sunday School at Ringshall Chapel. If the weather was particularly inclement, their father would deliver them safely in the horse and cart. This form of transport was quite usual in those days, and was much enjoyed by the children. It seems to have been a very happy childhood for them with firm discipline, lots of laughter, and a healthy regard for Christian beliefs. Wilfred's own children would later on benefit from his firmly held beliefs and good manners instilled in him by his parents.

Wilfred grew up to be a quiet, unassuming young man with a sunny disposition and an exceptionally helpful nature. Farm work didn't really appeal to him; so on leaving school he went to work in a grocery shop in Offton, helping with the deliveries. The family farm was eventually managed by his brother, Thomas, who married Joyce Preston of Naughton.

During the next few years Wilfred married Mercy Clover; was called up for war service (more details of this part of his life later), and had a young family, Leonard and Daphne. After the war he worked as a roundsman for Donald Potter who kept a grocery store in Mill Road, Battisford. He kept this job for a number of years, when unfortunately Donald Potter had to retire because of ill health. Wilfred then went to work for Swains of Stowmarket, in the shop. Because of his gentle manner and helpful nature he was always very popular with the customers. Ill health forced his early retirement from this job; and he died eighteen months later, in 1974.

The Baptist Church was always a very important part of Wilfred's life. After the war he became secretary to the Naughton Baptist Mission (the chapel was built in 1936 and is now a private house). This position was to be held by him for approximately thirty years. He continued to be dedicated to his chapel work until his death.

Mercy Clover (Leonard's mother), was born on Sunday 29 August 1909 to Jabez and Gertrude in Chelmsford, Essex. Jabez was a very active member of the Baptist Church, and sometime during 1917 the Church called him to the pastorate and they moved to Crowfield, Suffolk. By then the family consisted of Grace, Mercy, William and Ruth. Four more children were born during their years in Crowfield. After a very happy and secure young life, Mercy left home to go into 'service' with a family in the village of Henley. Her ambition had always been to become a nurse, but as the second-eldest daughter of a large family of a poor minister, this was not possible.

On 20 March 1940, Mercy Clover married Wilfred Le Grice, right hand man to Pastor White from Wattisham Strict Baptist Chapel. The happy couple started married life in a small cottage, "Lucky's Corner Cottage", Hitcham. The Second World War was now dominating everyone's life, and soon Wilfred was called up. Because of a childhood accident in which his right fore-finger was severed (the trigger finger), he was unable to go to the front line and remained in England doing very necessary work in the military stores.

Leonard Le Grice was born in Hitcham in 1941. During 1942 his mother took Leonard to Sunningdale, Surrey so they could be nearer to Wilfred. Almost immediately their small son developed alarming symptoms and was rushed into the intensive care unit of the local hospital. Meningitis was diagnosed. It was a terrible time for the young family and great was their joy and relief when Leonard made a complete recovery and they were assured there would be no brain damage.

Back in Hitcham and the young mother had much to keep her busy during those difficult days when war time shortages and rationing became an added burden to housewives trying valiantly to cope without the help of their men folk. An additional problem for country people was the lack of facilities in their homes. In those days water had to be collected from the stand-pipe by the roadside, and washing was done by lighting a fire under the boiler. Like many other families in country areas during the war, Mrs Le Grice 'took in' a young evacuee from London called Danny. Much to Leonard's regret, the family lost touch with this young boy after the war.

Tuesday 8 May 1945. The war in Europe was over and husbands, sons and daughters returned home. The ones who didn't will always be remembered. On 23 October 1947 Mercy Le Grice gave birth to a daughter who they called Daphne. The family was now complete, and during this time the family moved to Kelvedon House in the village of Stowupland. The two children were brought up in a very happy, stable home environment; and because of their father's connection with the Baptist church, the Bible was a most cherished possession.

A few years later, while the children were still young, Wilfred had a bungalow built for his family in Great Finborough. They named their latest home "Wilmerlenda". The young Le Grices spent their formative years in this bungalow. Bike rides round the country lanes were a very popular pastime for Leonard and Daphne, and their mother would enthusiastically join them on her 'sit-up-and-beg' bicycle. Picnics were also great fun, as was blackberry picking. The young friends of Leonard and his sister were always made welcome. Mrs Le Grice died in 1967.

In 1961 Leonard married Gwen Jones from "Watering Farm", Needham Market. They met through the Needham Market Young Farmers Club. They were married in Barking Church and subsequently came to live in Ringshall in 1966. First living in number one bungalow (tied property), and then moving to a cosy cottage with the delightful name of "Gardeners Rest" in 1975. Their only daughter, Alison, was born in 1967, but sadly died in 1971. Gwen has worked for the Hitchcock family on a part-time basis for well over twenty five years, and Leonard was the cowman for John Hitchcock. During his early years at Chapel Farm, it was the tradition to throw the young boys employed on the farm (even the students) into the moat on the event of their twenty-first birthday. One wonders if any got away without a drenching! Apparently this friendly ceremony was met with good natured laughter from the victims and much mirth from the older and wiser onlookers.

Mr Len' Le Grice working at Chapel Farm – circa 1973

A regular event in the nineteen-sixties was a gymkhana held in "Bakers Meadow" on the last Saturday in April. Leonard remembers one particular year when, due to unseasonably wet weather, several lorries became bogged down in the mud. Being of a helpful nature; Leonard, along with several other like minded chaps, did his best to get the lorries, and their drivers, onto more substantial ground. Evidently he did very well in tips handed out from very relieved drivers.

During their years in Ringshall, Gwen and Leonard have both given unstinting help and support to village activities. They remember with affection the Amenities Fund Committee. This was founded quite unexpectedly by the late Dennis Smith when he and his friends and neighbours decided to hold a Barn Dance to celebrate the Queen's Silver Jubilee. This was so successful they were left with a considerable amount of money, so it was decided to organise a mystery coach tour and take the senior citizens out for the day. The same group of people organised further barn dances. It took a lot of hard work and enthusiasm to get the barn scrubbed and decorated prior to the event. Sometimes trouble would break out between local lads, lads from Needham and lads from RAF Wattisham. To help quell the disturbances, chaps were brought in who were well practised in the 'art of defence'. Today they would be called 'bouncers'. Proceeds would go to various charities, such as The Gateway Club for the Handicapped in Stowmarket; the Scanner Appeal and Addenbrookes Hospital. On the death of Dennis Smith, his family and friends determined to

Gwen Le Grice giving a cheerful wave

continue his good work. The people concerned were Mrs Pamela Smith, Mrs Anne Buxton, Leonard Le Grice, Gwen Le Grice (Treasurer), Mr Jimmy Wilden, Mr Derek Smith (Chairman), Mrs Pauline Smith (Secretary), and Miss Julie Johnson (now Mrs Julie Smith).

On one memorable occasion the local children were taken to "The Barking Fox" for their Christmas party and had to stay overnight because of heavy snow. Gwen affirms that sleeping on the hard floor was no picnic. In the early hours, Leonard began his trek back to Ringshall through heavy drifting snow. Help was on the way, but in the meantime the tractor ended up overturned in a ditch, much to the chagrin of the driver. Eventually all children were returned safe and sound to their very relieved families.

Gwen and Leonard are keen whist players and work very hard, along with several other local people, to help organise various social events. Other stalwarts are Marian and John Thorpe, Angela Mitchell and Jean Laffling.

....

NOTE: Information concerning the life of Mercy Le Grice (Leonard's mother) was taken from the book "Price Above Rubies, The Story of a Suffolk Housewife", written by Daphne Swanson (sister to Leonard). Some of the information on Wilfred Le Grice was obtained from John Waspe who knew him very well when both were young men.

The machine, called a Stack Liner was driven by the power take-off of the towing tractor. Leonard Le Grice believes it to be the first machine to be brought into the country. It was fully automatic and would pick up 55 single bales. These could then be hydraulically tipped up and stacked. The length of the stack would be determined either by the amount of bales, or the length of the field.

Leonard Le Grice with his young daughter, Alison – 1970

Happy Memories of Ringshall

By Miss Barbara Goodchild

Although I didn't move into the village of Ringshall until October, 1962, I have happy memories of Ringshall from a very early age.

I was born in Willisham in 1924. My family moved to Naughton in 1928 and started farming there, and it was from there I was sent to Ringshall Sunday School which was held in the Free Church. Each Sunday I would walk the three miles from the farm with the Le Grice family from the adjoining farm. We all became firm friends. It was very pleasant walking through the lanes and meadows during the spring and summer months. Cattle grazed peacefully in the meadows and the lanes and hedgerows always had an abundance of wild flowers. Kingcups were a particular favourite of mine.

After Sunday School which was held each Sunday morning, my sister Daphne and I would visit our granny, Isabella Goodchild. She and my grandfather, Frederick Goodchild lived in the end cottage of the terrace of three, next to the Free Church. They brought up a large family in that cottage and remained there all their married lives. Grandfather was a church warden at St Catherine's Church and my grandmother helped to keep the church clean and polished. She would also invariably be called upon to assist when a birth was imminent in the village. Before leaving for home we were often each given a piece of chocolate and this was a great treat looked forward to with relish!

My father, Frederick William Goodchild usually collected us in his pony and trap after Sunday School. This meant we didn't have to walk the three miles back to the farm.

My father started work at "Ringshall House", which at that time was owned by Mr Makins. As small children we loved to hear stories about our father's early days in farming and the following is one such story. He told us how he and his brother, George, used to drive sheep from Bury St Edmunds cattle market. Along the way were certain meadows wherein the sheep would rest for the night, and the tired men would stay at a nearby Inn. Eventually, after a journey lasting several days, sheep and men arrived at Ringshall House. No A14 in those days! My eldest sister, Eva, also worked at Ringshall House, staying there for twenty seven years. She is now ninety two years old.

One of the 'highlights' for me as a child was the annual Good Friday tea at the Chapel and the Special Service. The Sunday School Anniversary was always on the first Sunday in June when the Chapel would be packed with people, with some having to sit outside. Children and helpers would sit at the front of the Chapel, special songs would be sung, and most of the children gave long recitations. On these occasions there was a special guest speaker.

The next event was our Sunday School treat to Felixstowe. As this was the only time we paid a visit to the seaside, this trip was looked forward to by both parents and children. During the war years such trips to the seaside were impossible, so instead a games afternoon and evening was organised when parents were invited to join us, and this they did with enthusiasm. This event was held in the meadow opposite the Free Church by kind permission of Mr Tom Gibbons. Some of the American servicemen stationed at RAF Wattisham joined us for Sunday worship, and they were delighted to join us for our games afternoon, becoming thoroughly involved in all the activities. Chocolate and sweets were rationed at this time, so the children were thrilled to be given an assortment of candy (sweets) by the American servicemen. A nice tea was provided by friends at the Chapel.

There followed, what later in life became to me the best social event of the year, the Harvest Festival Services. These were always held on the first Sunday in October, when fruit, vegetables, corn and flowers from field and garden were given to decorate the Chapel. How thankful we were to sing, "All is safely gathered in, Ere the winter storms begin!" One knew that, "All good gifts around us were sent from Heaven above" – and we were so thankful.

Miss Barbara Goodchild's bungalow in Ringshall – Summer, 1969. The property was then called "Underwood Grange". It is now called "Underwood" and is owned by David and Clare Secret who live there with their son, Adam

October, 1962. My mother and I moved to Ringshall, into a bungalow built for us on land which had previously been farmed by my grandfather many years before.

Mr George Grimwood was a near neighbour and was at the time leading the work at the Free Church. After many years of faithful service he asked me if I would be willing to take this on. For several years thereafter I was privileged to lead the Sunday School, and I was also secretary and caretaker of the Church.

No Sunday School existed in Willisham in those days, so several of the children, with the assistance of grown-ups with transport, were able to attend Ringshall Free Church. As well as the local children, we had a healthy intake from RAF Wattisham. It was a joy to see those children coming each Sunday. On special mornings, such as Easter Sunday and Mothering Sunday, when we had Family Services, the Chapel would be reasonably full. High ranking officers from the RAF would come to hear their children taking part. I still hear from a number of them and they refer to those days at Ringshall as 'Happy Memories'.

Each January a special tea was organised for the children when Mr Stanley V Gardner (of S.U.) would join us and put on a 'Jungle Doctor' film. Afterwards he would join in quiet games with the children.

Several willing helpers were involved in this work but specific names will not be mentioned for fear of inadvertently leaving some out.

Another special event was the Centenary of the Chapel on 27th-28th July 1968. This event was celebrated by a special weekend and a tea. The guest speaker was the Rev. T. McBeth Paterson of Enfield. Other Pastors took part and friends from the Chapel and others brought messages in song. Music was provided by the Band of Battisford Free Church who also composed and sang the following 'piece':

> *Happy Centenary,*
> *Happy Centenary.*
> *Happy Birthday, dear neighbour,*
> *Happy Centenary,*
> *May God bless you today,*
> *May God bless you today.*
> *May God bless you,*
> *And fill you, and keep you always.*

A report of the history of the chapel was given. The following points were mentioned in the text.

QUOTE:
(a) The ground was given by Mr. Beaumont.
(b) The chapel was erected by Mr. Edward Gibbons, of Ipswich, at a cost of £132.
(c) Eight Trustees were elected.

The first speakers of the chapel were supplied by the Methodist Chapel of Stowmarket. Mr Govan and Mr John London of Gt. Bricett would also take the services. Baptist ministers from Somersham and Wattisham conducted one week night service each month.

This arrangement continued until 1924 when Mr. Frederick Le Grice was appointed leader of the work. Mr. Le Grice formed a Sunday school and evening service, and remained in charge of the work for twenty-one years until he left the district in 1946.

Mrs Coleman of Ringshall faithfully cleaned the Chapel for many years. The old combustion stove was replaced by electric heating in 1963, the oil lamps having already been replaced by electric lighting in 1952. Throughout the history of the chapel, faithful preachers have always been ready to help, as have organists and Sunday School teachers. UNQUOTE

Thus ended a happy weekend.

The work continues today just as diligently. The jobs of treasurer, organist and caretaker are undertaken by Mr and Mrs Felix Wilding. Mr Cecil Welham is secretary. In September, 1998, Mr. Graham Steward was inducted as Pastor.

August, 1987. My mother passed away in her 93rd year.

March, 1988. Because of constant back trouble, my doctor advised me to move to a property with a smaller garden. With regret I left my bungalow in Ringshall and moved to Hitcham.

Miss Barbara Goodchild presented a beautifully handwritten text containing interesting facets of her life in the Suffolk countryside. She wrote the 7-page text between periods of hospital treatment on her eyes. Her dogged determination to 'put some of her story' on paper was much appreciated.

Ringshall Independent Chapel

In Lower Farm Road, set back slightly from the road, stands a small chapel. The following is a résumé of the history of Ringshall Independent Chapel written by Mr George Grimwood just before his death in 1965. He was a much loved and respected member of the congregation here for many years.

QUOTE: Ringshall Chapel built 1868. Trustees then were Mr Stockings who married Mr Beaumont's daughter, which gave this piece of land for the chapel to be built. Mr John Beaumont son of Mr Beaumont, which gave this piece of land was also Trustee and Mr E Gowen, Bricett Hall was also one, when he died his son Mr Arthur Gowen became Trustee and Mr W Waspe, Battisford was also one. Mr Garrod, Nedging was one of the first Trustees, Mr W Hitchcock, Ringshall was one, Mr James Wilding, Ringshall was one, Mr David Mann, Ringshall, Mr Harwood of Battisford Hall was one also when he died his son Mr A Harwood was one. Also Mr W Chinery, Shoemaker was the first Chapel Keeper, lived Middle Cottage near the Chapel, brother-in-law to Mr James Wilding who Mr Chinery worked for. Mr Chinery was the first one I remember to look after it, Mr John Kerridge, Ringshall, was the second one.

I was born at Ringshall on April 13th the year 1878, my parents attending the Chapel when they brought me. When I was 5 years old they moved to a cottage 4 doors from the chapel. Then I came often. In 1899 the Holy Spirit shew me to be a lost sinner the last week in December, 1899. On January 2nd, 1900 I saw Jesus dying for my sins and I saw my burden roll away and I have been saved ever since. It was after this happened I began to do a little in the Chapel. The Methodist, Stowmarket started to send a few Speakers a few Sundays in each quarter, morning and afternoon is when the services was, this is when Mr John Kerridge was Chapel Keeper and Mr E Gowen, Bricett Hall was alive and Mr John London of Bricett, both good speakers. We could very often call upon one of them to take the services when the Methodist failed us. The Baptist from Wattisham and also from Somersham then sent their Minister from here one week night a month and also one Sunday night a month from Wattisham and Somersham and continued till 1924, this is when the Sunday School started by a mission by Miss Norris and Miss Weir. Mr Kerridge turned the Methodist down and found all the speakers which has never failed us and have been much better this way. Sunday School in the morning and Gospel Services afternoon and night. The Chapel cost one hundred and thirtytwo pounds to build and start it going. Mr Gibbons, Ipswich built it.

Mr Emerson, Barking Tye, rake and handle maker, a young man, collected the money and he lived till I was a man grown. He and his family attended this chapel. Mr W Hitchcock when he died gave the deeds to his son. I asked him for them so I have put them in a safe place in Mr Hayward the Lawyer's office, Needham Market, in an iron safe bricked in the wall so they are free from fire or water because they would cost a lot to replace them if they were lost. Mr Beaumont which gave the piece of land had in Ringshall 2 sons and 3 daughters.   G Grimwood   UNQUOTE

Mr George Grimwood – born April 13th 1878. Circa 1930.

Mr George Grimwood was a member of the Ringshall Free Chapel all his life and was a much loved character in the village

The following has been taken from various diaries:

QUOTE: A copy of the plan for the Stowmarket Circuit for the primitive Methodist Church of 1923 gives their motto for 1923 as "Live at peace with all" Heb 12v 14. The Society steward for Ringshall is given as J Kerridge and the times of the services as 10.45 am and 12.15 pm. Places on the Circuit were Stowmarket, Old Newton, Wyverstone, Coddenham, Ringshall, Buxhall, Stonham, Ward Green and Stow Lodge. The speakers who came to Ringshall from this Circuit in October to December 1923 are as follows:

7th October	R Payne of Buxhall
28th October	W Waspe of Combs
4th November	F LeGrice of Naughton
25th November	J Q of Stowmarket (name not given)
2nd December	W Thorndyke of Wyverstone
23rd December	W Waspe of Combs
30th December	C Smith of Coddenham

On 4th November there was a Sustentation Fund Collection. A list of receipts shows Ringshall as having given 12 shillings, possibly over the last three months or was it over the year so far, ie, 9 months? A list of disbursements shows the Minister's salary as £62.10 shillings.

In 1921 Mr F LeGrice came to Naughton and in 1924 was appointed Leader of the work and started a Sunday School and evening service. He was in charge of the work for 21 years until he moved from the district in 1946. Special children's services were held at Ringshall Chapel on Sunday 24th August 1924 when the speaker was Mr N Bugg. During these years Mr G Grimwood was Secretary and held this office until the end of 1962, he continued to attend the Chapel until his death 4th April 1966 aged 88 years.

The Chapel was originally heated by a combustion stove and the lighting was provided by hanging oil lamps. During this period the Chapel was cleaned by Mrs Coleman who faithfully performed her duties for several years. Electric lighting was installed in 1952 and electric heating in 1963. The chapel was redecorated in March 1965 when new chairs replaced the then existing forms. A Faith Mission Prayer Union was formed in 1946 and Mr T Barton became representative, a position he held until his death in 1965, he was also Treasurer for a number of years. Trustees prior to 1962 included: Mr Rowley S Clark of Glemsford; Mr Frank Goldsmith of Combs; Mr John Buckle of Does Farm, Naughton; Mr Reg Rumsey of Buxhall Farm, Gt Finborough; Mr Nelson Bugg of 30 Sproxton Road, Norwich; Mr Frederick Grimwood of Willisham and Mr Robert Green of Willisham. Others in 1962 were Mr Harry Waspe of 123 High Street, Hadleigh; Mr Wilfred LeGrice of Gt Finborough; Mr Leonard Morphew of Gt Bricett; Mr Tom Barton of Gt Bricett; Mr Peter Caley of Ringshall and Mr Cecil Welham of Barking Tye.

There should not be less than 5 for a Trustee meeting.

Throughout the history of the Chapel, faithful speakers have always been ready to help, some have cycled several miles and even walked considerable distances to the Chapel.

A meeting was held at Ringshall Free Church on 11 February 1966 chaired by Pastor Hawkins of Wattisham Baptist Church. Those present were Mrs Barton, Miss S Caley, Mrs Coleman, Mr R Francis, Miss B and Mr R Goodchild, Mr and Mrs Morphew, Mrs Smith, Mr and Mrs C Welham and Mr and Mrs F Wilding. At this meeting Mr C Welham was appointed Secretary, Miss B Goodchild Sunday School Leader, and Mr F Wilding as Treasurer. These people would form a Council to oversee the business of the Church. Mr Francis would caretake the outside of the building and Miss Goodchild the inside.

Ringshall Chapel Sunday School treat, 1941 (Back left) Mr George Grimwood, (back right) Mr Le Grice

Ringshall Chapel Sunday School treat, 1943. (Back row from left) Mr Le Grice, Mr George Grimwood, Miss Barbara Goodchild and Miss Joyce Le Grice

Sunday School, 1951

Sunday School, Autumn 1965

Sunday School outing to Felixstowe July 1966 (from left) Micky, Peter, Colin and David

220

On 27th and 28th July 1968 Ringshall Chapel celebrated their Centenary with special services, the speaker for the weekend was Rev Tom McBeth Paterson of Enfield Evangelical Free Church. The first service was held on the Saturday afternoon at 4 pm, when the Chairman was Pastor P Day of Stowmarket Baptist Church. Prayer was offered by Rev Youdin Duffie of Ringshall Parish Church and Mrs T McBeth Paterson sang a solo. The hymns from Sankeys hymn book were No. 11 'O worship the King'; No. 253 'I love thy kingdom Lord', No. 206 'We praise Thee, we bless Thee' and No. 228 'The Church's one foundation'. Pastor Day brought greetings from Norfolk and Suffolk Strict Baptist Association and from his church at Stowmarket, Mr C E Welham, Secretary gave the thanks and notices. The Bible reading was Psalms 125 and 126 and the text Numbers 6 vs 24 and 25. Those present included: Mr and Mrs John Clover of Stowmarket; Mrs V Cooper; Mr and Mrs J Baldry; Mrs N Welham and Mrs Waspe of Battisford; Mr and Mrs C Ward of Framsden; Mr and Mrs Jennings of Woodbridge; Mr and Mrs Goldsmith of Combs and Mr W Denny of Needham Market who brought and played his electric organ. Much food had been prepared for the public tea to which about 70 or 80 people stayed.

The evening meeting took place at 7 pm, the Chairman being Pastor V Moss of Gt Blakenham Parish Church, the prayer was given by Mr C Ward of Framsden. Members of Wetherden Baptist Chapel, Mr and Mrs David Bannister and Mr and Mrs John Rushbrook sang a solo and duets. The hymns were No 23 'To God be the Glory', No.21 'Behold me O Thou love', No. 620 'It passeth knowledge', and No. 524 'Guide me O Thou Great Jehovah'. The Bible reading was Deuteronomy 31 vs 1-19 and the text Deut. 33 v. 3. Pastor Moss brought greetings from his church and Mr C Welham read a short history of the Chapel and also two letters, one from Mr Philip Butler formerly of the Friends' Meeting House, Barking; he and his wife wished 'every blessing on this notable occasion' and said they had 'many happy memories of fellowship with members for many years past'. The other was from Mr W J Porter, Superintendent of the Faith Mission work in East Anglia. He sent warm greetings and went on 'I know you have had a long association with the work of the Faith Mission and we have certainly appreciated all your help and fellowship in the work of the Lord. We rejoice with you in having reached this great milestone and we wish you every blessing as you seek to carry on the witness in His Name'. Those present at this evening service included: Mr and Mrs Mudd of Wattisham, Mr L Smith of Ipswich, Mr Crysell of Mendlesham, Mr K Woollard and Mr and Mrs R Garrod of Naughton, Mr and Mrs S Squirrell of Wattisham, Mr S Mayhew of Stowmarket and Mr and Mrs S Gardiner representing the Caravan Mission to Village Children. Offerings amounted to £27. 16s.

Rev Paterson was again the guest speaker for the afternoon and evening services on the Sunday. The Chairman for the afternoon service was Pastor Baker of

Mendlesham who brought greetings from his church. Battisford Free Church Band led the hymns and played two pieces, their choir also sang two pieces, before the service commenced they sang 'Happy Centenary' to the tune 'Happy Birthday' to their 'dear neighbours'. Mr John Clover of Stowmarket gave the prayer. The hymns were; No. 203 'All hail the power', No. 207 'Be glad in the Lord and Rejoice' and No. 357 'Sing them over again to me'. The Bible reading was 1 Kings 18 vs 36-46 and the text Psalm was 139 v. 5. Those present included Mr and Mrs John Waspe of Whatfield, Mr and Mrs James of Stowupland, Mrs Rose Bugg of Naughton and Mr and Mrs Strawson of Barking Tye.

The evening service was conducted entirely by Rev Paterson and Mrs R Wilding, and Mrs E Beckley sang a duet 'Shepherd of Israel'. The Chapel was only about half full compared with overspill into the portable hall loaned by the Faith Mission in the afternoon. The hymns sung were No. 271 'How pleased and blest was I', No. 902 'My hope is built on nothing less', No. 508 'Rejoice in the Lord' and No. 517 'God will take care of you'. The Bible reading was Ephesians 2 vs

Above: Summer 1967. David and Peter at Felixstowe

Right: Sunday School, 1968. Miss Barbara Goodchild, (far left)

Auntie Audrey with some of the children on Barking Tye. Games Session – May 1971

(From left) Joan, Barbara Goodchild and Linda – 1974

1-8 and the text 2 Corinthians 6 vs 2. Collections altogether amounted to £51. 4s. 3d. Those present Sunday evening included Mr W Ward of Battisford, Mr J Partridge of Kersey, Mr R Kemp of Ipswich, Miss G Ball of Offton, Mr P Caley of Stowmarket and Mrs Wheatley and Mrs Bentley of Ringshall. The weather remained fine and warm and a great time of fellowship and blessing was experienced.

For many years members of the congregation walked around the local villages carol singing at Christmas time. They collected for the Royal London Society for the Blind. In December 1970 a record amount was collected, ie, £27. 5s. In their letter of thanks the Society wrote: "We see that according to our records you first started collecting for the Society in 1953 and to date we have received from you a total of £287. 9s. 6d, which really is a substantial amount. Once again many thanks and our best wishes to all your members and friends". UNQUOTE

Graham Steward Arrives at Ringshall Free Church

The Chapel was first opened for services in 1868 (the 31st year of Queen Victoria's reign). It was built on land owned by Mr Beaumont at a cost of £132 and was erected by an Ipswich builder, Mr Edward Gibbons. In those days preachers would cycle, or walk, several miles to the chapel.

A Sunday School was organised (this always took place each Sunday morning), and it was well attended by eager youngsters from Ringshall and the surrounding areas. On Good Friday there would be a special service, followed by tea at the Chapel. The Sunday School Anniversary was always on the first Sunday in June when the Chapel would be packed with people. Sunday School treats were regularly organised, with a yearly trip to the seaside at Felixstowe. Such trips would continue until the nineteen seventies when the Sunday School ceased.

We now enter a new phase in this small Church's history by introducing Graham Steward, who is proud to have become its first pastor in 130 years. Until now the congregation relied on the services of lay preachers.

Graham Steward was born in Denham, Suffolk into a local farming family. When he was three years old his parents moved to another farm at Banham in Norfolk. Although busy on the farm, religion was not forgotten, and Graham's parents were stalwart members of the local Methodist church. To their young son, the love of God was a natural extension of family life. Nevertheless, whilst still very young, Graham questioned and rejected his parent's beliefs, although still attending church with them. As a teenager he became aware that the God he did not want to believe in, was in fact, stirring his heart, and at the age of sixteen he made a personal commitment to Jesus Christ. This conversion experience was to have far-reaching repercussions, as subsequently he would enter the Christian ministry as a free church pastor.

In the meantime, his father was now running a Nursery at Brockford in Suffolk, and on leaving school, indeed for the next thirteen years, Graham too would work in the nursery. The words "nitrogen, phosphorus, and potassium (potash)", would become as familiar as the alphabet. His faith was a continuing source of satisfaction during this time, and he was becoming more involved in the Methodist church. At the age of eighteen he began preaching regularly in local Methodist churches, as well as churches of other denominations.

As he moved into his twenties and early thirties, profound changes occurred in this young man's life. He met, and married Gwen Horrex who had been born and brought up in Battisford. In due time they had three children, Julian, Lyndsay and Vaughan. Life was happy and busy for the Steward family. Graham was still working at the nursery, and with three boisterous youngsters, life was never dull. However there was a growing conviction in Graham that God had other work for him to do. Having first discussed his feelings with his wife and with her firm support, the young husband, with no formal training in the ministry, accepted the pastorate of Stratford St Mary Evangelical Chapel. Shortly afterwards, their youngest child, Ysabelle was born. The family were to spend ten very happy, fulfilling years in this village. Gradually, Graham felt God wanted him to move on, explore pastures new.

Graham was concerned that there should be a continuity in the Ministry at Stratford St Mary and was pleased to be able to welcome a new pastor there even before his own future was certain. This meant spending another fifteen months in temporary rented accommodation whilst a new position was sought. During this time Graham undertook an itinerant ministry, leading worship in a variety of churches. During this time the door was opened to undertake his present ministry.

Graham was to become pastor of not just one church, but two. Some challenge! Ringshall Free Church, and Barking Chapel come under a shared ministry. With the former, history was in the making. For the first time since it was built, Ringshall Free Church would have its own pastor.

A house move to Battisford got under way for the Steward family, and arrangements were made for the new pastor to start his new post in September, 1998. All went well, not even a minor mishap – that is until Graham decided to go 'house to house' through Ringshall, introducing himself, hopefully, to some of his new parishioners. Accompanied by a colleague, he optimistically set out. The people he found in were very welcoming, his confidence grew. Unfortunately, the sight of two young men knocking on doors, made one resident highly suspicious, and the two embarrassed men ended up having to explain their situation to the local constabulary.

With a sure and steady hand, Graham hopes to increase the present congregation. People from Wattisham Airfield, and nearby villages will be welcome. Gwen, an enthusiastic supporter of his work, looks forward to working with young people. For many years, until the nineteen-seventies, this small chapel had fairly large congregations. It was a much loved Christian focal point for Ringshall and nearby villages. The new pastor hopes to encourage people of all ages into the Church. So far the majority of the congregation seems to hail from neighbouring villages, but hopefully more Ringshall residents will 'take a peep inside the door', before too long.

Having to divide his time between two parishes can be difficult at times, but the new pastor is keen to get to know the local people and hopes to produce a 'News Sheet' containing Church dates and items of interest for all age groups.

Hopefully this short introduction to the new pastor of Ringshall Free Church, will give some indication of his hopes and dreams for the future of his ministry here.

Recollections from Ernie Thorpe

When my parents were first married they lived for a short time in Ringshall in what was then called a 'double dweller'. My sister was born in that house. Sadly, this property was later demolished when the road diversion to connect with the Brick Kiln hill was made. In the ensuing years the Pumpkin Garage was opened by Mr Thompson, as was a café owned by Mrs Clement Hitchcock during the war years. This became quite an attraction both to the local people and personnel at the Wattisham Base. To get to Ringshall we had to go through the "Barking Farm" of the Ringshall Hall Estate. This was owned prior to 1925 by the Long family. My father, uncle and my grandfather were employed at "Barking Farm". My Uncle Harry and Grandfather John lived at the 'stone cottage', a 'double dweller' on the edge of Barking Tye.

I have a vivid memory of visiting Ringshall Hall as a child in the nineteen-twenties, with my father. On meeting Mrs Long, my father reminded me to say "Good morning, m'am". A polite child makes everybody happy. I believe the main reason for our visit was to collect some of Mrs Long's lovely golden butter. A further memory concerns their son Harold, or the 'boy Harold' as he was known. While jumping a ditch on his horse at Barking, he fell off. This mishap seemed to cause a certain amount of agitation on Harold's behalf, and nearby residents started searching the ditch. In my childish mind I decided they must be looking for money dropped from the hapless young man's pockets. Unfortunately there were no metal detectors in those days.

About that time, my father was given toys, books and a quantity of picture postcards etc, from Mrs Long. I was rather surprised at her parting with these, but by this time her husband was dead, her son Edward was farming in Stradbroke, and her other son Harold was farming at Creeting St Mary. She obviously felt the time was right for a 'clear out', and my father and his young family seemed a natural recipient.

The Ringshall Hall Estate, totalling 573 acres was eventually put on the market by Moore, Garrard and Son at the Crown and Anchor Hotel, Ipswich on 14 July 1925. The estate consisted of the following ...

>Ringshall Hall
>3 cottages
>Muckinger Wood (55.5 acres)
>The Bradley Farm (12 acres of Woodland and 141 acres)
>The Barking Farm (most) with Double cottage (stone)
>Plus 196 acres.

I believe Ringshall was withdrawn from sale at £2,350, approximately ten pounds per acre. It must be added that 'Rowley' Hitchcock states in his book "Rowley Recalls Farming, Fighting and Fun", that his father, William bought Ringshall Hall for about ten pounds per acre. There has always been confusion over the way farms have been sold. It cannot be said that the acreage gives the correct price when properties and buildings have to be accounted for in the final total. In later times we have seen prices rise to over £2,000 (two thousand) per acre, farms fragmented, boundaries altered, houses sold, and farm buildings adapted for housing and commercial purposes.

I must now tell a tale that was passed down to me.

A long time ago, Mr Long (of Ringshall Hall), decided to buy another horse for the forthcoming harvest. He picked out a fine beast that was supposedly 'quiet in all gears'. Unfortunately, the clatter of the binder behind the three horses caused them all to run away – still attached to the binder. My father was on the binder and when he, the horses and machinery eventually came to a standstill, a workmate cheerfully remarked "Thus right, bor, thus quiet in all gears".

Harvest time has always been a very busy part of the year, and I can well remember taking my father's 'beaver' over to him. This strange sounding item was in fact the usual late afternoon snack given to farm workers at that time. He was to be found 'shocking', which means he was standing up sheaves thrown out by the binder. Along with his fellow workers he would sit by the 'shocks' and eat his snack. Another memory is of seeing the three-wheeled water tank reversed into the pond at the Barking Farm. The eight horses that 'stood' were Kitty, Moggy, Captain, Short, Price, Doughty, Stormer and Scott.

As a schoolboy, I remember cycling to Ringshall and coming across farming equipment which had been distrained. It seemed Mr Waspe had not paid his tithe. From this disturbance a strange alliance was formed between our Chapel parson, who was secretary to the Suffolk Tithe Payers Association and Sir Oswald Mosely's 'Blackshirts'. This 'partnership' was unbelievable as Mr Butler (our parson), was an extreme pacifist and the 'Blackshirts' were not averse to a bit of 'rough and tumble'. Eventually, the substantial tithe charges were eliminated and therefore Mr Butler and his fellow campaigners 'won the day'. Queen Ann had directed that tithes, which were formerly paid to the State should be channelled to the church, which meant that parsons had a vested interest in the tithe being paid.

When the Long family sold the farm in 1925 it was bought by Mr William Mullett, a hat factor from Luton and step-brother to the Bugg family. In 1936 the farm was sold again, this time the owner was John Gibbons. Supposedly, it was he who then sold part of the farm to the Hitchcock family. I believe the Hitchcock family acquired approximately eighty acres and this was amalgamated with Chapel Farm. With this latest transaction, the lane to Muckinger Wood disappeared as did the site of Bowtell Hall. I became aware of this quite forcibly when on a 'first date'. The prime necessity for a small farmer's wife was 'staying' power. To this end I devised a long walk for my young lady. This would take us via Hascott Hill, the Valley Farm, and through Muckinger Wood. Alas, we found the familiar path had disappeared. This was the path my father had used when he was instructed by the Hunt people to 'block up the earths in your charge'. It was also the favourite path of his rabbiting expeditions. My girlfriend and I had to propel ourselves through Mr Hitchcock's wheat field. What one may ask, has the aforementioned story got to do with the history of Ringshall, but it must be remembered that the story of Alfred the Great burning those cakes, has certainly stood the test of time.

With the Long family gone, my father was allocated a nine acre holding behind 'Stone Cottage' and during the winter months would spend time 'rabbiting' in Muckinger Wood, with dog, gun and line ferret. In the nineteen-twenties farm wages were very low (twenty eight 'bob' a week). Even the rabbit skins were collected, nothing was wasted. Fred (Mick) Laflin, a woodman, was allocated an area in Muckinger Wood to clear. There was a demand for wood products at that time and even the thorn element was formed into 'shruff' faggots to form the sides of a 'shed'. In the nineteen-twenties, the true countryman born and bred, wasted nothing.

My schooldays were in the nineteen-twenties. I was a pupil at Barking School and some of my companions came from Ringshall, namely the Wildens and the Hambletts (Felix and Sidney Wilden and Philip, Wilfred, Kenneth, Brenda, and Monica Hamblett). These children had to walk the two miles to school and stay for lunch, while we local children were able to go home in fine weather. From this school children either left at fourteen to seek employment, or after 1930, the elder children attended Needham school. In country areas, brawn was considered more important than brains.

In the early nineteen-fifties, a new school was opened at Ringshall and children from Barking under the age of eleven went there. My own children attended Ringshall school and as it was over two miles away the Local Education Authority paid me to take them, along with one or two other pupils, in my car.

Children can no longer cycle with safety along these country roads, so buses are now used to convey the pupils. How country life has changed in the latter part of this century. Most villages have lost the village shop, the village blacksmith, local post office, etc, because of so called progress. No longer do local ladies collect in the 'shop along the road'. It is unusual to see people chatting animatedly at the garden gate now. Those precious days have gone, and we now go to the nearest big town in our cars for our groceries. Water is on hand in the home, no longer a walk to the village pump (thank goodness for this bit of progress). It must be admitted some progress is good indeed, but some of the good things in country life have disappeared for good, along with some of the characters who gave us all plenty of fun and laughter.

Up to the 1939-45 war, villages were almost self contained and the small local shops stocked up accordingly. One such shop existed on Ringshall corner and was run by the Hall family for some time. Long before the war most people in the nearby villages were aware of 'Fishy' Hall. He would drive his horse and 'dealers' cart through our village, singing at the top of his voice. He often worked at Ringshall Hall for 'Rowley' Hitchcock. In those days before the war, milk was collected from local farms until Chapel Farm started house deliveries. Harry Turner had an open touring car and he had an oval shaped container holding approximately three gallons. There was a pint scoop on the side ready to pour the milk into the ladies' jugs. In those far off days most houses were occupied during the day.

While Rowland Hitchcock resided at Ringshall Hall he went into the haulage business as a 'sideline'. It was said that Ringshall Hall was difficult to manage, which is probably why Rowland decided to have another 'string to his bow'. He carted my father's sugar beet for a time, first in an old Thornycroft and then in a 3-ton Bedford. In those days a ton of beet could be conveyed to the factory in Ipswich for six-shillings, loaded and unloaded by hand. Clement Hitchcock (brother of Rowland), also acquired a two-ton Bedford lorry and this was driven by Harry Turner. Rowland employed Edgar Largent as his driver and one year when the beet harvest at Ringshall Hall was behind schedule, I was pleased to become, albeit temporarily, the driver's 'mate'. Several other small farmers also gave willing help. The introduction of the 10/20 tractor helped the situation.

As a young boy I remember seeing a Gyro tiller at work at Ringshall Hall. This machine stirred out large roots by the hedgerows, and unfortunately it would sometimes dislodge drainpipes.

The old Fordson Standard, and International tractors seemed to spend much time in ditches so farmers were pleased when rubber tyres and steering brakes were fitted as tractors evolved over the years.

I would now like to mention a few of the people who have resided in Ringshall during the last hundred years.

When I was a young boy older people in the area would often talk about Rob Makens. He was a bachelor and lived at Hill Farm (now known as Ringshall House), with his sister, and was described as a farmer, brickmaker and cattle-dealer. He supposedly had farming connections in the Norwich area and was said to be one of the last farmers to use draught oxen for field work. As a young man he used to drive in his horse and gig on Saturdays to Norwich market, and drive home again on the same night. As Norwich is approximately forty miles away he and his horses must have been extremely fit. Although a bachelor he had a discerning eye for the ladies. He would be driven to church in his later years by Mr Barton, presumably the one who was known as 'Buskins'. In those days, shiny buskins were the final touch to a smart outfit. The body of their carriage finished as a chicken shed on my grandfather's premises. I believe Rob Makens died at the beginning of the twentieth century.

Mr Clement Hitchcock used to graze his sheep on the Tye in the charge of my cousin Fred Pearl. Fred was only four feet in height and delighted in the nickname of 'shepherd'. Barking Tye was very useful to the local small-holders and villagers who grazed their draught animals there for generations. Ringshall did not have a Common or Tye. Much luckier were the villages of Barking, Willisham and Battisford. Barking is the only village to retain the Tye more or less intact. The general administration of the Barking Tye is in the hands of the Mid Suffolk District Council.

Sidney Wilden was an able carpenter. He made two huts for my father and they are still standing, albeit rather dilapidated, seventy years later. They have been used as fowl huts and granaries. Quite a chequered past.

William Last had a small-holding near Ringshall Hall. His wife was formerly a teacher at the Ringshall village school (1905), and in later years ran a small shop and the village post office.

Herbert Gooding lived at Charles Hall and was apparently also a pig buyer. Earlier this century there were a lot of 'callers' at farms. Dealing in machinery, foodstuffs, poultry etc, was quite usual. With more prosperity among the farming community, such 'sidelines' were no longer necessary but even in this present time (1998) farmers are advised to 'diversify'.

Very little building went on in the villages in the late nineteen-thirties. The council houses at South View were built in 1935 and I was involved in their construction. The original concept of village council housing was to provide accommodation for farm workers. The large plots on which these properties were built contrasts starkly to the small plots on which modern properties are sited. Even the 'executive' type of housing cannot boast such large gardens as the country council properties. Maybe land was not quite so precious in days past. The rent for a council property in those days would be five shillings and sixpence a week (approximately one day's pay).

The last war changed village life as we had known it, for ever. In 1937, just prior to the outbreak of the war, I began working at Wattisham when preparations were being made for its future development as a large scale aerodrome. When the hostilities began, local lads went away into the various armed services. Some had never been away from their village before. As a young boy my own father would never allow me to join the Boys Brigade. My call up papers came and I was off into the Royal Airforce for five and a half years. Life changed for us away from home, and things changed for our families who 'found their war at home'. Chapel Farm had two prisoners working alongside the local men. Fernando was from Italy, and Ernst Gotcher was from Germany. They were, I believe, both excellent workmen and fitted in well.

The war ended, and the lucky ones came home, but life would never be quite the same again. They now had greater expectations. People had fought hard and won for freedom. More equal opportunities, and a more equal standing among the people was demanded. This generation that had experienced the utter waste of a Second World War this century, were no longer content with the sort of life taken for granted by their forefathers.

So where is the tranquillity that town people dream of? In fact there is less tranquillity than might be supposed with the cawing of the rooks, the crowing of a cockerel and the various sounds common to a farmyard; we have a lot more traffic along our country roads than we had thirty or forty years ago. The Suffolk countryside is 'alive to the sound of human life', but local people who have lived in it for generations, still hold memories of a bygone age close to their hearts, and have a far greater sense of belonging than town people. Maybe this is the biggest difference today; people in country areas feel closer to their roots and this is ever more important in our ever changing world.

With changing times most farms in this area are free of livestock, the farmers having gone over to arable farming.

What better way to finish my story than to mention the young folk of today. Ringshall School provides primary education up to the age of nine for the children of Wattisham airfield, as well as the local children. This interesting 'mix' means that the village pupils derive benefit from contact with youngsters who have lived in various parts of the country, some abroad. This broader based education produces a much more enlightened pupil than would formerly have been the case.

How Times Have Changed!

By Michael Hodgson

Let us go back in time to 1951. At that time, according to Parish Council minutes, the village near the church was known as Further Ringshall. St Catherine's Church stood proudly on a slight incline, some way back from the road but the outlook was rather different then. The road by the 'old' post office carried straight on, the right turn led only to the Battisford Straight Road. The houses known as "Coronation Glebe" hadn't been built in 1951. They were constructed after the Queen's Coronation in 1953. Remains of the original road can be seen as the track leading towards Wattisham airfield. The original road was slightly more elevated and passed two farms, "Box Tree Farm", and "Bradleys Farm". The former was farmed by Mr Stockings, the latter by Mr Bye. Both these farms were burnt and bulldozed out of existence to make way for the main airfield runway to be extended. It is believed Mr Stockings retired, but Mr Bye moved to Clopton to carry on farming. When we first moved into "Moat Farm", and for some time afterwards, we shared a 'party' telephone line with the Bye family of Bradleys Farm. Mr and Mrs Bye had a young family who obviously

How Fashions Have Changed!

Young Girl Dressed for Farm Work c. 1100

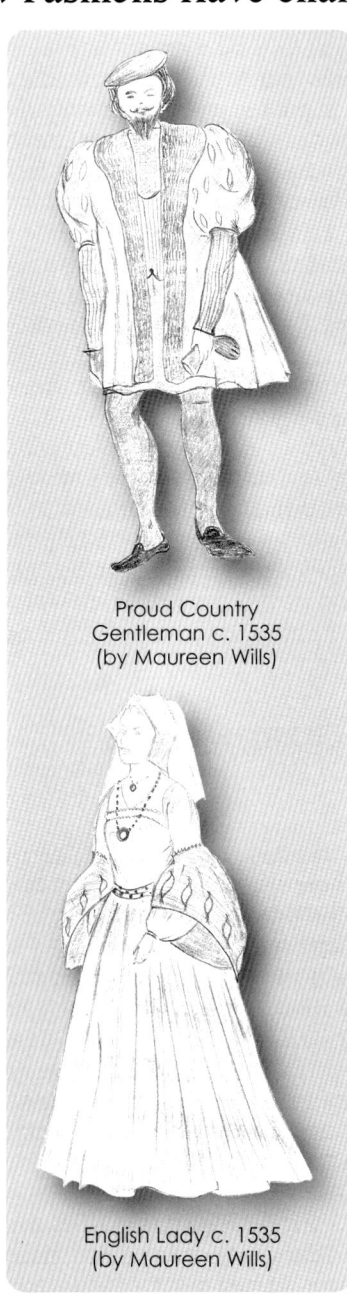

Proud Country Gentleman c. 1535 (by Maureen Wills)

Young Farm Worker c. 1100

Shepherd c. 1100

English Lady c. 1535 (by Maureen Wills)

English farmer c. 1335-1340

232

got immense enjoyment from playing with the telephone. On several occasions we found we couldn't use our telephone as their receiver was 'off the hook'. To rectify matters, we either had to get the car out or jump on a bike, whichever was around at the time, and make with all speed to Bradleys Farm. Having politely asked them to replace their telephone receiver, and with their apologies ringing in our ears, we would return home to make our call. It was some time before those young rascals got tired of playing with the telephone. In 1951 the airfield occupied the land on the left hand side of the road, as it still does today, and there were no buildings on the Battisford Road corner. The landscape was changed again in 1960 when the American Air Force built the Air Traffic Control Centre. At great expense, blast walls and hardened aircraft shelters were built at different times.

I will now try to recall what life was like in Further Ringshall in those increasingly far off days. By today's standards our existence was fairly primitive with no mains water, or electricity, perishable food was difficult to store as there were, of course, no fridges or freezers. Luckily, Vic Hubbard from Combs Ford came round twice weekly with meat, as did Emersons from Bildeston. Don Potter from Battisford delivered bread and groceries (bread 3 times per week), while a baker from Bildeston whose name I cannot recollect, delivered on the other days. His deliveries tended to be rather erratic and it was sometimes well into the evening before his knock was heard on the door. There were no supermarkets then to indulge in price cutting and our 'local' shopkeepers certainly did not inflate their charges to cover delivery, that was all part of the service. Hopgoods van would make regular deliveries of paraffin, all sorts of household requirements, and ironmongery, etc. We all enjoyed a service in those days that can be remembered with affection by older people, and envied by younger people.

There was an efficient bus service run by Cooper's Coaches of Battisford. Transport would take local people to Stowmarket on Thursdays and Saturdays, and to Ipswich on Tuesdays and Saturdays. It was even possible to catch a Corona coach at Bildeston to travel up to London. So called progress doesn't always seem to provide good service. In those halcyon days in the early 1950s Jesse Poulding still had his horse-drawn carriers cart at Wattisham, and would cover market days at Stowmarket and Ipswich. In the winter months we would hear the familiar clip-clopping of his horse as he made for home using paraffin lamps for light. He did eventually become mechanised when he bought a Ford van, but somehow it didn't seem quite the same.

As previously mentioned mains electricity and water were things other people had, not the residents of Further Ringshall! At "Moat Farm" we were not too badly off, we had the benefit of a deep bore (something like 80 ft deep) with a plentiful supply of water and an ex-army generator to provide illumination. Both water pump and generator were powered by a big single cylinder Lister diesel engine. Most of the time this engine behaved itself but every now and again the valves would start to stick and the wretched thing would be impossible to start. This generally happened in the winter months and as water was essential for the cows we kept, many were the times I had to work on the engine on a cold winter's night by the light of a Tilley pressure lantern, to be sure of the next day's water supply. Mains water came tantalisingly close in 1953 (I think) when Cosford RDC brought the mains up to the council boundary but it was another year or so before Gipping RDC started work and joined up to it. Water supply to Further Ringshall featured regularly in the Parish Council Minutes of those days. Electricity or the lack of it was another problem. Pressure to get a mains supply had started in 1950/51 and it was most frustrating to see all the lights on the aerodrome, on the runway and on the perimeter track and to know that we were dependent on either a generator or paraffin lamps (our very first refrigerator ran on paraffin). As with the water supply electricity was frequently discussed by the Parish Council but in fact we had to wait until 1963 before the mains came our way, we were connected a few days before Christmas.

The road from Wattisham village through to Ringshall and on to Needham was yet another problem. We had heard in 1957 that the road was to be closed to allow the main runway to be extended, and when that happened soon afterwards we were faced with a detour via Battisford of three miles. Needless to say, while work was in progress we often took a short cut across the airfield. Despite regular pressure from the Parish Council, it was 1960 before the new road was opened on its present alignment.

The more I write, the more the memories come flooding back. It caused quite a rumpus when Mother disappeared. She had been missing for some time and the family were getting seriously concerned over her safety. Suddenly, as we again searched round the farm buildings, unusual sounds were heard coming from the deep litter house. There she was, shut in! Evidently, while she was inside collecting eggs, someone (no one owned up to it), not realising she was inside, had bolted the outside door, leaving her to her fate. I don't think she was too happy!

One day we received a letter from the Parish Council stating a complaint had been made by a West Suffolk councillor regarding the hedge on the bend by Moat Farm. It was politely requested that the offending hedge be cut back. On close inspection, we could find no fault with the size of the hedge, especially as there was so little traffic. It was left to grow and beautify. Approximately one year later we received yet another letter from the Parish Council. The same West Suffolk councillor had made yet another complaint about our hedge. This time we duly trimmed it back. Incidentally, I am sure that particular hedge is no better today, still straggling beautifully and with a lot more traffic going past. Still on the subject of traffic, there was a noticeable increase when the Americans moved into their Air Traffic Control Centre, and unfortunately an even greater increase in the amount of litter thrown out of their cars.

In those days there was always aircraft noise and activity and many different types of aircraft were to be seen. The most unforgettable were the Hunters of Treble One Squadron, and the Black Arrows, with their aerobatics displays. The worst memory is of the time a Black Arrow crashed on our land, less than one hundred yards from where I stood. I feel sure that the pilot stayed with the aircraft to avoid hitting either the farm house, or Weir Cottage, and in so doing lost his own life. The noisiest aircraft must surely have been the Lightnings, especially taking off with afterburners on and climbing vertically.

When we indulge in nostalgia, we tend to remember only the good things, not the bad things. Would we really want to go back in time when water wasn't laid on to our homes, no electricity, and much longer working hours for manual workers. We were happy in those distant days, we didn't know a different life, but no one refused the improvements as they came along. How many would want to go back to the drudgery of sugar-beeting in the days before harvesters, or back to wash days with the copper fire having to be lit first thing in the morning? No thank you, the memories will do for me!

12
Wattisham Airfield

A Short History of Wattisham Airfield

The following article depicting a short history of Wattisham airfield was taken from manuscripts supplied to me from the Base. Most of the text was originally compiled and written by RAF personnel.

*Special thanks must go to **Warrant Officer Terry Betchley M.B.E.** of Wattisham Base who kindly supplied the above mentioned material, and gave my husband and myself a very informative tour of the Museum, and was always willing to answer my queries.*

My sincere thanks go to everyone connected with the following article, whose names are too numerous to mention. Without their literary compositions, it wouldn't have been possible for me to compile this particular story, and therefore share this interesting information with so many people. To you all, thank you!

"Mighty Oaks from little Acorns grow"

How it all began.

It is probably correct to assume that the formation of the Service we know as the Royal Air Force, took place just before the end of the First World War (1914-18). The Cabinet gave approval for the number of squadrons in the Royal Flying Corps to be increased to 200. This Service was then united with the Royal Naval Air Service to form the Royal Air Force on 1 April 1918. Major General Sir Hugh Trenchard was appointed as first Chief of Air Staff.

107 Squadron

This story begins at Lake Down, Salisbury on 15 May 1918 when Number 107 Squadron was formed as a day bomber squadron. The Commanding Officer was Major J R Howett. The Squadron was equipped with D.H.9 aircraft and was mobilised in just over two weeks. On 3 June 1918 the Squadron embarked for France. (Infancy was over, the formative years had begun.)

110 Squadron

On a typically damp day in November 1917, a young captain in the Royal Flying Corps reported to the Station Adjutant at Dover Aerodrome to discover the whereabouts of his Unit. The Adjutant was slightly perplexed. As far as he knew no such Unit of the name given to him existed at Dover, or, as far as he knew, anywhere else, either. The young man was becoming equally bewildered, and persuaded the Adjutant to look through his records, where to his surprise, and the young captain's relief, he discovered that a party of about forty airmen under Captain Erskine-Bolt had already left Rendcombe en route to Dover where it was to form the nucleus of the Unit. Captain S F Vincent was to preside over the formation of the new Unit which would be No. 110 Squadron, destined to be part of Sir Hugh Trenchard's Independent Force.

RAF Wattisham – the war years (1939-45)

On 1 April 1937, approximately 11 acres of land were purchased by the Air Ministry from Mr W Hunt. A further 450 acres were added over the next two years. Main contractors were Hippersons and John Laing and Son Ltd, whose task was to demolish three farms, namely Red House Farm, Crow Croft Farm, both owned by members of the Gooderham family, and Rookery Farm, and transform the land into a suitably enlarged air base. Local farmers gave able assistance by supplying tractors and other light machinery. Levelling and re-seeding took over a year. Everything possible was done to keep local upheaval to a minimum. Some roads were re-routed but the Roman road was retained as the approach road to the base. Ten thousand trees and shrubs were planted in and around the Station to make the site look a bit more attractive. Four type "C" hangars were erected and a grass landing formed.

The airfield was formally handed over to the RAF on 6 April 1939 having taken nearly two years to complete. First Station Commander was Wing Cdr O R Gayford, DFC AFC, later to become an Air Commodore. His family came from Hadleigh, and on his retirement from the RAF he lived at Naughton Hall, Naughton until his death in 1945. A plaque to his memory can be seen in St Mary's Church, Naughton. The Station Commander's house at Wattisham was named Gayford House in his honour.

On 11 May 1939, 107 Squadron and 110 Squadron were moved to RAF Wattisham, the Base from which they would begin to fight the threatening war. The first to arrive in the morning from Harwell were the air crews, ground crews, etc, of Squadron 107 with the short-nosed Blenheims Mk 1. During the afternoon the Commanding Officer of 110 Squadron, Squadron Leader Cameron, arrived from Waddington with officers and other ranks in their respective Blenheims. Most of the ground crews came by rail, or road, using whatever mode of transport they could muster. That evening the mess was surely the scene of much jollity as young men gathered together and drank to comradeship.

The original Blenheim was developed from the Rothermere Bomber. The prototype was sponsored and paid for by the newspaper baron of the same name, who foresaw the need for such an aeroplane back in 1935/6.

In the summer of 1939 the squadrons took part in the exercises designed to bring the RAF to a high degree of readiness as the war clouds gathered over Europe. The August exercises were the most realistic ever. They took the form of simulated formation bombing attacks on various Midland towns. Briefings would be held in the operations room. The routes generally taken were out into the North sea, down the Channel, re-crossing the coast, flying north somewhere around the Isle of Wight. During one of these exercises, Squadron 107 suffered its first peace-time loss of life.

Flight Lieutenant Barton led a formation down the channel and ran into low cloud and rain. Down he flew until the sudden appearance of a cross channel steamer immediately below made him realise how low he really was. At this point, Sergeant Farrow lost formation and entered cloud alone to make his way home. Unfortunately, at approximately 500 ft a reasonable height for the rest of the south coast, he flew into Beachy Head. Careering along the cliff top, he killed a woman walking along the grassy slopes, and then dropped four hundred and fifty feet down the cliffs onto the rocks below. Three aircrew were killed in that horrific accident. The mess was unusually quiet that night.

The time for practice was drawing to a close. Hitler's armies were poised on the borders of Poland. Capitulation and appeasement were at an end. On the 3 September 1939 the Second World War began.

A very high morale existed in both squadrons, and the young airmen didn't have to wait long for action.

The German cruiser "Leipzig" was known to be at the entrance to Wilhelmshaven, and the pocket battleship "Admiral Scheer" lay undisturbed in the Schillig Roads, (naval anchorage off Wilhelmshaven). Further out in the

Jadesbusen were four destroyers, and at Brunsbuttel were two more warships, the "Scharnhorst" and "Gneisenau". The Royal Air Force was ready for action! On the afternoon of 4 September 1939 nine Blenheims from Wattisham and fourteen Vickers Wellington bombers from another base, took off to bomb the German fleet. Pilot Officer Henderson and 110 Squadron being the first on the scene had the element of surprise on their side. Apparently some of the sailors on the "Admiral Scheer" were so unprepared for action they were leaning over the rails of the ship attending to their laundry. Pilot Officer Henderson brought the formation right into the bay a few miles north of the target from where the four aircraft attacked at a little above mast height. Flight Lieutenant Doran scored two direct hits from very low altitude. Neither of the 500 lb bombs exploded, crashing onto the deck, they immediately rolled overboard into the sea. Other bombs were near misses, and one aircraft failed to locate the battleship. One plane, N.6199 was lost, probably due to enemy fire. For his part in the raid, the first allied offensive of the war, Flight Lieutenant Doran was awarded the DFC. This was the first award of the Second World War.

107 Squadron was briefed to fly over the Schillig Roads at 500 ft and attack any ships sighted. The weather over the north German coast had worsened, the cloud was thick, and the rain heavy. With such bad visibility, the Squadron's progress was slow, and by the time they arrived the German ships were ready for action. Again the attacks were carried out from mast height, and below. One aircraft after another crashed in flames, four were lost, one aircraft with Pilot Officer Stevens, returned safely having become lost in the low cloud and rain, thus being unable to find the target.

Two of the crew of aircraft N6240 became the first prisoners of World War Two.

The gallantry of those courageous young men who set out from England on 4 September 1939 left a deep impression on the enemy. Several months later a conversation was overheard on a train going through northern Italy between a German sailor and a fellow passenger. Mention was made of this particular air attack, and the sailor commented on the bravery of the aircrews. Evidently he had been impressed with the close attack of the planes, and he also described how he had witnessed one of the aircraft blown up in the blast of a bomb burst. The eavesdropper to this conversation was an escaping prisoner of war.

The battleships, Scharnhorst and Gneisenau, anchored off Brunsbuttel were attacked by the Vickers Wellington bombers. No bombs found their targets. Two aircraft were lost, twelve returned safely to base.

The first battle of the Second World War gave an insight as to what was to come. "Never in the history of human conflict has so much been owed by so many to so few" – Winston Churchill.

After the 'phoney war' of the winter of 1939 and the spring of 1940, the fall of France and the 'Battle of Britain', Wattisham was consistently attacked. Many buildings, including barrack blocks and hangars 2 and 3 took direct hits resulting in many casualties.

Both squadrons were heavily involved in the action at Dunkirk, where the important evacuation of the remnants of the British Expeditionary Force took place. The smoke, half sunken ships and the motley traffic of boats would never be forgotten by those who witnessed it. The ground crews at Wattisham worked round the clock to keep the aircraft in the air. Many men and Blenheims were lost. The young men and aircraft that eventually returned to base looked a sad and sorry sight.

Among those shot down trying to defend Dunkirk was Wing Commander Embry. He had been assigned to make command of 107 Squadron in September 1939 and had proved an exceptional leader. Although captured by the Germans, with steely grit and determination he managed to escape and amazingly made his way home to England in little over two months. His adventures along the way would be recalled in his book "Mission Completed".

There was of course a lighter side to life on the Wattisham base. Well known entertainers, male and female, from this country and America, were warmly welcomed. An open air stage was erected on the Barrack Square. In the summer of 1944 Bing Crosby made an appearance, and Bob Hope, not to be outdone by his friend and 'partner' arrived later that year. The musical sound of Major Glenn Miller's AAF Band was also heard. Many other entertainers gave their time willingly to help cheer and encourage forces personnel everywhere who bravely risked their lives for freedom.

Local people in Ringshall and nearby villages also went out of their way to be friendly and helpful. Farmer's wife, Mrs Clement Hitchcock of Chapel Farm decided to open a small café supplying good, wholesome, homemade food. The Pumpkin Café proved a very popular venue for the RAF personnel at Wattisham. Mrs Hitchcock was ably assisted by Mrs Stockings, Mrs Smith and Miss Phyllis Gooderham. Later on, the American Service personnel would delight in the tasty 'cuisine'.

A popular venue for air crews from Wattisham during the war years was the "Swan Hotel" at Lavenham. Several years before these air crews had become 'regulars', the landlord had hit on a novel idea to keep his customers entertained. Public recognition would be given to anyone who could drink the contents of a glass wellington boot in record time. What an undertaking, and how keenly the challenge was taken up! The boot's capacity was 4 pints and the record in 1939 was about 1 minute 55 seconds held by a local farm worker. With some very thirsty young men from the two squadrons at the nearby air base frequenting the hotel bar, many more attempts were made on the record. Sergeant 'Spike' Robson knocked thirty seconds off the previous time. A jolly time would have been enjoyed by all on that occasion. His name was inscribed on the wall of the hotel bar. Wing Commander Sabine of Wattisham also temporarily held this much coveted record. The most memorable challenger was Pilot Officer Joe Culling of 107 Squadron. Quite a large young man, his very first attempt was awe inspiring. He downed the entire contents of the boot in fifty eight seconds. A night to remember! He probably didn't!

We next meet Flight Lieutenant Joe Culling in a German POW camp where he has been held for four years. He and other RAF inmates are watching a film show organised by their German 'hosts'. One of the features is a documentary showing the Yorkshire Dales, the Dorset coast, the Welsh mountains, and the picturesque villages of East Anglia. Suddenly there is a very familiar picture on the screen. Looming up in front of Joe is the interior of the Swan Hotel, Lavenham. Smiling into the camera is the landlord ......holding the infamous glass boot.

"Landlord .... I think... um.... I've....um...gulp...had enough". The bar at the Swan Hotel, Lavenham – circa 1940

The original glass wellington boot was unfortunately stolen in 1996, but there is a replacement, although somewhat smaller. Regular reunions of those wartime squadrons still take place at the Swan Hotel. Some of the older locals who gather round the bar today remember the young air crews who drank their ale with gusto, joined in the laughter and jokes, and generally became 'one of the locals' for a short time. Places like The Swan all over the country must have seemed like a safe, warm haven to those young men and women during those dark days of war.

On the night of 17/18 August 1942, eight Blenheims of No.18 Squadron were sent forth to attack the airfields at Theine, Trente and Vechta. All returned safely. This was the last operational flight by Blenheims in Bomber Command, and Wattisham had mounted the first and last Blenheim operation of the Second World War.

A momentous change took place at Wattisham Base on 12 June 1942. RAF Wattisham was transferred to the 8th Air Force of the USAAF (the 'yanks' had arrived!). During that year the grass air strips were replaced with hardened runways. The 4th Strategic Air Depot was responsible for the maintenance and recovery of all USAAF aircraft in the European war zone.

In 1944 Wattisham Base was provided with three Squadrons of Lockheed Lightnings, 434th, 435th and 436th. Colonel Kyle, the first Commander of the Group, was shot down near Paris and taken prisoner. He was later to return to become the only officer to command the Station twice.

After the war, 1946/47 the Royal Air Force returned to Wattisham. The famous Black Arrows of 111 Squadron, well known for the 22 aircraft loop, were also on the Base for a time. Land was purchased from Box Tree Farm and Bradleys Farm in the early nineteen fifties when the runways were extended.

The East Coast floods in February 1953 caused much devastation to properties, etc, and distress to families in these vulnerable areas. Felixstowe was badly flooded, and Wattisham personnel were sent to help. Many of the town's temporarily homeless residents were evacuated to Wattisham and lived for a short time in the barrack blocks. Men from the Base were dispatched to various coastal areas to help dam the breeches in the sea defences.

Aircraft from Wattisham took part in the flypast above the Mall on 2 June 1953 in celebration of the Coronation of Queen Elizabeth 2nd.

During April 1956 aircraft from Wattisham took part in a flypast at RAF Marham. The special guests were Soviet leaders Bulganin and Krushev.

In 1982 the Base was involved in the Falklands conflict.

The control of Wattisham was handed over to No.3 Regiment Army Air Corps on 1 July 1993. Nos. 653, 662 and 663 Squadrons flying Gazelle and Lynx helicopters arrived before the year was over. No.3 Regiment was joined in early 1995 by No.4 Regiment, 659, 669 and 654 Squadrons operating the same type of helicopters. 7 ES Bn REME also arrived at the Base. This specialised Royal Electrical and Mechanical Engineers Battalion provides second line aircraft maintenance support.

The Royal Air Force hasn't disappeared completely from Wattisham. Its presence remains in the form of a B Flight 22 Squadron operating two Sea King Mk III helicopters used specifically for search and rescue missions. They moved to Wattisham from RAF Manston in June 1994. In 1997 there were 80 helicopters operating from this Base.

March 1999, and Wattisham personnel were again lending support to NATO forces engaged in the attacks on Serbia. We all prayed for a solution to put an end to the hostilities. The story of this Base will continue.

Wattisham Air Base Museum

It was with some trepidation that I had originally telephoned the Wattisham Air Base and spoke to Lt Col Peter Coombe and explained my intention of including the history of the local airfield in my book about the village of Ringshall. I needn't have worried, everyone I contacted on the base was kind and courteous.

The comparatively small museum is situated in what was a Nissen hut. During the war years and for some time afterwards, the building was used as the chapel. The small vestry still remains, a reminder perhaps of young brave people of yesteryear, who found peace and solace when sometimes desperately frightened; and far from home.

Historical Note: A section of an old Roman road runs through part of the Wattisham Base and on to Coddenham.

We regard a museum as a place designed for the exhibition of antiquities, natural history, the arts, etc, and many such places can seem gloomy and austere; but not this one. There are several glass cases wherein are displayed medals and documents relating to the history of Wattisham Airfield. Many weapons adorn the walls,

Wattisham Base – 2000

as do military regalia. There is also an interesting display of parts rescued over the years from aircraft that sadly have crashed. Each piece of metal has a story to tell. Various photographs are on display which give a good, visual insight as to what life was like on the Base, past and present, plus pictures of many of the personnel associated with Wattisham.

Many places of historical interest seem to have a 'haunting', and Wattisham Museum is no exception. Several people on the Base have experienced very strange happenings in this building. Some of the personnel will not enter this room alone at night. Individuals working in the Museum have reported feeling a strange presence nearby. Eerie footsteps have been heard, making those inside this building depart rather hurriedly, with no backward glances.

The building is always securely locked at night, which makes the following incident very strange indeed. Preparations were being made at the Base for Armistice Day, and it was decided to leave some of the poppies in the Museum Vestry overnight in readiness for the Remembrance Day Service. A surprise awaited those who unlocked the Museum the following morning! The poppies were no longer in the Vestry, they had been removed and were on the top of one of the glass display cases in the Museum.

Too many people at Wattisham Airbase (some completely teetotal too!!) have experienced these 'ghostly' happenings for the stories to be treated with disbelief and disdain. Tangmere, another wartime Fighter Base in West Sussex is reputedly haunted by an airman, maybe two, so why not Wattisham? Who knows! Are these stories true, or have they grown more vivid with the telling? I certainly wouldn't care to enter the Museum during the hours of darkness to find out!

(Right) Warrant Officer Terry Betchley, M.B.E. with the author's grandson, Jonathan

Jonathan Baxter preparing for 'take off' in a Westland Lynx Mk9. Jonathan is the grandson of the author, and was given a special viewing of the helicopters by Warrant Officer, Terry Betchley on 10th October, 1997

Jonathan trying out a Gazelle for size – 10th October 1997

September 1999

The Parachute Regiment became part of the newly formed 16 Air Assault Brigade.

The Brigade will be centred on Colchester, with engineer assets in Woodbridge, and its helicopters based at Wattisham, including, soon to be issued, the Westland attack helicopter, the Apache.

On September 3rd, 1999, Prince Charles, Colonel-in-Chief of the Parachute Regiment, visited Wattisham Base, accompanied by his two sons, Prince William and Prince Harry, to view a display by the Air Attack Brigade.

Many thanks to Lt. Col. (Retd) Peter A. Coombe of Wattisham Base who supplied the above information.

13
Last – but not Least

This lovely letter was supplied by Mr Michael Poll of Ringshall.

About 1908,

Hearing Pastor Murlor & Dorothy Mudd are moving in to Brick Kiln Cottage Gt. Bricett brought back nostalgic memories of over seventy five years ago.

At that time the cottage was occupied by Mr and Mrs Fagg and their three daughters Lucy, Amy and Lily.

Two men and a boy were employed at the brickyard nearby making bricks. In the hollow there was a pump producing water for this purpose. I think I am right in saying there was no other pump or well in Ringshall, only ponds and drain water from the fields working during wet seasons. I lived near Ringshall Corner, Grandma from Leavenheath, who owned a well came to stay with us but wouldn't drink pond water and sent Uncle Jim to the pump for a pail of water. I think she was afraid of getting a goitre.

There were some delightful walks and several ways to get to the Brick Kiln field.

Primroses and delicious wild strawberries grew on the banks down the hollow.

Calico Meadow to the right produced buttercups, daisies, blackberries, sloes and hazel nuts in their seasons. We also found many larks' nests on the ground. Also to the right at the end of a long field there was a row of gooseberry bushes seemingly belonging to no-one. Naturally we found our way there when they were ripe.

Happy carefree days
Rosa Botwright.

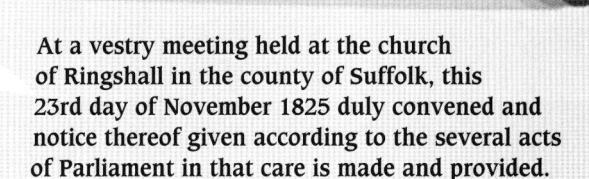

At a vestry meeting held at the church of Ringshall in the county of Suffolk, this 23rd day of November 1825 duly convened and notice thereof given according to the several acts of Parliament in that care is made and provided.

Rev. Charles Frederick Parker. In the chair.

It was resolved and we the inhabitants of the said Parish of Ringshall present at this meeting, do hereby authorise and empower the churchwardens and overseers of the said Parish for the time being to unassign and release all the right title estate and in interest of the inhabitants of the said Parish of Ringshall in and to all and singular the messuage or tenement-land and hereditaments with their and every of their appurtenances situate lying and being in Ringshall aforesaid late belonging to John Beaumont deceased and many years ago used or intended to be used as a common workhouse for the said parish.

And we further authorise and empower the said churchwardens and overseers for the time being to convey and assure all and singular the said hereditaments and all the right – and title of the said inhabitants of Ringshall as aforesaid unto and to the use of the executors of the said John Beaumont or their assigns or unto such person or persons as they may direct or appoint.

Chairman
Charles Frederick Parker

Thomas Hayward   Jonathan Crooks
Ebeneezer Hitchcock

Translated by Michael Poll, Ringshall

Certificate of Honour

presented to

Ringshall

Savings Group

in grateful acknowledgement of Successful Achievement in

SALUTE THE SOLDIER

NATIONAL SAVINGS CAMPAIGN 1944

I send my thanks to all concerned in this important National Service

P. J. Grigg
SECRETARY OF STATE FOR WAR

Extracts From The Parish Council Meetings 1951–1988

20-1-51
Mrs E M Last proposed that the Committee should approach the Gipping RDC to ascertain the position regarding the building of new council houses.

This was the year of the 'Festival of Britain' and Mrs Last proposed that a bore with tablet inscribed 'Festival of Britain' should be made in Further Ringshall at a cost of £250.

Another proposal related to the provision of electricity for the Ringshall Stocks area. Mrs Last suggested that Gipping RDC should supply drinking water for the old people at Further Ringshall.

The above indicates how life has changed in the village over the last 50 years.

1-9-52
A new manager was required for Ringshall school, which was in the course of erection.

4-2-52
The new school manager was the Rev Price-Jones.

27-6-52
Mrs Last informed the Council that residents of Further Ringshall are still without drinking water. Mr Jennings agreed to supply the water if the Council would meet the capital cost.

There were frequent references to the open sewer at 'New Bungalows'. This subject was raised at most meetings but it seems that an open sewer was not entirely unacceptable to the authorities even as recently as 1952.

7-7-52
Mr G Welham agreed to supply cart water to Further Ringshall.

26-1-53
The Council requested Gipping RDC to name the new council houses 'Coronation Cottages' to commemorate the accession of Elizabeth II.

19-3-53
A bench seat was to be bought for £12 to provide a memorial to the coronation. It would appear that the effect of the 'Cold War' had spread to Ringshall in that Mrs E Wheatley and Mrs M Last were appointed Civil Defence Billeting Officers. One assumes that in the event of an attack, these ladies would have been responsible for the accommodation of refugees.

19-3-58
Mr Price-Jones suggested that a bus shelter should be built at Ringshall Corner.

2-6-58
Mrs Last appointed school manager in succession to Mrs C Howe.

4-9-58
A plan of the proposed bus shelter was presented by the chairman. The Committee felt that a total expenditure of £168 on this project was too much.

3-3-59
A penny rate was proposed to fund the new bus shelter.

13-10-59
The new road replacing Ware Road (which was requisitioned by the Air Ministry) was discussed. It was decided to name the road 'New Ware Road'. It was hoped the new road would be opened by the Earl of Stradbroke.

2-2-60
Mr C Hitchcock objected to the site of the omnibus shelter and proposed an alternative.

30-6-60
The bus shelter is completed and in use.

22-1-62
It was reported that the bus shelter 'had been damaged by destructive persons'. Roof tiles and the drain pipe had been pulled away.

The above shows that nothing changes. Those 'destructive persons', or hooligans as we would describe them, may now see the error of their ways or perhaps they are languishing in gaol – who knows?

28-3-62
Rev Price-Jones said that he thought we ought to make a resolution concerning the 'new road' to pass the Pumpkin to the Red Lion. Mrs Wheatley and Mrs Last thought this was very necessary.

17-5-62
Mrs E Wheatley thought that Carter's Lane should be made 'one-way', but the other members felt this to be unnecessary. There was more vandalism by the 'destructive persons' who had damaged the bus shelter twice and the telephone box on another occasion, making the telephone unusable.

17-7-62
Electricity would soon be carried to Further Ringshall, having been requested in 1951.

26-6-63
It was decided to apply to Gipping RDC for permission to erect four bungalows and four houses. Rev Price-Jones was deputed to look for suitable sites.

7-10-63
The tenants of Coronation Glebe have requested that the ditch in front of their properties be filled and piped.

2-6-64
There was more discussion regarding the lack of sewage service at South View, this topic having been brought up on previous occasions. Yet another letter was sent to Gipping RDC.

7-12-64
A letter was received from D B Smith of Stocks Farm complaining about the increased volume of water coming from Wattisham Aerodrome, resulting in occasional flooding.

A letter from Gipping RDC stated that no new houses would be authorised for 1965. Rev Price-Jones said that we had had no new houses for 12 years and the lack of housing is driving the young people away to the towns. It was stated that the South View houses were in a bad state with no bathrooms, drainage or sewage services.

17-2-66
The Rev Price-Jones left Ringshall to take up the living at Horringer.

29-3-67
The Committee welcomed the new rector, the Rev Youden-Duffy and his wife to the meeting.

29-3-68
Another application submitted to Gipping RDC for bungalows for the old people.

16-9-68
It was expected that Ringshall would soon be served by a mobile library.

The Council presented a birthday gift to Mrs Last on the occasion of her 85th birthday.

20-1-69
A minute's silence was observed in memory of Mrs E Wheatley who had recently died. She had served the Council well for many years.

The mobile library was now visiting Ringshall.

31-3-69
The first street lights in Ringshall had been erected at the corner.

There were nearly 300 pupils attending the school. Children at this time stayed at Ringshall until 11 years old. They then transferred to Needham Market Secondary Modern or Stowmarket Grammar Schools.

31-3-70
The need for bungalows for the old people was expressed yet again but the District Councillor, Miss Gooderham, felt that it was unlikely they would be built until the main sewer was laid through the village. This seemed probable in the next year or so. (Maybe this comment was a little optimistic!!)

Mr R M Kemp had now decided to leave Ringshall after 20 years' service on the Council. He was deservedly presented with a cheque.

1-5-70
Following the imposition of age limits, Mrs Last was forced to relinquish her tenure as school manager.

1-6-70
C G Hitchcock appointed chairman. Mrs E M Last no longer a member.

19-10-70
Gipping RDC provided a plan of the proposed sewage scheme and stated that matters were well in hand. (They seem to have fallen out of hand subsequently!!)

25-1-71
Mrs Last retired as sub postmistress, the office being taken up by Mrs Pamela Smith.

1-6-71
Mrs John Hitchcock appointed vice-chairman.

25-10-71
The Parish Council again asked the County Council for a 30 mph limit through the village and again this was refused. The Coronation seat was now damaged beyond repair and removed.

25-4-72
As there was to be no speed limit, the County Council suggested that a footpath from the school, westwards to the limit of the properties would be considered.

The 'S' bend at the Pumpkin Service Station occupied much time at Council meetings but to the date of this meeting the County Council were not prepared to address the problem.

28-3-72
The Coronation seat was replaced by a timber and concrete bench.

Suffolk Local History Council asked the Parish Council to provide a person to act as recorder of items of historical interest for the Parish. Miss Elizabeth Bartlett was suggested for this post.

30-5-72
The County Council again proposed to build a path from the school to Walnut Tree Cottage.

The number of parish councillors was to be increased from 5 to 7 on the occasion of the 1973 election.

Miss Elizabeth Bartlett had agreed to act as Recorder to the History Council.

9-1-73
The Council discussed the ramifications of the Local Government Reorganisation which would take place on 1 April 1974. An informal meeting was to take place with Great Bricett Parish Council to discuss the possibility of amalgamation.

The clerk reported that the Area Joint Highways Committee had accepted the proposal to construct a footpath from the school to Walnut Tree Cottage.

19-6-73
Mr Pattle became the headmaster at Ringshall School.

2-10-73
East Suffolk County Council were willing to provide a footpath from the school to Walnut Tree Cottage and additionally would consider a 'walkable verge' from this point to RAF Wattisham.

27-12-74
The Rev H Cartwright was leaving the country and consequently resigning from the Council after 3 years' membership.

19-3-75
Consideration was given to renaming one of the two Bildeston Roads in the village. It was decided to recommend that the road from the Pumpkin Service Station to RAF Wattisham should be known as Lower Farm Road. The area known as Further Ringshall will be known as Mile End, Ringshall.

The autumn term saw only 144 pupils at the school due to two squadrons of Lightnings being transferred to other stations.

20-5-75
Mrs John Hitchcock declined to continue as vice-chairman. She was replaced by Mr N W Portway.

The renaming of the second Bildeston Road to Lower Farm Road was accepted by the District Council and the clerk was instructed to notify all concerned.

The age range of the pupils in the school is now 5-9 years.

21-10-76
As the Honorary Clerk was intending to give up the post after the 1976 council elections, it was decided to advertise for someone to take the job on a salaried basis. The proposed salary would be between £120 and £150 pa.

13-1-76
A salaried clerk (Mrs Portway) was appointed at £120 pa.

25-11-76
The Council discussed ways of commemorating the Queen's Silver Jubilee and decided to provide suitably decorated mugs. These were to be free for the children and 50p each for adults.

14-1-77
A street light had been placed in Lower Farm Road opposite the Sub Post Office.

Permission was sought to demolish Chestnuts Farm – a listed building – the Council had no objection.

12-5-77
The Council proposed to give a bench seat to the school in honour of the Silver Jubilee.

In response to a letter, Chief Inspector Walker attended the meeting. He expressed the view that a speed limit in Lower Farm Road was very unlikely as this would be very expensive and there had been no accidents on the road.

11-8-88
For several years the position regarding the Parish Room had been discussed. There had been no progress regarding a lease upon which depended the willingness of the Council to spend money on its refurbishment. At this meeting Mr Lightfoot (vice-chairman) suggested that the church commissioners might sell the building. The clerk was instructed to find out if this was likely and to obtain an approximate sale figure.

10-11-77
Mr J Willis stated that the Parochial Church Council would sell the Parish Room on condition it would always remain for use by the public. It was resolved that Carter Jonas should prepare a valuation of the building in order to commence negotiations.

The provision of a playing field arose at this time and it was known that the Education Committee was thinking of selling the plot of land next to the school. It was decided that contact should be made with a view to purchase or let.

More street lighting was desirable in the village, especially in Lower Farm Road according to Mr and Mrs Smith. Coronation Glebe would also benefit from more lighting. Mr Portway (chairman) undertook to obtain the views of the residents.

The Jubilee celebrations including the barn dance and outing had been successfully organised and Mr Portway thanked those responsible.

17-1-78
It appeared that the purchase price of the Parish Room could be £2,500, plus a further £4,500 for improvements. The condition relating to public use was not accepted as it was legally unenforceable.

The street lighting question was brought up. The residents of Coronation Glebe were unanimously in favour. Those of Lower Farm Road were apathetic. It was decided to contact the Electricity Board with a view to installing one or two lights at Coronation Glebe.

17-3-78
Miss E A Bartlett (Councillor and Village Recorder) submitted her resignation as she was leaving the area.

A letter was received from the Parochial Church Council stating that they would sell the Parish Room for £2,500.

11-5-78
The seat donated to the school was not yet in place. The likely inscription would be, 'Elizabeth II R 1952-1977'.

As the valuation of the Parish Room was greater than the asking price, the Council decided to buy the room at £2,500.

12-10-78
Of the three street lights suggested for Coronation Glebe, the Council felt that in view of the cost (£39.23) they would arrange for one only.

Following correspondence between Suffolk County Council and the Parish Council, a meeting took place at which it was suggested that a piece of land could be leased for a nominal rent for use as a playing field.

The contract for the purchase of the Parish Room was signed.

22-11-78
The Clerk had written to Mr Pattle enquiring why the bench seat was not yet in place. No reply was received.

A letter was submitted by the clerk offering her resignation.

Completion date for the Parish Room purchase was to be 2 January 1979.

13-12-78
Mrs Chapman appointed Parish Clerk at £120 pa.

11-1-79
A letter was received from Mr Pattle (Headmaster of Ringshall School) apologising for the delay in installing the seat. He would get this done as soon as possible.

The light at Coronation Glebe was still absent whilst the light opposite the Post Office was not satisfactory. The Electricity Board were asked to hurry things up.

Suffolk County Council wrote saying that the nominal rent for the playing field land would be £10 pa. The Chairman seemed to feel that this was too much so a decision was put off until the next meeting.

1-3-79
Mr Pattle wrote to say he had no further news regarding the Jubilee Bench. It was considered that he had allowed this matter to drag on for too long. The clerk was instructed to tell Mr Pattle to make the necessary arrangements, or to allow the Council to do it for him.

The residents of South View were supported by the Council in their request for a street light.

It was decided that the ground next to the school would not be used as a playing field as the existing school playground could be utilised providing the necessary permission was forthcoming.

The Council were now the owners of the Parish Room. It was decided to call the building 'Ringshall Village Hall'.

19-4-79
The Chairman mentioned the death of Mr Clement Hitchcock who had served the village for many years as Council Chairman. Gratitude was expressed for all that he had done for the village.

7-6-79
It was resolved that a bench should be provided by the Council and placed in the school grounds to commemorate the Jubilee.

It was proposed that rumble strips should be laid in the road near the school in order to slow the traffic.

12-7-79
The request for rumble strips was denied by the County Council.

The planning application for a bungalow at Stocks Farm was approved.

The proposed management of the Village Hall was discussed. The majority felt that this should be undertaken by the Council. The matter of independent management was to be investigated in that it may have been included in the terms of the sale contract.

The Parish Clerk's salary was increased to £175 pa.

26-7-79
The legal position was set out in a letter from the solicitors, Block & Cullingham. In short, the Village Hall had been bought by the ratepayers of the village. The result was that it was decided that a Village Hall Management Committee would be set up at a meeting set for 13 September 1979.

13-9-79
Permission had now been received for the school grounds to be used by the children in the school holidays and out of hours.

4-2-80
Planning permission for D B Smith to build a bungalow in Lower Farm Road had now been granted.

22-5-80
The Chairman paid tribute to Mr D B Smith who had recently died. The village had lost a true friend who had done much to improve the local amenities.

The Parish Council's Jubilee gift for the village was mentioned. The bench was even now still not in evidence and the flag pole which had also been approved was also conspicuous by its absence.

17-7-80
The street light had now been installed in South View.

Mr J Hitchcock said he could get a flag pole and put it in the school grounds if permission was forthcoming.

11-12-80
Mr Pattle wrote to say that he would be pleased to accept a flag pole for use at the school.

10-2-81
Mr J Hitchcock was hoping to erect the school flag pole shortly.

A planning application was discussed concerning an extension to Pumpkin Garage to form an MOT testing bay. This was approved.

14-4-81
The Chairman proposed that the day to day running of the Village Hall should be transferred to the control of the Village Hall Management Committee as from 1 April 1981. This was carried.

12-5-81
About 200 children in the village and RAF Station were to be given crown coins to commemorate the Royal Wedding.

24-11-81
Mr J Hitchcock reported that the flag pole was now in position at the school. Mr R Stevens (School head) thanked the Council for supplying and installing it. There had been a burglary at the school when £40 was stolen. The police had not made any progress in discovering who was responsible.

12-1-82
Mr J Hitchcock reported that the flag pole had broken off during the storm on 20 December. It was resolved that a suitable piece of timber would be obtained from Shrublands Forestry in order to make a new pole.

A letter of congratulation was sent to Mrs Jane Hitchcock on the occasion of her award of the British Empire Medal.

23-3-82
A tribute was made to the memory of Mr Harold Dagley who died on 16 January, only four days after chairing the last meeting.

A complaint was received from the Headmaster of Ringshall School regarding vandalism by some of the children using the facilities in the playground. A letter was sent to all residents and to the RAF reminding them of their responsibilities with regard to the behaviour of their children.

25-10-83
Mr J Hitchcock reported that the new flag pole was now in position in the school grounds. A suitable plaque would be fixed to it in due course. The School Headmaster insisted that all children playing on the school field should be accompanied by an adult as there had been many unfortunate incidents resulting in damage to property. The Council members were disappointed that the privilege extended to the children had been abused. A letter would be sent to all residents informing them of the new rule. The police were unaware that anything had happened.

Mr Johnson asked if a 30 mph limit could be instituted in Lower Farm Road. PC Hunn, for the police, said that this would not be possible.

31-1-84
Mr J Hitchcock repeated his suggestion, made at a previous meeting, that Ringshall should have a village sign.

22-5-84
Mrs S Portway gave a report of the meeting held at the school on 2 May. No damage had occurred for the last 10 months. Children were still to be supervised by an appropriate adult. The Council wrote to the Education Department requesting that the children should no longer have to be supervised as there was no other safe place for them to play.

22-1-85
The plaque relating to the Jubilee Flag Pole was now in place on the school wall.

26-3-85
A letter was received from Mid Suffolk District Council to the effect that the land near the school would not be used for Council housing but would be sold.

4-11-85
The Education Authority gave permission for the children to use the school playing field unaccompanied, once more.

The Village Hall Management Committee had had its AGM, all officers being re-elected. Funds in hand amounted to £800.

13-1-86
Further to previous discussions regarding improvements to the Village Hall, the clerk read the minutes of a special meeting held on 25.11.85. The architect, Mr Cleverly sent his table of charges showing that he would expect 13% of the cost plus £300-£400 for preparing preliminary plans. This was considered to be more than the Committee wished to pay so a letter was sent to Mr Cleverly asking him not to proceed. Two builders had provided estimates for the work required – principally refurbishment of the kitchen – which, in each case, amounted to about £9,000. Further discussion took place in relation to funding the project by fund raising, grants, etc.

28-1-86
The financial aspect of the Village Hall building work was discussed. It was agreed that £5,000 would be made available by the Parish Council and that a grant should be sought from Mid Suffolk DC. A sub-committee comprising Messrs Willis, Hitchcock and Johnson was set up. A rate levy of 3p was agreed which would raise £4,125 for 1986/7.

12-5-86
Mr Willis reported that the sub-committee has accepted an estimate of £6,735 + VAT for the rebuilding of the kitchen by Mr Ames.

3-11-86
A 50% grant had been awarded to the Village Hall Management Committee towards the costs of building work at the Village Hall.

26-1-87
There had been yet another traffic accident at Ringshall Stocks junction. As a result of previous incidents the Council had written to Suffolk County Council asking for the road to be improved. The reply from Suffolk County Council stated that it would be at least another 15 years before any work would be done.

More problems with the Village Hall – Mid Suffolk DC had informed the Council that the footings were too close to the ditch. The weather turned bad and held up progress. A large crack had appeared in the brickwork which would cost £200 to repair.

A letter was received from Mr J Hitchcock outlining a provisional plan to provide a piece of land for recreational purposes and a small housing development in Lower Farm Road.

18-5-87
Planning permission was requested by Mr A Sands of Pumpkin Garage for erection of a forecourt canopy.

The clerk reported that Mr Ames had completed the work on the Village Hall to a very high standard.

2-11-87
Mrs Chapman relinquished the post as clerk after eight-and-a-half years. She was replaced by Mr Pearce.

The Village Hall had been valued for insurance purposes at £47,301. £500 was donated to the Village Hall Management Committee.

Mr Norwood raised the question of footpaths along Lower Farm Road. Mr Wallis believed that these were scheduled for 1989/90. A letter was sent to the Highways Department asking for information on this subject.

11-1-88
The Village Hall had been burgled between 16 and 19 December when 2 Calor Gas heaters were stolen.

Mr Johnson asked if there was any information regarding mains drainage. The Clerk was to write to Anglian Water to find out if there were any plans to provide this facility.

3-2-88
This meeting was called to discuss the repair work which had been instigated without the full knowledge of the Council. The Chairman of the Village Hall Management Committee tendered his apologies regarding the lack of communication on the part of the Committee. Prices had been obtained with regard to damp proofing. The existing floor needed to be replaced. The Chairman asked that all work should be delayed until further reports could be obtained.

Parish Council Chairmen from 1951–1988

Mrs E Wheatley	prior to 1951-1968
Mr D Jennings	1969-1970
Mr C Hitchcock	1970-1976
Mr N Portway	1976-1979
Mr H Dagley	1979-1982
Mr R Willis	1982 - to beyond 1988

All extracts and table above were compiled by John Wills and typed by Andrew Toomey.

Extract from "The Evening Star" Dated 31 May 1994

"Last Post For A Village's Post Office & Stores"

A VILLAGE store and post office is to close this summer – because not enough local residents shop there.

Richard and Anita Pearce, who run the business at their home in Ringshall, say they can no longer afford to stay open.

Now villagers will face an eight mile round trip to Needham Market for post office services unless a replacement can be found.

Mr Pearce who took over the shop in Lower Farm Road eight years ago, said it would probably be closed within three months.

"I always wanted to run a small shop in the country and we had one or two good customers, but unfortunately not enough of them", he said.

Paul Diggens, a Post Office spokesman said they were advertising locally for someone to run a local service.

"We always try to find a replacement and if all else fails, we could try to find a community office which would open four hours a week".

The shop was originally owned and run by Dennis and Pamela Smith of Stocks Farm, Lower Farm Road, Ringshall. When they decided to 'retire' from this business they sold to Richard and Anita Pearce. There is now a post office available at Wattisham Airfield.

Miscellaneous News

The following extracts taken from "The East Anglian Daily Times"

Dated 30th December, 1983
Villages unite to fight ruling over jet noise grant

QUOTE: RINGSHALL PARISH COUNCIL is joining Wattisham in support of residents who appeal against the RAF's decision not to allow them noise insulation grants.

The councils have announced they will back people who fight for a share of the RAF's one million pound scheme announced in October, which will go towards shutting out noise of fighters from RAF Wattisham.

Many villagers from communities around the base are unhappy at being told they do not qualify for a grant. The eligibility boundary line passes through some such as Ringshall, so that half qualifies and half does not.

Ringshall Parish Chairman, Mrs Susan Portway said yesterday ... "As far as I am concerned the line was drawn arbitrarily, though it must be difficult to decide what the limits should be". Parish clerk Mr Richard Pearce said a letter had been sent to Central Suffolk MP Mr Michael Lord expressing the council's disappointment at how the insulation grant scheme rules were worked out.

A spokesman for Barking said nobody in the village would get grants. Armed Forces Minister Mr Roger Freeman had written saying there was no appeal against the decision.

The village had not fallen within the "continuous decibel level" as set by the MoD.
UNQUOTE

Dated 2nd August, 1962
New Road at Ministry Cost – Part of Airfield Compensation

QUOTE: RINGSHALL IS TO HAVE a new length of road to help make up for that lost when Wattisham airfield was extended under war emergency regulations. It is to run between Ringshall School and a Gipping Rural Council housing estate, and will be paid for by the Air Ministry. The airfield extensions took in an entire farm, the farmhouse being demolished in one day, and one locally important road and several lesser rights of way were stopped up. One of the compensatory rights of way would have been a cycle track near Wattisham parish church. Because of objections, however, this plan has not been approved.

The Finance and General Purposes Committee of Gipping Rural Council was told that a Ministry of Transport letter recalled objections that had been made to the proposed order. The objections made had caused the Ministry to refer the matter to the War Works Commission for a report.

After considering the draft order in the light of the objections, the Commission was satisfied that there was too much interference with agriculture to justify the construction and presence of a cycle track.

The Minister of Transport has decided to accept the Commission's report and to modify the order as recommended by them. UNQUOTE

Dated 10th November, 1988
Planners Support Conversion of Barns

QUOTE: SCHEMES FOR THE CONVERSION of two barns into homes at Ringshall Hall, Ringshall, received the support of Mid Suffolk councillors yesterday.

The Council's southern area development control sub-committee approved an application to Mr P Dahl to convert one barn to a home.

They agreed in principle to Mr Dahl's plan to convert into two homes a late 16th Century barn described by principal planning officer Mr Stuart Brooks as a most important listed building. Now Mid Suffolk planning officers will embark on further discussions with Mr Dahl aimed at retaining the character of the 16th Century barn. UNQUOTE

Dated 4th August, 1988
Village to Gain Playing Field Site

QUOTE: THE VILLAGE OF RINGSHALL is to gain a playing field and five new houses.

Mid Suffolk District Council's southern area development control sub committee yesterday approved an outline planning application by C G Hitchcock and Sons to build the homes at Chapel Farm, Ringshall, with a playing field on nearby land.

Mr Michael Shave said it was a very generous gesture of the applicants to donate the playing field area to the village. Mr Roland Wallace told councillors that the playing field site was close to the village hall.

"This is in the right place, it is an opportunity to help young people in this area and the parish council has the resources and will carry out the maintenance and long term planning of the playing field", Mr Wallace said. UNQUOTE

Harvesting Methods Over The Years

Originally the cereal crops were cut with sickles and threshed with wooden flails. Scythes were also used for cutting. A gang of men would travel from farm to farm performing this very hard work. They would start at six o'clock in the morning with breaks for refreshment during the day. On a good day, an acre of barley would be cut.

The first reaper was developed in Scotland in 1828 by the Rev. Patrick Bell. The first commercially successful reaper was constructed by Cyrus McCormick, in America, in 1831. It was thirty years later that the self raking, or sail reaper, came into use. In some cases the reapers were destroyed by men who feared they would lose their jobs. The next development was the self binder which cut and tied the crop into sheaves.

A Lance Oil Bath Binder was imported in 1946 by the Black family at Bacton. This was driven by the tractor's power take off shaft. The binder was rebuilt in 1984 and is, to this day, used to cut long straw for thatching.

The reaper thresher which combined the cutting and threshing was introduced in America in 1936. Fifty years later Daniel Best developed a fifteen ton machine which required 40 horses to pull it. Lighter, more advanced examples appeared which were powered by horse, steam or tractor and were now generally known as combine harvesters. The Case Model Q bought by Mr Percy Cooper at the 1936

Harvesting with the scythe, taken around time of First World War

Suffolk Show cost £500. There were fewer than 50 in the country at that time so there was enormous interest in the machine. Pecks, bushels and coombs were the units of capacity of the sacks used to transport the various crops.

The self propelled combine harvester was the next development. The Massey Harris 21 combine was the first of this type. 1,500 of these Canadian machines were imported between 1941 and 1948. They can be driven at a speed of 1.5 to 4 miles per hour. The first British Massey Harris combines were made in Kilmarnock in 1948. In the 1950s the combine finally replaced the binder and threshing machine. The Massey Harris 780 was an improvement on the M.H. 21 with a working speed of 1 to 7 miles per hour. In 1957 this machine could be bought for £1,475. More than 28,000 were made. The 902 was the first self-propelled combine made by Ransomes, Sims and Jefferies of Ipswich. It would work at a top speed of 11 miles per hour and was introduced in 1958. It could harvest up to 6 tons of wheat in an hour. The 300 horsepower Massey Ferguson 40 brings us up to date.

The Case Model Q could thresh about 27 tons of grain on a good day, whilst the Massey Ferguson 40 can harvest up to 300 tons in a day. The most remarkable feature is its satellite global positioning system which enables the farmer to make a detailed yield map of each field.

The field map disk can be used in the tractor's on board computer, also linked to the satellite system and this is used to vary seed rate, fertiliser application and spray treatment according to the potential yield in different parts of the field. The operators of the latest combines, sitting in air conditioned cabs, undoubtedly earn their money, but one wonders how many of them would care to go back to harvesting with a sickle.

By kind permission of Old Pond Publishing and Brian Bell, M.B.E
Old Pond Publishing, 104 Valley Road, Ipswich IP1 4PA

A Horseman – circa 1935

Not Manchester United – Yet!

By Roy and Angela Green,
6 South View, Ringshall

It started by Roy Green placing an advertisement in the local Parish Magazine asking for any interested parties wishing to help organise a village football team to get in touch with either himself or Nick Banks.

On Saturday 5 November 1994 Roy and Nick waited hopefully, but with some trepidation, on the local playing field. Seven enthusiastic young players turned up that morning. It was the beginning of an amateur football club that would be called "The Ringshall Rovers".

On 14 April 1995 a sponsored run was organised to raise funds for a football kit. The grand sum of £235 (two hundred and thirty-five pounds) was raised. All was now ready for their first game, and that took place against Oakwood School, Stowmarket. It was a friendly match and Ringshall lost 3-1. Carl Gibbs scored for Ringshall and the other players were ...

>Simon Thorpe
>Stephen Thorpe
>Andrew Favargue
>Mathew Strawson
>Don Smith
>Philip Brooker
>Colin Shann
>Craig Green
>Oliver Pinson-Roxburgh

On 10 July 1995 Ringshall joined the Waveney and District Youth 'seven-a-side' league, for the 1995-6 season for the under 14s.

On 5 August 1995 a meeting was held and it was decided the team would be known as "The Ringshall Rovers", and team colours would consist of red shirts, black shorts and black socks. Their first game in the league was a 'home' match against Woolpit. Ringshall lost 2-0. The team for this match was...

> Stephen Thorpe (Captain)
> James Summers
> Scott Thorpe
> Oliver Pinson-Roxburgh
> Garry Strawson
> Paul Laflin
> Wayne Smith
>
> Substitutes were...
> Gary Laflin
> Shaun Thorpe
> Hadley Parsons

Although Ringshall struggled in their first season, eventually finishing bottom of the league, they were awarded the "Sporting Award".

In the 1996-97 season it was decided to run two teams in the league, one for the 'under 10s', and one for the 'under 14s'. The former were managed jointly by Neil Smith and Duncan Anderson, the latter team by Roy and Angela Green.

The village can now boast two very enthusiastic and well organised Junior League football teams. Both teams won the "Sporting Award" for the 1997-98 season. Ringshall has also been running a Senior side for the last three seasons, competing in 'friendly' matches.

Let us hope that with good facilities, much enthusiasm from local youngsters, and the more 'senior' local youngsters, and with stalwart help and guidance from Roy, Angela, Neil Smith, Duncan Anderson, Debbie Kempson, Julie Smith and Rose Laflin, the Ringshall Rovers will go on to better and greater things. Good luck!

"Ringshall Rovers"
Waveney Youth 7-A-Side League
1998-99 Season

Submitted by Roy Green

Under Eleven   Finished League Runners Up

Under Thirteen   Losing 1-0 A.E.T to Combs
                    In League Trophy Final
                    Winning Sporting Award

The Under Thirteen Team...

Front Row (left To right): Ashley Turner, Stewart Arnold, John Willis
Missing are Andrew Card and Jonathan Molineaux

Back Row (left To right): Dale Smith (Capt), Tom Goodchild, Jake Chinnery, Chris Allen, Joe Jackson, Gary Laflin

The Romanian Connection
From Rosabel and Alan Peck

Two very remarkable people live in Ringshall.
They are Rosabel and Alan Peck of 5 Coronation Glebe.
Theirs is quite an exceptional story.

Alan Peck was, and is, a workaholic! A prosperous business man in the construction field, he and his family enjoyed a good standard of living. He was aware, however, that many people in the world led much less privileged lives, and a growing desire to help such people took hold. Alan felt he should repay some of the dividends back into life that success had brought him and his family.

In 1991 an opportunity arose for him to help refurbish an orphanage in North Eastern Romania. Together with his wife, Rosabel, and forty volunteers whom they recruited, a very successful mission was eventually accomplished. The beginning of any 'project' is often strewn with problems. When Alan and his band of dedicated workers arrived in the commune, consisting of four villages, they were appalled at the pitiful conditions of the inhabitants. The team was galvanised into action, and determined to try to make life better for these people whose culture is so different from that of the western world.

On returning home to England, Alan, Rosabel and a few friends started their own charity group, namely, Suffolk Romanian Connection. On returning to the commune, they decided to live in one of the villages, Goesti, for several months. By living with these people and sharing their lives, Alan, Rosabel and their helpers were in a better position to establish a rapport, and by doing so would

Goesti School – Nursery room.
Photo: R Peck

Crucea 1996 – Village children enjoying play area while work in progress. Photograph – R Peck

Goesti 1995 – Kindergarten room. Photograph – R Peck

find out how best to help the community. "The best laid plans of mice and men,".... The 'several months' turned into three years. During this period they formed another charity group over there, to twin with the English group here. A charity shop was opened in one of the villages, and sufficient funds thereby gained for much needed improvements to the community to be carried out.

It was decided to start with the four schools which were very neglected. The Victorian style classrooms were dark, dismal and bare. The toilets were indescribably disgusting. Work soon got under way, and in a short time the first school boasted a new toilet block. Classrooms were repaired, and made cheerful by bright, new colour schemes, toys were installed in the nursery rooms, with play equipment outside. The western world takes such things for granted, in poor countries, such things are a luxury.

Each year saw another school transformed, and they are still 'beavering' away after eight years, returning each year for four months with a small band of very dedicated people. Four of these people are from the original group.

With love, care and much help, maybe the next generation won't suffer the indignities of past generations. Alan, Rosabel and their motley group of helpers hopefully will continue this very necessary work which cannot succeed without willing contributions from caring persons here. The Oxford English Dictionary defines the word "determinism", as "Philosophical doctrine that human action is not free but necessarily determined by motives, regarded as external forces acting on the will". With regard to these unique people, how apt is that description.

Rudyard Kipling must have the last word, "To win the lottery of life is to be born an Englishman".

A New Butterfly for the Third Millennium
By Mr Andrew Toomey

It is unusual to report that any species is increasing its range by spreading into such an intensively managed landscape as that of Ringshall. Nevertheless this is just what has happened. The Speckled Wood (Pararge aegeria) butterfly has never been recorded in the parish before but this year I have found colonies in two separate sites.

The Speckled Wood butterfly - drawing by Mr Andrew Toomey

To monitor the abundance of any butterfly, the country is divided up into squares whose sides measure 2 km. When a butterfly is spotted it can be marked as present in the square covering the area where it was seen. In Suffolk there are about 1000 such squares.

The Speckled Wood butterfly was present in only 53 of these squares in the 1982 Butterfly Survey. In 1998 it had been recorded in 353 squares and now, as our parish lies over two squares, the total is 355.

The butterfly is mainly brown with white and cream speckles. It lives in woodland and is difficult to spot because its colouring helps it to merge well with the background. The caterpillars feed on the grasses Cock's-foot and Common Couch. Both are very common in Ringshall. The adult butterflies can be seen on the wing from April to October. Overwintering pupae hatch in the early spring. Caterpillars may overwinter and pupate the following year. These will hatch in June. In favourable years a second generation will be produced.

Ragged Robin *is a plant I didn't expect to find in Ringshall. It is a plant of wet ditches and damp places. It is easily crowded out by the coarser vegetation, which is normal in our ditches.*

You can imagine my delight when I found a small colony of Ragged Robin in a damp spot in a meadow in the parish. It is now five years since my discovery and I am pleased to say that it is still thriving. I hope that it continues to do so.

(Lychnis flos-cuculi). Drawing by Mr. Andrew Toomey

In the past one hundred years, Ringshall, like most of Suffolk, had its share of unimproved grassland. That is grassland that has not been 'improved' by treatment with fertilisers, insecticides or selective weedkillers. These grasslands supported a huge variety of plants and animals. Like most of Suffolk, Ringshall has lost these grasslands - well almost.

As with many villages, the lost flowers and animals can still be found. In some villages the churchyard is managed as a wonderful reservoir of wildlife. In all villages some of the roadside verges are really rich in plants and invertebrates. Ringshall is lucky enough to have a very good example of such a verge. In a scheme which involves co-operation between Suffolk County Council and Suffolk Wildlife Trust this verge is managed as a Roadside Nature Reserve. The management is straightforward. It involves cutting the vegetation on the verge after the plants have seeded each year. The cuttings are removed to prevent them from enriching the soil. The rewards are more than worth the effort.

Represented on this reserve are the plants that one would expect to find in the local soil. They are not overgrown with docks and nettles. This is because the cuttings are removed and no fertiliser is added to the soil. It is too much fertiliser that causes the stronger plants to grow well and suffocate the weaker, more desirable species. Some of the plants on the Ringshall Roadside Nature Reserve are not only rare in Suffolk, but are nationally scarce. One such plant is the Sulphur Clover. The Reserve supports a large colony of Bee Orchids and the very, very rare Man Orchid.

A colony of Common Blue butterflies thrives on the abundant Bird's-Foot Trefoil. With luck and the popular will, this reserve will survive into the next millennium. The plants will be conserved ready to spread into and to enrich the surrounding countryside when our land management practices change.

In addition to the designated reserve, some of our other verges support an interesting and diverse flora. It is likely that these will continue to survive whilst their growing conditions remain unchanged. I find it a refreshing thought that our interesting natural history may persist for future generations to enjoy.

The above photograph taken by Mr Andrew Toomey of 3 Bakers Corner, Ringshall shows the Bee Orchids on the Ringshall Roadside Nature Reserve

Compiled and written by Mr Andrew Toomey

Printed 1878

Haughley Bushes
Dagworth Hall
Harleston
Tot Hill
Halfway House
Columbine Hall
Gipping Town-house
Earl Stonham Town Barn
Saxham Street
Thorney Green
Newton Bridge Farm
Mount Pleasant
Chilton-hall
Chilton House
House of Industry
Star House
STOWMARKET
Station
Stow-upland
Crown Inn
Park Farm
Hammond's Corner
Earl Stonham Mills
Waterloo House
Broad Green
Shepherd & Dog
Sheep Gate Hall
Braziers Hall
Raydon Hall
Red House
Creeting Green
Hill Farm
Wilderness
Great Finborough
Boyton Hall
Combs Lane
Creeting St. Peter or West Creeting
Camp Farm
Five Acre Grove
Horse pasture Grove
Combs
Combs Wood
Holy Oak
Gorse Cover
West Creeting Hall
Creeting All Saints Hall
Creeting St.
Jockys-hall
Ash Grove
Park Cover
Grove Farm
Ravens Bridge
America
Badley
Badley Green
Hall
Little Finborough
Kimberlee Hall
Johns Grove
Newton Field
Needham Market
Station
Battisford Tye
St. John's Manor House
Battisford
College Grove
College Farm
Barking
Charles Hall Wood
Ringshall
Hall
Charles Tye
Honeypot
Parsonage
Bowcell-hall
Barking Tye
Darmsden
Ten Wood
Whitefield-house
Red House
Glebe
Chapel Farm
Ringshall Stocks
Ditch Wood
Baylham Hall
Goddards
Willisham Tye
Round Wood
Breakfield Farm
Great Bricett
Crow Croft Grove
Hall or Priory
Bricett Park
Glebe Barn
Out Wood
Bowerland's Grove
Green Street Green
Willisham
Middle Wood
Lower Farm or Well Farm
Nedging Tye
Waller Farm
Pot ash Farm
Offton
Little Bricett
Rookery Farm
Nettlestead
High Hall
Weetley Green Farm
Naughton
Brick House Farm
Mackles Hall
Tithe Barn
Castle
Parsonage
Little Blakenham
Charles Gardens
Greyhound Inn

This photograph shows the site of Ringshall brickworks. It stood opposite Ringshall Hall. The remains of the kilns were destroyed in the 1950s when the site was bulldozed in order to enlarge a field. I could not find much of the history of the brickworks. Apparently the bricks made here were stamped with the word 'RINGSHALL'. Some were used in the construction of Great Bricett School. *(Photograph – A Toomey)*

This copy of an original invoice to Mr Makins, Brickmaker, Ringshall was obtained by Mr Michael Poll of Ringshall

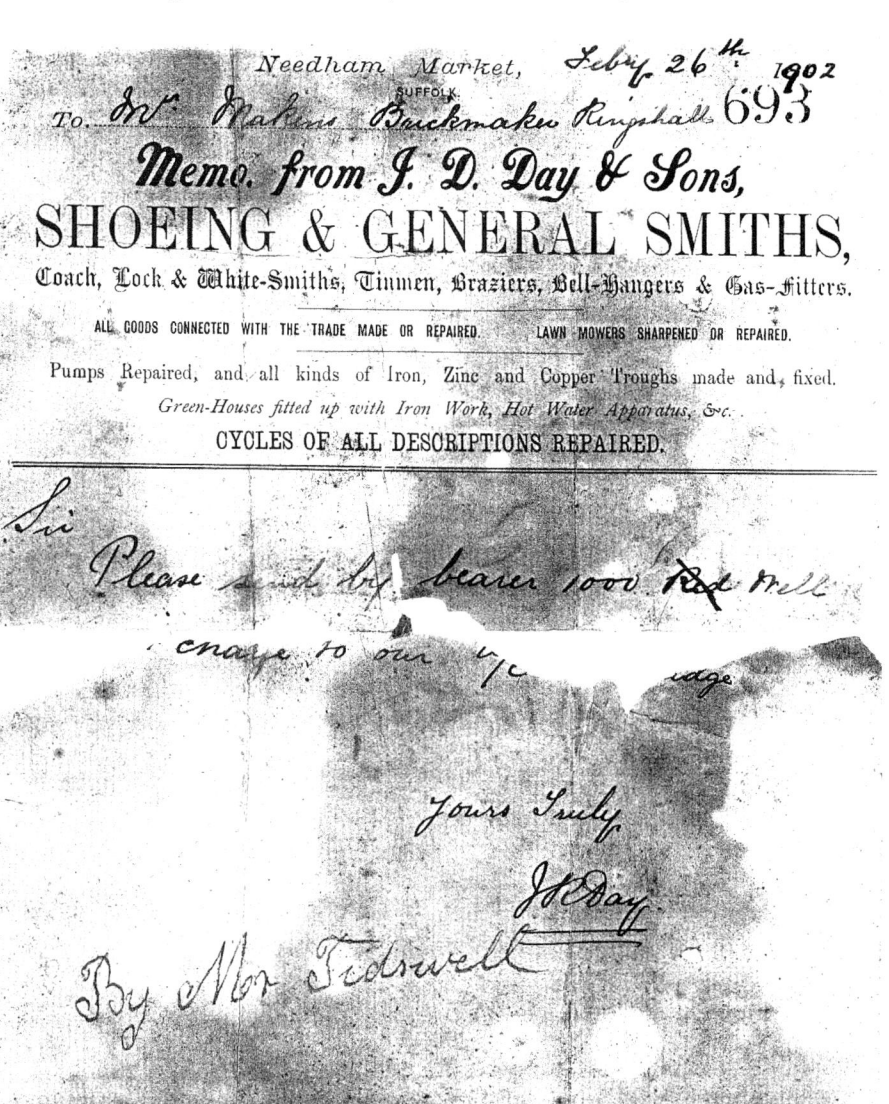

Needham Market, Feby 26th 1902
SUFFOLK.
To Mr Makins Brickmaker Ringshall 693

Memo. from J. D. Day & Sons,
SHOEING & GENERAL SMITHS,
Coach, Lock & White-Smiths, Tinmen, Braziers, Bell-Hangers & Gas-Fitters.

ALL GOODS CONNECTED WITH THE TRADE MADE OR REPAIRED.   LAWN MOWERS SHARPENED OR REPAIRED.

Pumps Repaired, and all kinds of Iron, Zinc and Copper Troughs made and fixed.
Green-Houses fitted up with Iron Work, Hot Water Apparatus, &c.
CYCLES OF ALL DESCRIPTIONS REPAIRED.

Sir

Please send by bearer 1000 *** well

charge to our a/c

Yours Truly

J R Day

By Mr Tidwell

Ringshall Map – 1905

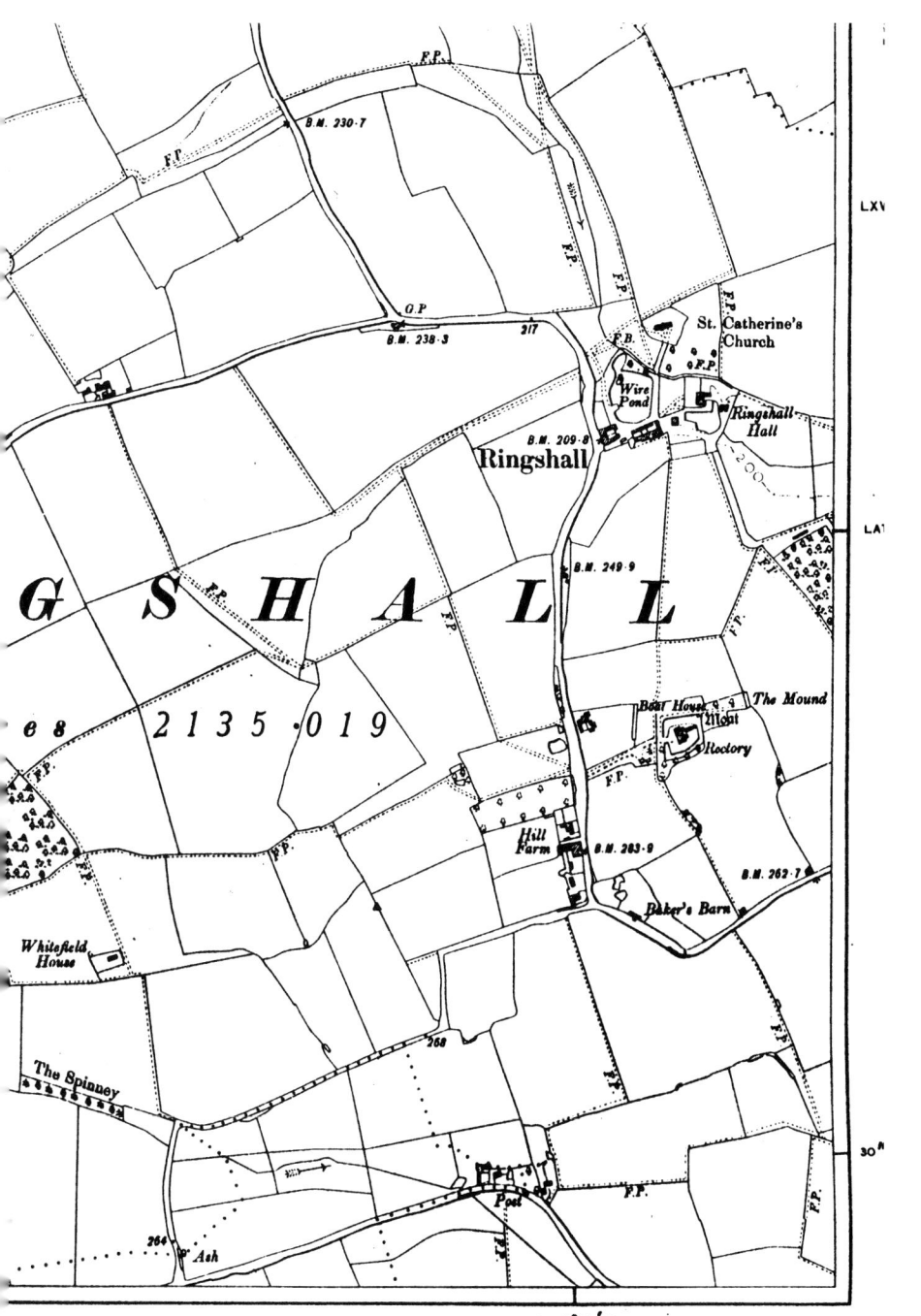

Ringshall

St. Catherine's Church

Wire Pond

Ringshall Hall

G S H A L L

2135 · 019

Boat House
The Mound
Moat
Rectory

Hill Farm

Baker's Barn

Whitefield House

The Spinney

Pool

Ash

LON. 0° 59′ E.

Marian Cole taking a break from her word processor. Her help was invaluable

All finished! Now I can relax, hope you enjoyed the book!